LEGAL DEFENSE HANDBOOK

FOR CHRISTIANS IN MINISTRY

Carl F. Lansing
Attorney-at-Law

NAVPRESS
BRINGING TRUTH TO LIFE
NavPress Publishing Group
P.O. Box 35001, Colorado Springs, Colorado 80935

The Navigators is an international Christian organization.
Jesus Christ gave His followers the Great Commission
to go and make disciples (Matthew 28:19). The aim of
The Navigators is to help fulfill that commission by
multiplying laborers for Christ in every nation.

NavPress is the publishing ministry of The Navigators.
NavPress publications are tools to help Christians grow.
Although publications alone cannot make disciples
or change lives, they can help believers learn biblical
discipleship, and apply what they learn to their lives and
ministries.

Library of Congress Catalog Card Number:
     92-81119
ISBN 08910-96833

This publication is designed to provide accurate and
authoritative information concerning the subject matter
covered. It is sold with the understanding that the author
and the publisher are not engaged in rendering legal
or other professional service. If legal advice or other
expert assistance is required, the services of a competent
professional in your state should be sought. *From a
Declaration of Principles jointly adopted by a Committee
of the American Bar Association and a Committee of
Publishers and Associations.*

All Scripture in this publication is from the *Holy Bible:
New International Version* (NIV). Copyright © 1973,
1978, 1984, International Bible Society. Used by permission of Zondervan Bible Publishers.

Lansing, Carl F.
     Legal defense handbook : for Christians in minis-
try / by Carl F. Lansing.
        p.   cm.
     Includes bibliographical references.
     ISBN 0-89109-683-3 : $15.00
     1. Church management—Law and legisla-
tion—United States.   2. Clergy—Legal status,
laws, etc.—United States.   3. Christianity and
law.   I. Title.
KF4865.L36   1992
349.73′08′82—dc20
[347.300882]   92-81119
                                                   CIP

Printed in the United States of America

FOR A FREE CATALOG OF
NAVPRESS BOOKS & BIBLE STUDIES,
CALL TOLL FREE 1-800-366-7788 (USA)
or 1-416-499-4615 (CANADA)

Contents

For my patient and understanding family
who is always there at the right time
with a word of encouragement.
Thanks Sally! Thanks Kirsten!
Thanks Casey! Thanks Chris!

Acknowledgments

A note of recognition is warranted for some special friends who have supported me and kept both me and this project in their prayers over the past two years: Lumpi and Cree, Jon and Nancy, Doug and Margy, Al and Debbie, and good buddies Bob K. and Jerry M.

My editor at NavPress, Steve Webb, is a genius in his vision and skills as a writer. God has also given Steve large doses of patience, which made him a perfect match for me.

My law clerk and legal assistant, Sonja Rawls, has been a priceless contributor with quality insights and analysis from the moment this book was a rough outline on a legal pad. Finally, Sharon Phillips, Mary Ellen Phillips, and Terri Decker were each divinely selected to help a computer-illiterate lawyer type, revise, edit, and proof the work that follows. God bless you all!

Preface

It may be apparent to nearly everyone in Christian ministry that the legal system has become as much an adversary as an ally. Nonetheless, my personal and professional experiences tell me that churches and ministry organizations have yet to respond effectively to the challenges currently upon them. Hundreds of hours of legal research also support such a conclusion.

A number of considerations for this failure are discussed in this book, but two primary causes have repeatedly surfaced and deserve special attention. First, too many of us Christians make the ill-fated assumption that serious legal problems could never happen to us. This supposition may belie a more serious misapprehension that would say, in so many words, lawsuits are reserved for those of lesser faith or suspect theological foundations. "With God for us, who can be against us?" sums up this approach to what is considered a worldly concern.

The second cause of this failure to respond effectively to the legal challenge stems simply from the lack of helpful, practical information on how to take steps to protect your church or ministry legally. There is an enormous void within many Christian organizations and churches when it comes to legal defense skills. Those who have a desire to become more knowledgeable have had nowhere to go to begin the process of becoming more legally skilled.

My goal in this book is to tackle these two root causes in a practical, readable fashion. I have always kept in mind the small church pastor, the typical board of elders or deacons, and the parachurch staff member administering any one of the thousands of independent ministries serving, for example, youth, teenagers, the poor, the hungry, or the sick or elderly.

So whether you serve in any of these capacities or on the staff of a megachurch, you should benefit from the practical, timeless legal defense principles and strategies found in the following pages. I think they will serve well those who are in the business of God's Kingdom. Without that as my driving goal, I'm convinced this dream of many years would never have come true.

CARL LANSING
EASTER 1992

PART ONE

A Legal Storm Brewing for Ministries

CHAPTER ONE

The Changing Legal Winds for Ministries

The legal winds in the United States for churches and parachurch ministries have been changing direction of late. These winds have eroded the old landscape. New attitudes and a whole new playing field have emerged from the erosion. The old, comfortable ballpark has been replaced with a far less inviting playing field. In the Windy City, Cubs baseball fans affectionately refer to their old ballpark as the "Friendly Confines of Wrigley Field." Well, the new legal arena, to which pastors and ministry staff are being introduced at an alarming rate, is far from friendly. These new venues in which Christian organizations have become involuntary guests are the courtrooms of the United States. The numbers of lawsuits and other legal actions being brought against those in Christian ministry have caused this field to emerge as one of the most rapidly expanding "growth industries" for lawyers.

"You don't need a weatherman to know which way the wind blows," wrote Bob Dylan.[1] Indeed, the most obvious circumstances should be the most readily observed. But this is not always the case in the human equation. More often than we like, the truth manages to escape our comprehension even when it looks us straight in the eye. Unpleasant realities are the first to be denied and the last to be confronted. Our nature is much more willing to embrace comforting delusions than to face honestly the winds of unwelcome change.

This wind change is not a spring breeze that has been particularly selective in blessing those on whom it decides to blow. Instead, it's a harsh, cold, penetrating wind that blows in all directions without advance warning. No religious denomination or parachurch or ministry focus is immune from its destructive power. In the last couple of decades, the public's general respect for and reverent confidence in religious organizations have been severely eroded along with many other previously highly regarded professions.

For example, not long ago even elected officials in government were highly respected, rather than made the butt of jokes. Obviously, Watergate had a lot to do with the diminished level of honor given to politicians. But somehow religious leaders have joined politicians, doctors, and lawyers as favorites of a "bashing" form of disrespectful humor.

THE CHURCH AS A TARGET

With the fall of political service, medicine, and law from their prior plateaus of high esteem, the winds of change seemed to scan the horizon for other institutions upon which to thrust derision. The "church" has become the latest target. Sadly, it appears that America's intellectually disconnected and ethically unattached culture has brought us to the place where even church members and pastors—yes, pastors too—have joined outsiders in bringing lawsuits against the local church. And it's done as readily as if the church was a business establishment whose service or product failed to adequately perform.

Don't misunderstand me; I do not advocate that churches and ministries should be exempt from legal responsibility for the wrongs they inflict. To the contrary, everyone, including churches, Christian organizations, ministers, and staff, should be held accountable when a harm is clearly committed. But my main concern is that we now live in a society, within both the larger Christian community and the evangelical subculture, that has deteriorated to the point where deference, forgiveness, grace, and compromise seldom enter into the decisions of people who consider litigation. "What are my rights?" seems to be the overriding, if not single, concern of too many Americans, including an alarming number of Christians.

Much of the banter in social conversation and superficial writings lays the blame for the American litigation explosion at the feet of lawyers. No question, lawyers play a significant role in the widespread use of unnecessary lawsuits to settle differences. But people must remember that in *every* case in *every* courtroom, *every* lawyer has a client to represent. Clients never say no to the opportunity to receive large sums of money and most often are willing participants in their own lawsuits. Although "ambulance chasing" by lawyers remains an ongoing problem confronting the profession, the client nearly always seeks out the lawyer. A symbiotic relationship of greed is on the rise between the public and the legal profession.

Lawyers make money by suing people. This has always been the nature of what we do, and it surprises no one. What is new and different in the United States is the willingness, moreover the desire, of so many people to bring a lawsuit with the view of becoming rich. Compensation for a wrong is not the driving force in many of these lawsuits. Getting back to status quo is not the aim. Rather, to gain and to improve one's lot through the legal system seems to be many litigants' chief goal.

A fairly common law school illustration may bring home the point of how much our society has changed. Twenty years ago someone standing on a street corner whose elbow was brushed by a passing truck would likely exclaim, as he brushed the dust from his shirt sleeve, "Thank God, I'm alive!" Now a person in the same circumstance would shout, "Thank God, I'm rich!" The way things are headed, there may even be some people out there who are praying to be hit by a truck (a small one owned by some wealthy company) so they too can cash in on the American legal jackpot.

To further illustrate this point, we would not be surprised to read a newspaper headline about a corporate manager who filed suit against his employer for what he perceived to be an improper layoff after many years of service. In fact, such a case would not even warrant a headline, since employment lawsuits are now very common in corporate America. All states have developed labor laws to the point where business employers can no longer reduce staffs or transfer personnel up and down the corporate ladder without exercising great care.

CHRISTIANS JOIN THE RANKS OF LITIGATORS

But that is corporate America, the business world. We can't imagine the clergy or their staff claiming similar "rights" to job security. After all, isn't being a pastor or minister a "call" from God rather than merely employment at a job? That assumption may have been true twenty years ago, but it is no longer appropriate. A few decades ago it would have been unthinkable, let alone unbelievable, that a minister would sue his own church and governing denomination on the grounds that he was wrongfully discharged after forty years of dedicated service. Certainly he would have experienced deep feelings of rejection and pain, much embarrassment, and perhaps even depression. Harsh and heated words might have been said with regrets in private meetings held behind closed doors. Letters from supporters may have been sent to question, or even challenge, the unusual decision to let this senior leader go. But never would the pastor bring suit claiming that his church "mutilated his contract rights, tarnished his reputation, and ruined his emotional health."

In 1988 the Christian and Missionary Alliance (CMA) faced such a lawsuit brought by one of its pastors (Natal) who had served the CMA for nearly forty years.[2] The plaintiff minister not only shocked his church with the notion of a lawsuit and its odd-sounding secular allegations quoted above, but he also surely interjected a strong element of fear by his request for one million dollars in compensatory damages *plus* punitive damages with no maximum amount to punish the CMA and make the denomination an example for others. On top of all this, the court case reports that Pastor Natal's wife also joined in the lawsuit claiming her own damages of $200,000 for "loss of business and mental anguish." Apparently, the pastor's wife operated a religious bookstore in the church annex and was asked to leave the premises when her husband was relieved of his duties.

All the facts of what transpired are not publicly known. As with most reported court cases, many of the personal reasons for the resulting bitterness are left untold. Obviously, Pastor Natal and his wife felt betrayed and treated unfairly. Since the lawsuit was dismissed prior to trial, the public may never know whose side justice and common fairness favored.

The most revealing fact this case provides is that the courthouses of the United States are increasingly becoming forums where churches and religious organizations find themselves attempting to resolve legal issues and disputes. If the current mood in religious society is one in which ministers find it more readily acceptable to sue their own churches, surely we can expect secular interests to be even more willing to consider litigation against ministries as a viable option to gain redress for perceived wrongs. No longer is a lawsuit against a church or Christian ministry socially unthinkable.

A Universal Phenomenon

The *Natal v. CMA* case is by no means an isolated, unusual occurrence. Such cases, which would have recently been considered shocking, now happen at an increasing rate. For reported court case examples, consider the following:

- ◆ A minister sues his denomination, claiming age discrimination as the reason for "being denied a rightful promotion" and for breach of contract for "failing to move him to a congregation more suited to his training and skills and a more appropriate level of income."[3]
- ◆ An ordained faculty member files a civil suit against a theological seminary of the Reformed Church of America for being denied tenure by the seminary president, a fellow ordained minister who was also named as a defendant.[4]
- ◆ A pastor sues his own church and its board of elders, challenging the elders' authority to amend church articles and bylaws and seeking an injunction to prevent them from "interfering with the performance of his duties on behalf of the church."[5]
- ◆ Twelve church members bring a "class action" lawsuit against their church pastor, deacons, and trustees for a financial accounting of the Pleasant Green Baptist Church.[6]
- ◆ Board of Trustees of First Union Baptist Church of Alexandria, Louisiana, file suit to prevent the church pastor from continuing as pastor. Shortly thereafter, a rival board

of trustees of the same church joins the lawsuit to argue
that it is the true governing board and has "reinstated" the
now controversial pastor.[7]

◆ A church's membership becomes divided over the issue
of moving to a new building. The majority of the congregation votes to move to a new building and change
the church's name. A minority resolves to stay in the old
church building. In the midst of the dispute, it is alleged
that two church trustees secretly deed the old church property to themselves personally as "trustees" for the majority
group and then grant a mortgage to a local savings and
loan to borrow money for the new church purchase. The
minority group of members and deacons file suit against
the rival trustees for the new church, seeking to set aside
the deed and mortgage.[8]

◆ A family sues its church, O'Fallon United Church of Christ,
for paralyzing injuries suffered by their fifteen-year-old son
who fell from a tree that he had climbed at a church fellowship picnic. His parents reportedly watched him climb the
tree and even warned him that it was dangerous and to be
careful. His parents were twenty-two feet from the tree
when he fell. Finally, the Illinois Supreme Court overturns
two lower courts and rules in the church's favor after
years of complex, expensive litigation.[9]

◆ The assistant principal of a private Catholic high school
sues the school, the Catholic diocese, the Catholic bishop,
and the school's principal for the school's decision to not
renew her one-year written contract as a school administrator. Even after accepting an alternative position at the
school as a teacher, the lawsuit commences, alleging "bad
faith discharge, breach of employment contract, negligent
discharge, intentional and negligent infliction of emotional
distress and damages for loss of consortium (marital privileges) for her spouse." Actual compensatory and punitive
damages are both sought.[10]

This small number of representative cases should be enough to
convince anyone that we now face a changed religious culture that

no longer gives much deference to churches and religious institutions when it comes to exercising the great American right to litigate for damages. Add to that the reality of an already hostile, litigious greater culture and it's understandable why some now say that suing one another rivals baseball as the national pastime. Unfortunately, the American fever for the courtroom has not escaped American ministries and churches.

As these cases reveal, no faith, denomination, nor parachurch organization is exempt. No religious group can claim superiority. No one is untouched. If anyone in Christian ministry believes that "this cannot happen to us," I respectfully and sincerely believe that such an attitude will only add to that organization's future legal problems.

Every church and ministry must steer into these winds of change and confront the challenges head-on. Statistical analysis shows that the probabilities of being sued are on the rise and that the days are numbered for most every organization. "Will you be legally prepared?" is the question for those in Christian ministry.

LEGAL STRATEGIES AND PRINCIPLES

◆ The church has become the latest target of the litigation explosion in the United States. Americans' fever for the courtroom has now expanded to include Christian ministries and churches of every faith and denomination.

◆ Along with politicians, doctors, and lawyers, those in Christian leadership positions have become the latest subjects of deteriorating public respect. Ministries must prepare for the fact that deference, forgiveness, grace, and compromise seldom are factors in the minds of people considering a lawsuit.

◆ "Will you be legally prepared?" is the question for ministries in the nineties.

CHAPTER TWO

The Litigation Avalanche Hits Ministries

All the necessary weather conditions are present for a long and bitter legal storm against ministries and churches. The increasingly impersonal nature of society is breeding a diminished lack of respect for religious institutions. More people are becoming lawyers and for all the wrong reasons. The American legal profession faces an unprecedented challenge within its ranks on fundamental questions of ethics and professionalism. Far too many people seek to become lawyers with little or no interest beyond personal monetary gain.

When one adds the newly discovered facts that churches and parachurch ministries are often quite financially secure, while at the same time legally stubborn, naive, and vulnerable, we have the makings of a serious, long-term legal blizzard coming across the horizon.

Common sense says that the ever-increasing, even staggering numbers of lawyers in this country will necessarily find ways to keep themselves busy—professionally, that is. In 1990 in my home state of Colorado, population-wise a relatively small state, we added 993 new lawyers to the profession, making our total 19,010. In 1980 Colorado licensed 672 new lawyers and in 1974 only 210. In California, the country's largest state, the number of licensed lawyers rose to 108,531. In New York the number of lawyers doubled from 59,679 in 1980 to 97,970 in 1990. Illinois experienced similar growth, increasing from 35,509 to 59,628 from 1980 to 1992.[1] Any way you approach it, practicing law in the United States remains one of the high-growth industries.

IT'S RAINING ATTORNEYS!

One would think that sooner or later the United States would finally hit a supply-and-demand saturation point for people joining the legal profession. Free-enterprise theories would dictate that with more and more lawyers, salaries and the cost of legal services should sooner or later decline. Not so thus far. While temporary, minor dips in lawyers' average salaries occur every so often, many indicators show most lawyers' income on a steady rise.

For example, a 1985 survey of 150 medium to large law firms with an overall total of 5,000 lawyers found that the incomes of both associates and partners in the firms increased at approximately the same rate as the consumer price index between 1975 and 1985.[2] On balance, sole practitioners, small firm lawyers, and other professional groups did not fare as well in keeping pace with inflation during this period. Nevertheless, none of us lawyers would find a sympathetic ear if we claimed that our incomes were no longer attractive in the 1990s. In spite of increasing numbers of bodies, incomes are maintaining their relatively high levels.

The Proliferation of Law Schools

In spite of the mind-boggling growth in the number of lawyers, American law schools presently face even higher, record-breaking numbers of hungry applicants. This is not a good sign. No let up in the storm here! The *National Law Journal* recently reported that the nation's 176 American Bar Association-approved law schools were experiencing their *fourth* consecutive record year in applications for admission.[3] More than 94,000 people applied for 44,000 seats in entering classes at ABA-sanctioned schools in 1991. These figures do not include the applicants to *non*-ABA approved schools, of which there are thirty-seven in California alone.[4] These numbers represent about a 7 percent increase over figures in 1990, which was the third of three straight years of unprecedented growth.

The same article indicated that there are no detectable patterns regarding those desiring to become lawyers. Big schools and small schools, highly regarded and lesser known schools, are all being deluged with applications. In 1991, American University's Washington College of Law received 6,300 applications for only 325 first-year openings. Even tiny Mercer University Law School in Macon, Georgia, had 1,600 applicants hoping to be one of 142 successful candidates for admission.[5]

The Wrong People in the Wrong Place at the Wrong Time

Law school personnel handling admissions can't readily explain the relentless surge of people seeking entry into the legal profession. The "L.A. Law Syndrome" might be a contributing factor but can by no means account for such unusual numbers. More likely reasons for the influx of would-be law students are the recessionary economy and mid-life crises. As one law school admission official asserted, "People are saying, 'I can't get a job, I might as well continue my education.'" "I think we're getting more people changing professions," another added. "People are getting tired of what they're doing, so they go to law school."[6]

If these assumptions are accurate in the characterization of even a portion of this growing group of lawyers, it may explain the increased lack of professionalism among lawyers. Being a lawyer has become just another job or career change alternative, because it is "interesting" and is a lucrative business. Becoming a trusted, respected professional who helps people with serious problems motivates fewer lawyers. More entrants into the legal marketplace are driven by unclear and uncertain goals at best, or pure greed at worst. No wonder lawyers are a favorite target of off-color humor.

SOCIETAL DISRESPECT
FOR RELIGIOUS ORGANIZATIONS

In the United States we have seen a diminishing lack of respect for the church and its clergy across the denominational board. Historically in American law, dating back to English roots, pastors and ministers were extended unique privileges of the highest regard. Such privileges were sometimes known as "benefit of clergy."

Initially, benefit of clergy referred to the exemption accorded to clergymen from the jurisdiction of the secular, governmental courts.

Later, the privilege became an exemption from punishment by death for the clergy. This was later expanded in scope to include all those who were connected with the church.[7]

Interestingly, as a means of testing one's clerical character, the person who claimed the privilege was given a psalm to read before the judge. Usually the Fifty-first Psalm was used. Upon merely reading the psalm correctly, the person was transferred from the secular courts to a church tribunal to be ecclesiastically adjudicated. In the late eighteenth century and the beginning of the nineteenth century in the United States, the specific benefit of clergy privilege saw its demise and ultimate abolishment in criminal law.

While the process may have been slow, we are at a point where almost no formal legal privileges nor unstated deferences are given to those in churches and religious pursuits. The United States has come full circle judicially, morally, ethically, and spiritually from a blind total confidence in the institutional church to the current trend of little or no regard for the church as being anything special or favored. It seems strange today to think that once in our American heritage a person could be released from secular court jurisdiction simply by reading the Fifty-first Psalm. Such was sufficient proof . of being a godly and spiritual person, thereby placing the defendant under the sole responsibility of the church for punishment.

Great trust in the institutional church to administer justice and resolve legal disputes was obvious. It is not anymore. In fact, we currently have organizations whose sole purpose is to urge Christians to work out their differences within the church or within the guidelines of Christian mediation and reconciliation instead of in the civil courts.

THE REFUSAL TO APOLOGIZE

Why have Americans, even Christians, become so comfortable with suing one another? The answer often suggested is money, or more precisely, *lots* of money. But money alone cannot explain the phenomenon of church members, even pastors, suing their churches and fellow parishioners in the public courts. Arbitration, mediation, and conciliation can all lead to substantial monetary settlements. So why such a readiness to go to the public courts? Can it be that society has become so impersonal that people are essentially unable to confront conflicts and face disputes with one another without the use of hired agents (lawyers)? Can it be that the corporate Christian experience is such that Christians cannot seek a remedy for wrongs done to them without bringing in a hired secular gun?

Noted Denver trial lawyer Joyce Seelen, who specializes in malpractice cases against psychologists and who in September 1991 won a $1.2 million jury verdict against the Episcopal Diocese of Colorado and Episcopal Bishop William Frey, is surprised at how *unwilling* the churches she has sued have been *to face up to the wrongs their staffs have committed and to apologize.* In an interview for this book, Seelen acknowledged that "lawyers (herself included) make so much money because people will not simply apologize."

In her representation of clients harmed by the professional negligence of psychologists and counselors, Seelen claims to have "never met a money-hungry victim." She says, "Most of these people sincerely believe they have been mistreated or neglected, and monetary compensation is not anywhere near the top of their list when they retain a lawyer." Nonfinancial goals are also very important. Seelen claims that the church defendants she has sued have been unusually unwilling to seek out a settlement or even interject a simple "We're sorry this happened to you" into the process.

The proliferation of church-related lawsuits is not isolated to the grounds of clergy malpractice. Instead we face a startling indictment of the institutional church that pronounces reconciliation among people as one of its chief aims for existence yet refuses simply to apologize when involved in wrongdoing. From her litigation experience with various churches, Seelen claims that "churches are far less willing to make attempts to mitigate their losses when a harm to others has occurred. Businesses, in comparison, seem much more able to affirmatively face up to difficult situations and take steps to minimize the ongoing harm caused by their people or their products."

If Seelen's observations are indicative, the church community must immediately alter its course and learn how to resolve conflicts that stem from allegations that the church was wrong. Christians must become more able, in the collective sense to say they are sorry. They must learn how to respond to an injured plaintiff in ways that acknowledge that person's hurt. Christian ministries must become creative in seeking ways to resolve the serious controversies facing them. If a sincere apology or gesture toward reconciliation would, to a large degree, salve the wounds of a potential litigant, Christian ministries should be the first to adopt such a posture.

While the American legal system appears to be the fairest of the world's systems, it is not automatically "fair." It may result in more justice than others, but that does not mean it *is* in itself just. The church must come to the point where it realizes that the American courtroom is the worst place to find itself resolving a dispute. Therefore, it makes sense that every effort should be made and every alternative explored to settle differences in other ways.

In any event, Christians in ministry must face the facts and learn how to conduct themselves in this relatively new cultural environment where the odds of being sued successfully are against them. The climate foretells that more minor skirmishes, if not out-and-out battles, are in the future. Not only is the secular atmosphere ready, society is producing more enthusiastic "warriors" who are apparently less concerned with the straight line than they are the bottom line. Christians must be ready, or more of us will be the subject of cartoons like this:

LEGAL STRATEGIES AND PRINCIPLES

◆ Ministries must be prepared to face lawsuits, because there's no end in sight for the record numbers of lawsuits nor in the glut of lawyers who must find work to sustain their higher and higher salaries.

◆ Law schools in the United States are receiving record numbers of applications for admission. More and more entrants into the legal marketplace are driven by unclear and uncertain personal goals. Ministries need to prepare now, as a further decline in legal ethics and professional standards will likely occur.

◆ Christian organizations and churches have also been an important contributing factor in the legal mess in which we find ourselves. We must become experts at resolving disputes out of court. Corporately we need to learn better how to say we are sorry and acknowledge people's hurt.

◆ Any reliance we may have on the American legal system to produce justice in an efficient manner is probably misplaced. Beginning immediately, our churches and ministries must implement creative policies and programs to avoid getting sued and to reach reconciliations as quickly as possible.

PART TWO

The Perilous Course
of the Legal Storm

CHAPTER THREE

The Storm System: Understanding Legal Origins

In the last few decades we have seen a dramatic shift in the nation's response to injuries suffered by people as a result of the actions of others. It is possible, I suppose, to envision a society in which one person could cause harm to another without consequences. But such an environment would cause more and more destructive behavior. While saving the administrative costs of a compensatory system as well as those of compensation itself, none of us would seriously advocate such anarchy in which harms could be inflicted, intentionally or carelessly, without the perpetrator paying for his or her conduct.

Generally, every society has some system to deter harmful, objectionable, and unacceptable behavior and actions. The American system attempts to order society by applying both *criminal* and *civil* consequences to actions it wishes to prevent.

CRIMINAL LAW

Criminal law is rooted in the belief that an intentional effort to cause harm to people and property or to otherwise intentionally seek to violate a legal mandate is essentially a *wrong against all members of the society*. Some actions are not specifically intentional but so patently careless as to closely approximate intended behavior. The state often views such careless actions and those people who show a total disre-

27

gard for consequences of their actions as "criminal" as well. Extreme negligence that causes serious harm to others or their property is often considered a "crime" against the people of that state.

Criminal acts, as defined in the various states across our country, are actions deemed harmful not only to the specific victim or victims involved, but against you and me as well. Let me illustrate. Most of us who drive have been issued a traffic ticket at one time or another. On my last one it stated, "The *People* of the State of Colorado vs. Carl Lansing." The state says going forty miles per hour in a thirty mile-per-hour zone is a criminal violation of the rights of all the people in the state of Colorado.

The more flagrant the criminal act the easier to understand why crimes not only require justice for the specific victim, but are accompanied by a strong sense of outrage in society as well. Daily murders, rapes, and beatings create strong emotional feelings for all of us. Such emotional resentment is the reason why serious crimes are handled differently in the United States (and all countries, for that matter).

CIVIL LAW

Now let's look at the other branch of the American judicial system, civil law. A private party civil lawsuit places its primary attention on the person who commits an inappropriate or undesirable act and the person or persons who suffer from that act. Like the criminal law system that uses punishment (fines and incarceration) to attempt to control behavior, civil law uses monetary compensation to try to regulate people's behavior. In addition to taking a look at the perpetrator's conduct, civil law in the United States has historically sought to provide compensation to the victim as an individual. Civil law, therefore, serves two purposes. It is both a tool of policymakers to create ways to alter the future conduct of people and a device to make victims whole again, to the extent that monetary compensation can restore such wholeness.

To understand the American civil legal system and be able to operate within it effectively, you need to know the two primary bodies of law and legal theory. One is contract law and the other is called "tort" law. The lion's share of the lawsuits we read about and should prepare ourselves for arise under one of these areas.

Most civil lawsuits are premised upon the argument that the

other person failed to perform (or in legal language, breached) a certain obligation (duty) owed to the person who brought the lawsuit. In other words, most civil suits require proof that the plaintiff who brought the lawsuit was harmed in some way as a result of the defendant doing something he should not have done or not doing something he should have done. The *should* is the duty element of every kind of civil lawsuit.

This duty can arise in two different fashions. These are the features that distinguish contract law from tort law. In contract law the duties of the parties have been agreed upon in the contract. Under tort law duties are imposed upon people implicitly as a result of their activities and the obligation not to harm others.

Contracts

Contracts are nothing more than promises flowing back and forth between two people or companies. These promises, once agreed upon, are the essential ingredients to every contract or agreement. They may be made in either written or verbal form (oral agreements are considered binding). Once these mutual promises are made and a bargain is struck, the failure of either side to do as promised gives grounds for a lawsuit for breach of contract. The most important point to learn is that the *should* (the promise) is the specific duty that every contract lawsuit alleges to have been breached.

In a breach of contract lawsuit, one does not claim that some overall, general societal obligation of care has been violated. Rather, the claim is that a specific promise agreed upon was not performed properly. So, if I contract (agree with you) specifically to paint your church bus using a brush, that is what you have bargained to receive. That is the duty I owe you, to paint your church bus with a brush. The fact that your bus turned out to look inferior when compared to those painted with a spray gun is not justification for you not to pay me. If I otherwise paint your church bus completely and properly, I have performed my *duty* to you, in that regard, by use of a brush.

Torts

In tort law things are much different. The duty owed—to do or to refrain from doing certain things—does not arise from promises made nor anything agreed upon between the parties. The duty found in tort law is imposed by society to treat one another and to act generally with due care and prudence. In other words, we all have an obligation (a duty) to act appropriately and carefully. We all have a basic duty to refrain from negligence or carelessness, because our actions may impact each other's rights and property. To harm someone or his property carelessly is a "tort."

This duty "to act carefully" is a nebulous notion. What is the careful thing to do, or refrain from doing, in a certain set of circumstances? This question can be the subject of greatly divergent opinions. Alter the circumstances just a little and what is considered the careful and prudent thing to do can change drastically. Since determining what level of care each of us owes to each other in certain instances can often be impossible to determine by any safe consensus, the law applies what is called the "average, reasonable man" standard. More concretely, to determine what type and level of care any particular person owes as a duty to any other person, the courts will attempt to answer the question, "What would the average, reasonable man or woman with the same or similar background and experience have done under the same set of circumstances?"

Now let's revisit the church bus painting example. Since we agreed I would paint your bus with a brush, no duty is breached by the mere fact that no professional bus painter would paint a bus with a brush. But let's assume we only discussed color and price. It never crossed our minds to consider "agreeing" upon the *method* of painting. All our contract contained were two elements: I promised to paint your church bus yellow, and you promised to pay me $1,000.

If I paint your bus yellow using a brush, you can claim that I did *not* perform my duty of care owed to you. When thoroughly disappointed with the appearance of your bus, you could defend against paying the price with evidence that no reasonable *person*, let alone a reasonable bus *painter*, would use a brush. If you can demonstrate that the reasonable standard of care for painting buses in your community is using a spray gun, you have a sound defense against paying the agreed-upon price. Furthermore, you would also have an affirmative tort case against me for negligence (breach of my duty of due care to you) and the resulting harm to your bus.

At this point we can see how our legal system has gone awry. If you are a typical plaintiff today, you will be asked by your lawyer whether you suffered any emotional distress, mental anguish, or severe loss of reputation arising from the fact that you could not afford to rent another bus and were compelled to drive this eyesore around town and endure the corresponding humiliation. Suddenly your lawyer is hinting at a possible six-figure case and you're shocked. Then you are tempted. If you're the "average, reasonable client," you will say in response, "How soon can we get the case filed?!"

UNKNOWN LEGAL RISKS

The subtle, yet important, differences between contract law and tort law claims should be evident. Contract duties are more clear-cut and easier to focus on in detail. On the other hand, the duties that can underlie negligence suits are often difficult to ascertain, and whether they were breached adds a slippery aspect to tort law. These two widespread unknowns give all people in ministry many sleepless nights. *What* am I supposed to do? *How* am I supposed to meet that obligation? These are the legal questions of our time.

Even contract law has presented serious problems in recent years, contributing to the uncertainties of the litigation avalanche. The courts have severely diluted the ability of two people to freely and knowingly enter into binding contracts. Serious problems develop when parties to contracts are not quite sure whether the other person is actually bound to what he promised. Such uncertainties create mistrust and premature protective actions, which in and of themselves often lead to broken agreements. These defensive breaches of contract can be avoided by the legal certainty that a deal is a deal. A contract in the United States has become in the minds of many an "option" to perform instead of a duty to perform. Obviously, many societal problems and controversies exist today because no one's word is worth much anymore, even in the eyes of the law.

But contract law disintegration still cannot hold a candle to the societal turmoil caused by the last three decades of upheaval in tort law. In this area, Christians in ministry must diligently learn what is transpiring and the changes that are rapidly occurring if they are to maximize legal protection for themselves and the work of the Kingdom. Knowing why the courts are now acting as they are is the first lesson in becoming legally shrewd.

LEGAL STRATEGIES AND PRINCIPLES

◆ Criminal violations are wrongs committed against all other members of society. Civil liabilities on the other hand are violations of the rights of a particular person, business, or organization. When a recognized obligation or duty is not performed, the person for whose benefit the duty existed can seek monetary legal compensation from the violator.

◆ The particular obligations and duties all of us owe to one another arise out of two basic bodies of American law. Voluntarily we create obligations and duties for ourselves each time we make an agreement with someone and exchange promises. These duties come under "contract law." Involuntarily we also have societal obligations that arise from our actions and circumstances. Society requires each of us to treat one another with appropriate care and prudence and thereby not cause harm to others. These duties are broadly called "tort law."

◆ Contract obligations are fairly easy to determine by reading the terms of what we signed. However, tort obligations—acting with due care—are difficult to determine and are always changing. What amount of carefulness toward others is enough? As our circumstances change from day to day, our duties will also change. This is the inherent slipperiness of tort law and the root of nearly all contemporary legal fears.

◆ The only solution for properly discerning tort law is a better understanding of *why* the courts are acting the way they are. Ministries must begin to see how our conduct and programs will be viewed through the eyes of a secular judge and jury. They will be the final litmus test of whether we acted with sufficient carefulness and thereby met our tort law obligations.

CHAPTER FOUR

Enterprise Liability Theory: Opening Deep Pockets

Through the end of the nineteenth century, contract law had always determined responsibility for injuries that arose from the workplace, commercial relationships, and the use of products and property. To determine whether a duty was owed from one to another, the courts had always looked first for some type of consensual or contractual relationship.

If any form of an agreement could be found, the elements of that agreement would govern the questions of whether someone was legally responsible to his fellow contracting party. If no such agreement could be found, many claims went without a remedy because no duty was evident. This often lead to certain harsh results by today's standards. If an injured worker could not prove that his employer had agreed to provide certain safety measures, it was held by the court that full responsibility for one's own safety in the workplace fell on the worker. Tort duties of care were not nearly as widespread as they are today.

But after the turn of the century, as the United States developed into the complex, industrialized society it is today, the rules began to change. Fewer and fewer workers could truly bargain with their bosses. Individuals could not deal face-to-face with the maker of a defective product, as small businesses were overrun by large, impersonal manufacturers. Purchasers of goods and services saw their strength in bargaining diminish. It began to make sense that the legal system needed revision. The idea of determining liability primarily on the questions of freely and fairly negotiated contractual relationships came under pressure. True inequities were developing and serious injuries were going without any recourse simply because a victim could not prove a contractual commitment from the defendant, either directly or indirectly.

Furthermore, victims commonly overcame the threshold of proving an agreement only to find that the party with whom he or she contracted did not have the financial resources to provide meaningful compensation. Insolvent businesses left victimized people out in the cold. Too many empty pockets motivated judges and legal scholars to move toward new legal principles that would help injured victims find a "deep pocket" more able to restore them to where they were before the harm occurred.

ENTERPRISE LIABILITY TAKES ROOT

According to the *American Law Institute*, "The foremost culprit for today's litigation crisis is the 'Enterprise Liability' theory of tort law that took root in the fifties. It is commonly believed to have been *the major influence* in the expansion of tort liability from the mid-sixties onward"[1] (emphasis added).

An understanding of this fundamental concept is essential for every Christian organization that hopes to function into the twenty-first century. While the pendulum may be swinging back to balance the abuses of this theory, it may take a decade or more to appreciably correct America's passion for litigation.

The experts in legal public policy concur. In addressing the effects of the much heralded "tort reform" that swept the country a few years ago, the *American Law Institute* put it this way, "It is interesting to observe that none of the tort reform legislation of the eighties overturned any of the major judicial innovations in substantive liability standards . . . , state legislatures have only whittled away at the margins of these doctrines of enterprise liability and related concepts."[2] While so-called reforms were cheered on many fronts, they left untouched the root causes. The result is a lot of fluff with no real weight.

Essentially, the enterprise liability theory seeks to intentionally and directly spread the cost and expense of injuries across entire industries or enterprises. By spreading the expense caused by a small number of perpetrators over an entire industry, this legal theory reaches its goal of finding a true remedy for every wrong. Relatively small numbers of careless or intentionally harmful people in various commercial activities have raised the price of products and services throughout their particular industries as a result of this thirty-year-old public policy.

THE CHANGING ASSUMPTION OF RISK

The courts have expanded the scope of every person's particular tort duties so much that all forms of liability insurance are now a common need, regardless of price. According to the American Law Institute, "Judges who believed that risk distribution was desirable, were inclined to use litigation over serious injuries to expand the reach of tort liability to fill the insurance gaps."[3]

More specifically, several time-honored legal defenses to tort liability went by the wayside during the last few decades. The concepts of "contributory negligence" and "assumption of the risk" were either eliminated or severely restricted. The departure of these two concepts from the legal arena is the underlying reason the public is so disenchanted with the system. Let's take a closer look.

Total Personal Responsibility: Contributory Negligence

For centuries contributory negligence was a most effective defense to claims of carelessness and enjoyed a long history in both English and American jurisprudence. It barred injured plaintiffs from recovering compensation from others if the plaintiffs themselves had, even in part, been responsible for their injuries. In other words, one person suing another based on allegations of negligence had to be free from negligence himself. This was personal responsibility at its highest level.

Let's look at another simple example. Let's assume you and I had a typical, garden-variety car accident. I was carelessly looking over my shoulder toward the rear, and you were daydreaming about your upcoming vacation and not paying attention. Each of us "contributed" to our own injuries and to the damages suffered by our respective cars. With the old doctrine of contributory negligence in force, neither of us would have had grounds for a negligence suit against the other. Even if you could demonstrate that you contributed only 1 percent of the combined negligence that resulted in the bump on your head and I was responsible for the other 99 percent, you still would have no case against me. When viewed through the eyes of percentages in this way, it seems like an unfair principle. Most people today would agree.

Contributory negligence has been replaced by what is termed "comparative negligence" theories that apportion monetary damages along with percentages of negligence. Remember that the overarching goal of the enterprise liability theory is to find a remedy for every wrong. Thereby, through insurance, personal monetary losses are spread out over a large number of policyholders so that a few do not bear the full brunt of an unintended harm. (It is pertinent to note that it is typically not possible to buy liability insurance to insure one's own *intentional* acts of harm.)

Juries are now required to somehow determine the respective (comparative) percentages of negligence for which you and I are accountable and then award damages accordingly. So, if a jury decides the bump on your head is worth $100,000 in damages and I was 99 percent negligent in the cause of the collision, it would award you $99,000 in damages.

If you think this apportionment of percentages of people's negligence is in any way clear-cut, consider the following civil jury instruction from Colorado for use in applying a multi-defendant comparative negligence standard:

> If you find the plaintiff was damaged and that the plaintiff's damages were caused by the negligence of the plaintiff and one or more of the defendants, then you must determine to what extent the negligent conduct of each contributed to the damages of the plaintiff, expressed as a percentage of 100 percent.
>
> If you find that the plaintiff and one or more of the defendants were negligent and that the negligence of the plaintiff was equal to or greater than the combined negligence of all the

defendants, then the plaintiff will not be allowed to recover.

If you find that the plaintiff and one or more of the defendants were negligent and that the negligence of any one defendant or the combined negligence of more than one of the defendants was greater than the negligence of the plaintiff, then the plaintiff will be allowed to recover as against each of the defendants found negligent.

Also, as against any individual defendant whose percentage of negligence is equal to or less than that of the plaintiff, the plaintiff will be allowed to recover only that percentage of his damages that is represented by the percentage of that defendant's negligence.[4]

The 99-percent-versus-1-percent situation might be an easy one for a jury to handle. When the carelessness of one person is so extreme, the process has a chance at justice. But normally the division is a much closer call. It would be a rather unusual case that went all the way to trial and landed in the hands of a jury if, in fact, either side had been 90, 95, or 99 percent at fault. Usually an early settlement is reached when one side's carelessness far outweighs the other. It's the much closer calls that tend to end up in jury deliberations. Is it sixty–forty, or maybe fifty-five–forty-five?

The close calls draw into question the wisdom of adopting comparative negligence apportionments and the elimination of total personal responsibility. If you and I are *both* significantly negligent in not keeping a proper outlook in our driving, is it really so inequitable for the law to completely bar any monetary recovery for someone who truly contributed to her own predicament? With the old clear-cut rule in operation, I suspect people exercised more care and prudence in their affairs. A far less negligent world seems to have been the result. And in turn, careful people having nothing to do with the situation, apart from being in the same industry class or a policyholder with the same insurance company, did not share in the expenses caused by the careless few.

Taking Your Own Chances: Assumption of the Risk
The defense of "assumption of the risk" was the other time-honored doctrine that preserved each person's individual legal

responsibility. Defendants could defend against claims of negligence by simply demonstrating that the plaintiff suing them had freely and knowingly assumed all the risks of injury that might result from the activity in which the plaintiff had engaged. It was considered just and sensible to prevent someone from suing for injuries that he incurred from an activity that presented obvious risks of harm. The person chose to go forward in spite of the potential harm, thereby taking the personal risk to face the consequences of what might ultimately occur.

The concept of individual autonomy has also been subsumed into the prevailing comparative negligence theory. Activities that presented inherent and obvious dangers formerly came with the warning to "proceed at your own risk." This can no longer be said in many areas of the law. The ball never crosses into the other person's court. It is next to impossible due to the pervasive effects of enterprise liability thinking to put the risk of harm with the risk taker. There are two primary points at issue in these cases. The first question is whether you or your organization benefits in any way from the activity that presents risk to others. Second, even without a direct or indirect benefit, if you permit a *dangerous* activity to occur that you have the power to prevent, it is no longer an absolute defense that the other side chose to take the risk for its own personal benefit.

Individual Waivers of Liability

Last, another significant area of diminished personal responsibilities under the umbrella of enterprise liability is the strict scrutiny placed on *individual waivers of liability*. Even though a person signs a release of liability to another, most courts have found any number of ways to obviate their effect.

While most lawyers still highly recommend the use of waivers by property owners and operators of public activities, we also know that very little reliance can be placed on these waivers as a means of legal protection. The strength of the individual's word and commitment is no longer respected when he signs a waiver releasing, for example, his church-sponsored little league team from liability in exchange for his son's opportunity to participate in summer baseball. The courts are most reluctant to allow an intelligent person to freely and openly agree to look only to his own resources or the insurance he may already personally have rather than sue the church for an injury. In other words, the courts say they know better than everyone how to allocate losses due to unfortunate accidents.

Somehow the binding effects of personal commitments are shuffled to the side when the judicial system must make the hard call and force the seriously injured individual to live with the consequences of his or her earlier decision. The courts have found it easy since the fifties to rationalize how the big church, the big business, or the big insurance company is in the better position to juggle the financial burdens of a serious injury. It can be passed on to a large group, so *no one person suffers a lot, while many suffer a little*.

THE HOUSE OF CARDS COLLAPSES

As the crowning glory for enterprise liability theorists, the American liability insurance industry suffered such serious doses of "juggling" in the eighties that an enormous financial crisis confronted the nation. Insurance companies began declaring bankruptcy left and right. Many stopped selling insurance products, and some *enterprises* faced the unforeseen problem of possibly not being able to buy liability insurance from any source.

With a vast increase in the numbers of lawsuits to settle, expensive law firms to pay for their defense, and large monetary awards granted by juries, insurance companies began to crumble under the weight. Between 1969 and 1985, 125 property and casualty insurance companies nationwide were *liquidated*. The remaining *solvent* insurance companies were assessed $872 million under new insurance licensing regulations for claims of policyholders of the bankrupt companies. In 1986 seventeen more national insurance companies failed, with total assessments to the balance of the industry of $533 million. In 1987 eleven more went broke, including one large insurance group that alone ultimately accounted for almost $1 billion in assessment to the balance of the industry.[5]

Lest we believe the much publicized national effort to reform the tort laws in our states (called "the tort reform movement") in the mid-1980s had much immediate effect, the insurance industry saw more of the same in 1988 and 1989. In 1988 seventeen more insolvencies of insurance companies occurred, with twenty-three more going broke in 1989. According to one expert, sixty-eight insurance company failures occurred from 1986 to 1989, relegating approximately $1.5 billion in assessments to the so-called solvent remaining organizations.[6]

For three years in the mid-1980s, general liability premiums increased from $6.5 billion to more than $19 billion. Medical malpractice premiums soared from $2 billion to more than $5 billion.[7] As insurance costs skyrocketed, more businesses, professionals, and organizations either could not afford enough insurance or any insurance at all. A common response to double and triple liability insurance rates is for the purchaser to buy less coverage in order to keep the premium level constant and within budgets. The staggering increase in premium rates during this period does not necessarily mean that the dollar amounts of coverage remained constant. More likely, the public paid more for less. Enterprise liability expanded legal remedies to such a broad group that it backfired and caused a smaller insurance pool for those who were truly injured to access.

VICARIOUS LIABILITY

To make enterprise liability theories actually work, judges must find more ways to impose liability, vicariously, on other people or entities. This occurs in instances where the person or organization that directly caused the harmful act is *not* in a financial position to adequately compensate the injured victim.

If all active people in our society were millionaires or carried million-dollar liability insurance policies, enterprise liability theorists would have had no reason to expand the scope of potential defendants beyond those *directly* causing harm. But most people and small businesses do not have such substantial net worths or high limits of insurance coverage. Therefore, those committed to finding a real financial remedy for every wrong became highly motivated to expand the group of possible defendants until deep enough pockets *do* become available to compensate victims.

To make other people and entities available to answer for injuries caused by others, the courts began to expand the concept of vicarious liability. Judges impose vicarious liability most often on one person for the acts of another who is under the person's "direction and control." We again see the idea of people not being fully and completely responsible for their own acts. The focus of a lawsuit against a careless delivery driver who causes a collision is minimized by the court's attempt to attach vicarious liability on the deep-pockets employer under whose direction and control the delivery was made.

I'm quite certain there has never been an employer who "directed" her drivers to operate their vehicles recklessly and with disregard for the rights of others. To the contrary, in nearly all cases, an employer directs employees to act carefully and responsibly. But ultimately no employed person could be considered truly under the employer's direction and control. To hire and fire is the only real control an employer has.

But the law has made the employer "vicariously" liable for the negligent acts of employees while on the job. The articulated reason is that the employee is under the employer's direction and control, and the employer receives the benefit of the employee's delivery services—with the benefits should come the burdens.

It sounds superficially logical, but anyone who has ever employed or supervised people knows them to be independent, free agents who act as they please for the most part. In all honesty, one must admit that an employer neither directs nor controls a delivery driver who chooses, against company policy, to have a couple of beers at lunch and, in his tipsy state, later causes a serious accident. Since it is unlikely the employee has the assets to compensate his victim for medical bills, lost earnings, and so forth, a wrong could go unremedied unless the law finds a way to make the employer indirectly liable.

Enterprise liability has therefore expanded the ease with which an injured victim can successfully sue others not directly involved. Such suits are based on some relationship that gives rise to a loose application of the "direction and control" analysis. Typically, these vicarious liability rules are applied to the relationships of employer and employee and the broader category of principal and agent.

MINISTRIES AT RISK

Every church, parachurch organization, and other Christian ministry employs personnel that regularly, or at least occasionally, make deliveries as in the previous hypothetical case. Therefore, they are at risk of vicarious liability for any motor vehicle accidents that occur while the delivery person is on the job. This is true whether the personnel are paid staff members or volunteers. Level of pay is insignificant. That seems simple enough for most churches and missions to manage. Unfortunately, vicarious liability does not stop there. Let's take a look at an even more threatening expansion of the use of this doctrine against an organization.

The Samaritan Counseling Center in Alaska employed a counselor, Pastor John Garvin, who, it was claimed, entered into sexual contact and ultimately sexual intercourse with one of his female clients. She sued the church-based counseling center for "substantial emotional and psychological damage" resulting from the pastor's conduct and his negligent handling of the phenomenon of transference (see chapter 19) that had developed during counseling. The Samaritan Counseling Center is probably typical of many similar centers around the country in that it combined counseling "with the traditional healing practices of the church."[8]

The center and its board defended on the basis that the pastor's sexual contacts with this woman were:

1. Outside the scope of the pastor's employment at the center.
2. Not motivated by a desire to serve his employer, the center.
3. Not occurring within work hours nor on the premises of the employer center.
4. Not authorized nor sanctioned by the employer center.

This sounds like a good attack on the underlying principles of "direction and control" that provide the foundation for employer vicarious liability. As a result, prior to trial the judge dismissed the case, agreeing with the center's position that it would be inequitable to hold it responsible for Pastor Garvin's alleged sexual conduct under these circumstances.

The Supreme Court of Alaska disagreed on April 27, 1990. Alaska's highest court reversed the lower court and ordered that the case proceed toward trial. In making this decision, the court stated:

The basis of [employer vicarious liability] has been correctly stated as "the desire to include in the costs of operation inevitable losses to third persons incident to carrying on an enterprise, and thus distribute the burden among those benefitted by the enterprise." Employees' acts sufficiently connected with the enterprise are in effect considered as deeds of the enterprise itself. Where through negligence such acts cause injury to others it is appropriate that the enterprise bear the loss incurred.[9]

Amazingly, the court found that liability could attach to the center in spite of the court's own qualifiers in the language above. How can it be that sexual intercourse of a pastor with his client is "inevitable," "incident to" or "sufficiently connected" to a church-based counseling ministry? This recent decision of such a distin-guished court demonstrates vividly how the desire to find a deep pocket through the enterprise liability doctrine remains alive and well and does not respect organizational missions.

Enterprise liability does not resist attacking nonprofit, chari-table, or religious "enterprises." Deliberate precautionary measures must be utilized in Christian organizations and churches to max-imize protection against the expansion of the enterprise liability theory. Now that we have seen the basis for the onslaught of legal uncertainties and the growing use of lawsuits in social engineering by judges and lawmakers, we will take a look in the next section at how Christians have not kept pace with these far-sweeping cultural changes in the United States.

LEGAL STRATEGIES AND PRINCIPLES

◆ "Enterprise Liability Theory" is a key culprit for America's current litigation crisis. The policy decision of the courts to spread the cost of tort injuries across entire industries has caused many careful people to pay for the wrongs caused by a small number of negligent individuals.

◆ The risk of bearing the consequences of one's own

careless conduct has been intentionally shifted from the individual to the enterprises he or she comes into contact with in life. Personal responsibility has given way to industry responsibility.

◆ As an enterprise, every church and organized ministry has become a potential target as a "deep pocket" of financial resources from which individual harms can find monetary solace.

◆ As a "deep pocket," our churches and ministries will be held vicariously liable for every action of our volunteers and staff that is deemed insufficient in meeting the applicable standard of care determined by the judge and jury in court.

CHAPTER FIVE

The Christian Response Thus Far: In the World But Not of It

It is at least possible that the Christian community is choosing to emphasize one set of truths about the Christian life to the exclusion of equally important truths simply because the differences are difficult to synthesize or reconcile. The Scriptures command Christians to be as little children. They are to be like sheep, meek and mild. They are to turn the other cheek, to be forgiving. They are to be peacemakers, patient, kind, gentle, and long-suffering. Foremost, they are to love their neighbor, and this "love" is defined in 1 Corinthians 13 as being courteous, not self-seeking, not easily angered, and keeping no record of wrongs. Love always trusts, always hopes, and always perseveres.

Obviously, these commandments and truths about God and the Christian gospel are not readily compatible with the day-to-day workings of the American legal system and particularly not with the world of civil lawsuits. The American legal scene has become a very tough, hard, aggressive, unforgiving, argumentative, combative, self-serving place to find oneself.

Many Christians, therefore, have drawn the conclusion that legal matters are not the kinds of issues with which people of faith should be concerning themselves. To become sophisticated in legal affairs might tie one too closely to "the world." After all, Christians are to be "in the world but not of it."

We will next take a look at some of the more pertinent scriptural principles that govern how Christians are to conduct themselves in legal affairs. In the next chapter I will focus on a couple of actual headline-making lawsuits that will allow us to see up close the components of a killer lawsuit.

SHOULD CHRISTIANS SUE?

Scripture makes it perfectly clear that Christians are not to sue each other in any form of lawsuit. The Apostle Paul admonishes believers against starting a civil lawsuit to resolve a dispute:

> If any of you has a dispute with another, dare he take it before the ungodly for judgment instead of before the saints? Do you not know that the saints will judge the world? And if you are to judge the world, are you not competent to judge trivial cases? Do you not know that we will judge angels? How much more the things of this life! Therefore, if you have disputes about such matters, appoint as judges even men of little account in the church! I say this to shame you. Is it possible that there is nobody among you wise enough to judge a dispute between believers? But instead, one brother goes to law against another—and this in front of unbelievers! (1 Corinthians 6:1-6)

Many who claim the Christian faith take no heed to these abundantly clear and forceful words from Paul. We have already seen that even ministers, let alone the common believer, can rationalize their way into retaining a lawyer and walking boldly through the front door of the courthouse.

It seems clear that if Christians follow scriptural mandates, they are never to be on the offensive in legal disputes among believers. In other words, don't start a fight with other believers that nonbelievers will referee. But what about defending yourself in court or before a lawsuit is started? Can you put up a vigorous defense if hailed before the "pagan" judges? Are you required to confess judgment, to admit liability, where justice and equity seem to urge you to put up a fight?

Here, too, we find some scriptures that seem to indicate that

Christians are not to defend themselves. For example, in 1 Corinthians 6, Paul goes on to imply that it may be better to suffer an injustice than to allow nonbelievers to judge matters among believers:

> The very fact that you have lawsuits among you means you have been completely defeated already. Why not rather be wronged? Why not rather be cheated? (verse 7)

Jesus Himself could be cited convincingly for the premise that Christians should not defend lawsuits. Christ's own stunning refusal to defend Himself against His accusers is itself the best argument for Christians to be passive when sued. (A word of caution should be given to anyone considering legal passivity as a course of action. All insurance policies require the insured to cooperate with, and participate in, the defense of any litigation as a prerequisite to insurance benefits being payable. Therefore, any conduct or statements contrary to such insurance requirements may be grounds for the insurance carrier to deny coverage. As a result, you may be faced with paying a civil judgment without benefit of insurance.) But Jesus also expressed the Father's will on this issue of whether Christians should defend themselves in civil courts. In the Sermon on the Mount, He stated:

> "You have heard that it was said, 'Eye for eye, and tooth for tooth.' But I tell you, Do not resist an evil person. If someone strikes you on the right cheek, turn to him the other also. *And if someone wants to sue you and take your tunic, let him have your cloak as well.*" (Matthew 5:38-40, emphasis added)

While these particular scriptures and others raise serious questions as to whether Christians should even defend themselves in civil lawsuits, let alone ever start one, my purpose in this book is to help Christians in churches and ministries who desire to stay out of court altogether. I'll leave the biblical interpretations and theological questions for those better trained in such matters than I am. Nonetheless, it can be said that preventive legal measures that keep Christians out of court are not prohibited anywhere in the Scriptures. Christians can always watch out for legal trouble and take appropriate steps to avoid danger. Many Christians have taken these scriptures too far and erroneously equated legal awareness and preventive measures as somehow becoming tainted by the world's system.

Mules can be useful creatures when one learns how they work best and what causes them to be productive as opposed to stubborn. But learning where not to stand near a mule can save you from being kicked and suffering the painful consequences. The American legal system is, in many ways, now an unchosen partner in Christian ministries, and our ministries need to learn how to use the system's strengths to accomplish ministry goals. We also need to become aware of how to avoid being kicked.

BE YE SHREWD!

Is it permitted or even required to use every proper means to protect yourself and your church and ministry from legal problems and challenges that may be lurking down the road? I think the use of appropriate protections in the law and being sophisticated in this aspect of both religious and secular life is not only permitted but is commanded. But we enter the world of paradoxes.

Can Christians be sophisticated and savvy in worldly business and legal affairs? Won't developing a legal "toughness," so to speak, be contrary to the striving to be meek, mild, and long-suffering? This is not the first place that two seemingly opposite qualities must coexist in the Christian life. Let's look at a couple of God's exhortations that compel Christians and their institutions to become more adept at operating "in the world" of the 1990s.

In His instructions when sending out the twelve apostles in Matthew 10, Jesus specifically cautioned the apostles:

> "I am sending you out like sheep among wolves. Therefore *be as shrewd as snakes* and as innocent as doves. Be on your guard against men." (verses 16-17, emphasis added)

In this passage, Jesus Himself interjects what on the surface is the troubling command, "Be as shrewd as snakes"! Upon reflection, this phrase may bring to mind untypical images. Culturally, snakes are associated with being sly, slippery, cunning, and even cold-blooded.

Satan himself is the "serpent" in the garden. No wonder the command to be like snakes troubles many Christians and results in confusion. The confusion then leads to inaction, which is why so many Christians and Christian organizations are currently vulnerable to attack.

The secular legal community is becoming well aware of this vulnerability and has effectively declared "open season" on churches and religious organizations. The legal community is even promoting national legal education seminars, which are useful in learning how to more effectively sue churches.[1] To survive the onslaught, Christians must become shrewd as snakes.

The use of the term *shrewdness* is nearly as awkward for Christians as the snake metaphor. In modern conversational use, people normally associate "shrewd" with shady and underhanded business practices. *Webster's 9th New Collegiate Dictionary* defines "shrewd" as "marked by clever discerning, awareness and hard-headed acumen; given to wily and artful ways of dealing; stresses practical judgment."

Christ may have intended for us to experience the very reaction we have as we try to associate shrewdness and snake-like behavior with sacrificial love. In his commentary on Matthew 10:16, D. A. Carson states, "Jesus pictured his disciples in a dangerous place, defenseless in themselves." Sound like us today? Carson goes on, "In several ancient Near Eastern cultures, serpents were proverbial for 'prudence.' But prudence can easily degenerate into cheap cunning unless it goes with simplicity. They must prove not only 'shrewd' but 'akeraioi' (innocent). Yet innocence becomes ignorance, even naiveté, unless combined with prudence."[2]

Is this scriptural reference a one-of-a-kind item that could be minimized for its singular existence? I don't think so, because we can find both a parable that exalts "shrewdness" and a psalm where being shrewd is an attribute of God the Father. In Psalm 18:25-26 (also 2 Samuel 22:26-27), David sang to the Lord in praise:

> To the faithful you show yourself faithful,
> > to the blameless you show yourself blameless,
> to the pure you show yourself pure,
> > *but to the crooked you show yourself shrewd.*
> > (emphasis added)

God the Father, when dealing with the world, reveals Himself as a "shrewd" God—or, in Webster's terminology, a clever, discerning, aware, wily, hard-headed, and artful God. To you it may seem unusual to refer to Christians, let alone God Himself, with such qualities, yet as a lawyer I now strongly sense that there is a dimension of this "shrewdness" that Christians often ignore in their daily business dealings. As we approach this current period of lawsuit mania, it is critical that we draw upon that shrewdness, just as Jesus commanded.

The Shrewd Manager

Let's look at one of Christ's parables that is among the few in which His message seems to run directly counter to the universally accepted aspects of the gospel of love. I'm referring to what the *New International Version* calls "The Parable of the Shrewd Manager." In Luke 16:1-9, Jesus told His disciples:

> "There was a rich man whose manager was accused of wasting his possessions. So he called him in and asked him, 'What is this I hear about you? Give an account of your management, because you cannot be manager any longer.'
>
> "The manager said to himself, 'What shall I do now? My master is taking away my job. I'm not strong enough to dig, and I'm ashamed to beg—I know what I'll do so that, when I lose my job here, people will welcome me into their houses.'
>
> "So he called in each one of his master's debtors. He asked the first, 'How much do you owe my master?'
>
> "'Eight hundred gallons of olive oil,' he replied.
>
> "The manager told him, 'Take your bill, sit down quickly, and make it four hundred.'
>
> "Then he asked the second, 'And how much do you owe?'
>
> "'A thousand bushels of wheat,' he replied.
>
> "He told him, 'Take your bill and make it eight hundred.'
>
> "*The master commended the dishonest manager because he had acted shrewdly. For the people of this world are more shrewd in dealing with their own kind than are the people of the light.* I tell you, use worldly wealth to gain friends for

yourselves, so that when it is gone, you will be welcomed into eternal dwellings." (emphasis added)

Obviously, the manager acted with deceit and against the interests of the master to whom he owed a duty of loyalty. In fact, the text even refers to the steward as being "dishonest." Jesus does not use this story to commend graft but to encourage the prudent use of material wealth. The *Expositor's Bible Commentary* sums up the passage by saying, "Christians do not belong to this evil age, but they can nevertheless make responsible use of worldly wealth."[3] Another commentary agrees that the steward's fraud is not Christ's focus, but rather the manager's resourcefulness:

He (the Master) did not praise his (the steward's) unjust and fraudulent act as such, but the "worldly wisdom" with which he acted towards the debtors. It was His object to use the parable to call attention to the "wise" and diplomatic manner in which worldlings generally act towards their fellow-men in order to achieve their own selfish aims.[4]

It is also widely accepted in theological circles that Christ was not telling His disciples that "the end justifies the means." The parable praises and highlights the steward's *skill*, not the product of that skill's exercise, which in this instance was used for wrong. But something else still nags at us as we more closely consider the highlighted skill.

The adverb form of *shrewd* used in Luke 16:8 is the Greek word *phronimos*. While the adjective form of phronimos is used numerous times in the gospels, the adverb form of *phronimos* occurs only in this parable in Luke. The *New International Dictionary of New Testament Theology* notes, "Both forms as used in the Gospels are confined to parables or figurative language and refer to that wise, judicious behavior which should characterize those in the kingdom of God. The Old Testament idea of wisdom is involved, not just ordinary common sense."[5]

Consider these challenging thoughts of Fred Craddock, professor of preaching and New Testament at Emory University's Chandler School of Theology:

Many Christians have been offended by this parable (Luke 16:1-8), and on two grounds. First, some find it a bit disturbing that Jesus would find anything commendable in a person who has acted dishonestly. . . . The second and related offense in this parable is the use of words such as "shrewd" and "clever" to describe people of the kingdom ("children of light"). The words have so commonly been associated with self-serving behavior, if not ethically questionable behavior, that it is difficult to speak of a "shrewd saint." Of course, part of the problem lies in the anticerebral bias in the church and the unwillingness, if not inability, of many to conceive of thinking as a kingdom activity. Apparently, to be childlike is taken to mean naive, even though Jesus is said, according to Matthew 10:16, to have alerted his disciples to be "wise as serpents and innocent as doves."[6]

Craddock, in a somewhat critical way, hits the nail on the head concerning the customary response of Christians and Christian organizations to the myriad of legal pitfalls, complexities, and dangers that modern American society presents. Mere child- or dove-like innocence is not enough to fulfill all of the commandment to "be as shrewd as snakes and as innocent as doves." Christians must face the unpleasant legal issues confronting ministries with a clever, discerning awareness and with hard-headed acumen and wily, artful ways of dealing. I didn't say it, Jesus did.

NAIVETÉ IS THE NORM

My first ten years in private law practice were entirely in the secular world of business clients. Other than helping someone in Christian ministry with an occasional speeding ticket or preparation of a routine will for a couple who recently had a baby, my practice focused entirely on nonChristian business clients. Small, medium, and large corporations provided my livelihood, as they do today. Though I had not planned it that way, I earned close to zero legal fees from churches, parachurch ministries, or individual pastors or managers in Christian organizations during my first decade as a lawyer.

My primary area of emphasis was as a general corporate and

business adviser to companies with small groups of individual owners. The legal and business communities call businesses like these "closely held" companies because ownership and control are contained within a small group of people. My secondary involvement as a lawyer was in commercial litigation, namely bringing and defending lawsuits involving my business clients. Needless to say, in ten years I was exposed to a broad variety of approaches to business and legal issues through many types of clients.

Approximately four years ago I was retained, rather out of the blue, to defend two prominent Christian leaders in an unusual lawsuit in my hometown of Denver. As the practice of law sometimes goes, that case led to another similar case and other assorted advisory projects with several Christian ministries. These new clients have given me quite an eye-opener into the types of naiveté that D. A. Carson referred to in his quote mentioned earlier in this chapter: "Yet innocence becomes ignorance, even naiveté, unless combined with prudence [shrewdness]."

At first, I was surprised at my fellow Christians' naive approach to legal matters. While quite astute at nearly every other executive management skill, some lacked even the most basic understanding of legal issues. The contrast between a typical businessperson and a typical staff person or leader in ministry can be rather dramatic. Not surprisingly, the men and women involved in secular business pursuits tend to be more pragmatic, bottom line, and results oriented. They normally have little interest in pursuing legal negotiations or battles that have low probabilities of a successful financial outcome.

Many Christian ministry leaders, on the other hand, find settlement a very difficult concept to discuss meaningfully. They operate in a world in which moral principles mean everything, and rightly so. They will ask, "How could we possibly settle for one-half, when we are 100 percent in the right?"

Christians must learn that valuable financial resources, time, and personal energy are wasted when they spend enormous amounts of effort and legal fees pursuing relatively insignificant points of principle. As most of the real-world cases in this book demonstrate, Christians are defending every day against clear losers and unimportant challenges to unimportant principles.

Secular brethren would have long before negotiated a reasonable middle ground and gone back to business. Like them, Christians need to begin to prudently minimize the number of and time spent on legal challenges. Only then will they maximize their time, energy, and resources in ministry. Becoming skilled at knowing when and how to mitigate losses is an important part of being shrewd.

Not all of what we see happening among Christians and their churches is the product of legal and business naiveté. Instead, a certain amount of the cause can be attributed to two other fundamental characteristics: (1) a misplaced reliance on the true strength of the constitutional protections of "freedom of religion," and (2) a conscious lack of commitment to being shrewd in business strategy and legal understanding on the part of Christian leadership. Let's look at these two problems in more depth.

THE LIMITS OF FREEDOM OF RELIGION

Christians make an erroneous assumption when they think that since they are involved in church or other spiritual activities the constitutional guarantee of religious freedom protects them sufficiently in all that they do. While "freedom of religion" may have been a barrier to many legal exposures in the past, Christians have little to lean on anymore as American society heads toward the twenty-first century. An obvious direct protection comes from the First Amendment to the Constitution of the United States: "Congress shall make no law respecting an establishment of religion, *or prohibiting the free exercise thereof*" (emphasis added). Similarly, all of the fifty states have articles in their constitutions protecting the free exercise of our religious beliefs.

The less obvious, and sometimes subtle, unwritten protections to legal attacks came in the traditions of trust our society dearly held. These traditions began to erode in the sixties when no sacred cows went untouched. For nearly two centuries, American traditions taught people to respect and trust those in professional endeavors, including public service, medicine, law, and religion. By and large, politicians, doctors, lawyers, and ministers were part of a class protected by unwritten rules of tradition. Until recently, it would have been socially unthinkable to sue the family doctor or lawyer.

Likewise, suing a church or pastor was socially unacceptable. To sue your minister was tantamount to suing your mother or father. The social consequences were too severe. Thus, American heritage created a safety zone around churches and others in Christian ministry. However, we now live in an age in which children sue their parents for such things as "negligent parenting." Cultural impediments have all but disintegrated, and now we see a rapid erosion of the fine line of religious constitutional protections.

RELIGIOUS FAITH AND DOCTRINE

Generally speaking, constitutional safeguards have been interpreted to exist primarily in the areas of religious faith and doctrine. It is well established that civil courts may not interfere in matters of religious beliefs and practices. On the other hand, the courts can intervene in secular matters, even those involving a religious institution.

In a recent case, a professor brought suit against the seminary where he taught that is affiliated with the Reformed Church in America.[7] The school failed to grant him tenure that he contended was to take place under an agreement with the seminary's former president. An appeals court in New Jersey carefully noted that the case did involve issues of religious "customs" and religious church "practices," which are off limits under constitutionally protected freedom of religion. Yet in spite of the recognized fact that practices and customs of religion had a lot to do with tenure at a seminary, the New Jersey court ruled on the case in favor of the teacher.

Generally, churches and other religious organizations are left free from governmental entanglements in their religious customs, beliefs, and practices so long as a more important, overriding constitutional right of another person is not being violated. It's important to mention that constitutional protections such as life and liberty, in theory at least, take precedence over religious freedom. Many far less obvious constitutional protections also have been held to take priority. But in activities deemed primarily secular, protection under freedom of religion cannot be found.

The intervention of civil law into the "purely secular service" by a church employee is typified by an employment dispute concerning the church janitor. There is no religious freedom upon which to rely. Courts have held consistently that there is no religious freedom protection when the employee's job description possesses no duties even remotely related to religious beliefs or responsibilities.[8] In other words, there is no Methodist versus Presbyterian versus Baptist way to vacuum the carpet or mow the lawn. Faith and doctrine are irrelevant in these cases, so secular law applies.

Every church and other religious employer needs to use caution when hiring, promoting, and firing anyone in the organization whose job requirements would be considered purely secular in nature. While it is quite appropriate to quiz a prospective Christian education director concerning his or her theology, the same would not be true of the groundskeeper or shuttle bus driver in most instances. Seeking timely, competent legal advice in these "secular" areas is a must. A good rule of thumb to determine whether you are outside any scope of religious protection is to consider whether the job, activity, or pursuit is one also found in the secular world. Janitors are also employed in businesses. Little League umpires are also found in secular youth leagues. Ministers per se are only found in churches and parachurch organizations.

Selling Christmas trees to raise money for the church is also an activity done by secular groups. Offering psychological counseling in a church counseling center, in the sense that it is psychological versus spiritual in nature, is also an endeavor found in nonreligious groups. Christians can expect very limited protection from doctrines of constitutional religious freedom to the extent that they involve themselves in traditionally secular pursuits.

CHRISTIAN DISINTEREST

The second characteristic I have detected among certain Christians in churches and other ministries is a deep-seated lack of commitment to excellence in business and legal matters. This is really not surprising in that the values and interests of the typical person drawn to full-time Christian ministry are quite different from those that motivate the typical business manager, accountant, lawyer, or entrepreneur.

The common person in many church ministries would likely score high on personality tests in the areas of empathy, caring, and service, whereas business decisionmakers more often score well in areas of organization, analysis, and objectivity. Many ministry people do what they do because they have a primary attraction for people and the personal and emotional concerns of life. It's not amazing then that they generally do not prefer office time and business paperwork. These tasks can often be left at the bottom of their list of priorities and fail to receive appropriate attention.

While a student at a small Christian college in the early seventies, I found myself as one of a handful of students choosing a "worldly major" such as political science or business. In contrast, the "helping and caring" majors of psychology, sociology, education, and of course, religious studies were much greater in number. While some of these tendencies may have changed, the norm in Christian colleges is nonetheless for most students to dedicate themselves to the caring professions.

Seminaries, like the average Christian college, have not done much better at exposing their graduates to the legal and business side of the profession they are entering. In an unscientific poll of ten prominent seminaries in the United States, not one offered, let alone required, a course that would be the equivalent of an all encompassing "business law for ministry" class. Though many offer legal philosophy, church management, and church versus state courses and a few single focus legal issue courses (e.g., Fuller Seminary offers courses in family and counseling law requirements), none apparently recognize a need to ground their students in the ever-expanding legal framework of ministry in the nineties.[9] The institutions most prolific for producing church and other organized ministry workers have not themselves perceived legal awareness as any great concern. Christians should desire to perform ministry in a legally competent fashion. Now, whether we like it or not, ministries will be compelled to a much higher degree of legal shrewdness, if only by the fear being created by courtroom adversaries.

In the 1990s, we will finally see more and more religious colleges and seminaries offer and require courses such as "church law" and "clergy malpractice." It's a catch-up game, however. Much diligence and intentional changes of habit will be necessary to convert Christians' lack of interest and naiveté to a religious culture that is informed, mature, and shrewd in its legal involvements.

LEGAL STRATEGIES AND PRINCIPLES

◆ Jesus commanded His followers to be "shrewd as snakes" while having the innocence of doves. He also taught about the master who commended his dishonest manager for acting shrewdly. Our churches and ministries have been too slow to become legally shrewd.

◆ We must change for the future and be certain that our worldly innocence does not mask an ignorance or naiveté by our failure to include prudence and practicality in all that we do.

◆ The constitutional protection of freedom of religion, found in the First Amendment, is giving churches and ministries less and less protection. Only matters purely tied to religious beliefs, customs, and practices receive constitutional protection, while churches and ministries expand their influences into new areas of activity such as mental health counseling.

◆ Christian colleges, Bible schools, and seminaries have not kept pace with the need for more legal and business training for those heading into ministry work. The law and the courts have become new partners in ministry. We did not choose them, but nonetheless, we must take them seriously in all aspects of what we do.

CHAPTER SIX

Could a Killer Lawsuit Happen to You?

Joyce Seelen, the plaintiff's lawyer from Denver, believes from her experiences that certain churches and Christian ministries operate with as much arrogance as naiveté. Seelen, as you recall, won a jury verdict of $1.2 million after a three-week trial on behalf of a woman who claimed to have suffered great mental anguish resulting from a sexual affair with the Episcopalian priest whom she had seen for marriage counseling.

CONSIDER LOSING THE LAWSUIT

The jury's award was against both the Episcopal diocese and high-profile Bishop William Frey for his reported failure to intervene adequately and take disciplinary action when he learned of the affair from the woman and her former husband. After the jury's verdict was announced, Bishop Frey was quoted in the local press as saying, "I'm disappointed in the verdict, and I'm surprised by it. I think I'm probably guilty of being *naive* . . . but I'm not conscious of being malicious"[1] (emphasis added). Bishop Frey has now learned something about the legal differences in being negligent (in his words, naive) versus malicious. Merely seeing ourselves as being pure from any harmful intentions is not enough. Simple carelessness (or simple naiveté) can have a very high price tag as well.

Seelen, when interviewed for this work, indicated that she has found religious organizations to be much more than naive in their worldly dealings in court. She says churches are often totally unwilling to even consider for a moment that they might have committed a wrong. In secular litigation with no religious overtones, each side will hypothetically discuss the possibility of losing the lawsuit. They will readily consider how a settlement or compromise might be a better alternative than the risk of losing.

Some would advise, in fact, that when people wholeheartedly believe they did absolutely nothing wrong, then they should not allow themselves to be lured into any kind of settlement discussions founded upon utterly false allegations. Such advice may be noble counsel in the world of purely secular values, but I would contend that Christians in ministry are called to much higher standards. Jesus said, "Blessed are the peacemakers, for they will be called sons of God" (Matthew 5:9). How can you or I hope to be peacemakers if one of us is perceived to be arrogant and uncompromising in our affairs? Ministries cannot afford to be guilty of even the appearance of arrogance. While naiveté is not necessarily a value to be coveted in most respects, it is nonetheless a far better sentence than being rightly charged with arrogance while at the same time confessing Christ as Lord.

I'm sure in my own mind that Bishop Frey is by no means an arrogant person. Nor in all likelihood is the rest of the Episcopalian leadership. Joyce Seelen is entitled to her sincere opinions, and they are helpful here to illustrate how those in ministry can come across as taking an overly defensive posture toward allegations of impropriety.

WHAT ARE YOUR OPTIONS?

I've stated before that Christians need to reevaluate their conduct in worldly arenas like law. They must take seriously Jesus' admonition to be shrewd. We've examined the basic scriptural principles that govern Christian conduct, and we've looked at the consequences of failing to act shrewdly. With an understanding of the perceptions of others, perhaps Christians will be moved to take stock of their behavior in these critical arenas and actually begin to take action.

What causes Christians' behavior in these situations and results in wrong perceptions on the part of others involved? (Remember, many other people are involved in any given lawsuit that may involve Christians—judges, attorneys, witnesses, court clerks, juries, bystanders, and often, law-enforcement officers.) I think there are at least six options that explain such behavior. (Please note that these are only the most practical explanations I could find; they don't include the more sophisticated psychological and sociological possibilities.)

1. Christians' total confidence in God comes across as arrogance.
2. Christians are just as naive and gullible as they appear.
3. Christian churches and organizations have poorly trained, poorly prepared staff who are uncomfortable and insecure in dealings in worldly matters.
4. Christians are incompetent and try to overcome this by dependence on God to make up for their gaps.
5. Christians really are arrogant, having replaced confidence with pride.
6. Some combination of two or more of the above.

Psychological and historical explanations of these options can be explored by someone else. The fact is that many Christians, churches, and parachurch organizations are stumbling in their affairs while claiming to have their eyes fixed on God.

I wholeheartedly believe that God asks Christians to look to Him, and Him *alone*, for their spiritual and material sustenance. In other words, I believe Christians should have total confidence in God to meet their needs. But I do not believe that their trust in Him should—ever—move Christians beyond the same humility Jesus displayed in His earthly ministry. That is, Christians cannot afford attitudes or behaviors that portray an air that they are untouchable. A confidence in God that assumes He is always on the side of Christians is the flip side of tempting Him. It can have the same sort of consequences. Christians must avoid such spiritual snobbery.

Dealing with Legal Sin
At the same time, Christians must follow three simple rules in dealing with their sin in the legal arena.

First, they must broaden their legal vision. We all benefit from peripheral vision. Imagine an athlete like Michael Jordan without it. Its absence would result in massive numbers of missed opportunities and missed points for Michael's beloved Chicago Bulls. Imagine a big-game hunter without peripheral vision. He might miss that lion or tiger or bear just to his right. Such lack of vision could be deadly. By the same token, Christians must use their peripheral vision to take note of the changing legal climate and the distinct possibilities that some legal obstacles along their way may need to be stepped around instead of assumed to be automatically in their favor. Any lesser view could result in missed opportunities.

Second, when someone in a Christian organization steps on another's toes, or worse, does another person serious harm, shouldn't the organization be able to recognize, evaluate, and respond appropriately on a human, as well as legal, plane? In other words, Christian ministries must realize their mistakes and admit when they're wrong. And when they do, they must be prepared to pay the price for their own wrongdoing, or that of someone in the organization.

Third, ministries must balance shrewdness with humility in all their business dealings. Let's look at a final case that illustrates the need for such a prudent course.

THE CASE OF PASTOR BLAIR

Immediately preceding the headline-grabbing case against Bishop Frey and the Episcopal church, the Denver media kept readers apprised of a class action lawsuit against Pastor Charles Blair, his church Calvary Temple in Denver, and J. Allan Peterson of Family Concern in Wheaton, Illinois. A class action lawsuit is a seldom-used procedure whereby a small number of people bring a lawsuit on behalf of themselves and a very large group of other people who experienced the same kind of personal harm or financial losses due to the defendant's wrongful actions. As a result, every member of the "class" receives compensation if the representative plaintiffs win the case or collect a settlement.

Charles Blair had a very successful ministry at Calvary Temple as its pastor for more than forty-three years. The church had approximately 6,000 members at its zenith. Then, in the mid-sixties,

Calvary Temple commenced an ambitious multi-million dollar project to construct a 500-bed holistic center for treating the aged and infirm physically, spiritually, and mentally.

While millions of dollars were raised and one-half of the "Life Center" actually opened its doors, a number of financial and legal disasters led to the early failure and formal bankruptcy of the Life Center project in the mid-seventies. Liquidation of assets and related bankruptcy proceedings were not completed until the mid-eighties when Dr. J. Allan Peterson, president of Family Concern, entered the picture. In 1986 Peterson felt compelled to find a way to repay the remaining $4 million of financial obligations that had gone unpaid and actually had been legally extinguished in the excruciatingly long bankruptcy of the Life Center.

Reports from the church indicated that from nearly 3,000 people who were owed $18.5 million at the beginning of the bankruptcy in 1974, Peterson and Blair calculated that it would take only $3.9 million to pay off 787 remaining creditors who had not been made whole after the bankruptcy liquidation. A short time prior to the lawsuit, Blair and Peterson claimed these numbers had been reduced to 268 people still owed $1.16 million.[2]

Peterson and Blair commenced a high-visibility, national fundraising campaign called "The Second Mile" to do the unthinkable. They planned to raise, gratuitously, monies to repay creditors whose debts had been fully, completely, and legally discharged by the federal bankruptcy laws and by a court order from a federal judge.

I would think that each and every one of those 268 people would be thrilled at whatever measure of success Peterson and Blair might have in this seemingly insurmountable task. I say insurmountable because this fundraising program had no positive goals to promote such as the need for a new building or dorm, money to buy food for starving masses in the Third World, or support for a missionary endeavor. According to Blair and Peterson, the fundraising effort's chief aim was to help clear the tarnished name of Christ and the church by repaying legally canceled debts incurred by a now-defunct ministry.

In a bizarre turn of events, instead of unanimous appreciation for Blair's and Peterson's efforts, a small handful of these canceled creditors brought suit because they had not yet received their payments while others had been paid in full. The four plaintiffs claimed to represent the balance of the unpaid creditors. The lawsuit sought a complete, detailed explanation of each and every dollar raised and where it was spent, and for good measure, added claims for fraud, criminal theft, breach of trust, and punitive damages. These plaintiffs apparently thought it would be appropriate to punish Blair, Calvary Temple, and Peterson for the act of trying to raise money to benefit these people and the class of others purportedly represented. Life is stranger than fiction.

Obviously, the efforts of the Second Mile Campaign came to a screeching—let me emphasize, *screeching*—halt.

During the three years that this highly unusual lawsuit developed toward a final trial, Charles Blair and Calvary Temple took a beating in the local papers. After each court hearing along the way to resolve some esoteric legal point, the newspapers would grab the public's attention with headlines such as these:

Blair faces flock, denies wrongdoing
Congregation: 'Amen'
'I have never stolen a penny or misappropriated a dollar.'
—The Rev. Charles Blair

EMBATTLED PASTOR ON TRIAL AGAIN

Blair faces trial in suit charging theft

Blair proclaims his innocence to congregation

Witnesses say Blair stole from the elderly
Needy creditors were first in line for funds

PASTOR DEFENDS PAYOFF

No final judgment or decree had been entered, nor would one ever be entered, yet Blair and his congregation were already the losers in the community. This case provides the vicarious truth that "innocent until proven guilty" applies only within the walls of the American courtroom. It has no relevance or meaning on the front pages of newspapers.

In an interview for this work, Blair confirmed that the lawsuit, which came at a time the church was regrouping after the bankruptcy debacle, was "utterly devastating." The case was finally settled out of court, according to Blair.

Blair indicated that the church agreed in the settlement to pay a total of $700,000 in three payments over a two-and-a-half-year period. According to Blair, the opposing lawyer was to receive about $140,000 of that total, leaving only about $560,000 to go to the class of remaining elderly plaintiffs and other expenses.

Sadly, Blair says, the church *also* incurred legal fee charges of nearly $300,000 to its own attorneys, with another $40,000 in accountant's fees for financial audit services. Nearly $350,000 in hard cash was spent to reach the point of an expensive $700,000 compromise. Both of these payouts were uninsured, according to Blair. Some would say hindsight is twenty-twenty. Others would say Blair and Calvary Temple's leadership should have struck a settlement earlier, solely because of their history of legal problems in Denver that foretold that a big loss was inevitable.

Not only are Blair's headlines and huge monetary losses a lesson in themselves, but they are all the more painful when we realize that they might have been avoided with some simple legal steps. The Second Mile Campaign was never separately incorporated as a nonprofit corporation. That is, it had no separate legal existence apart from the church and the notable committee members who organized the effort. Therefore, the personal assets of Blair and his friends whom he brought into the campaign, along with the assets of Calvary Temple, were all put at risk in the lawsuit. The stakes ultimately were too high to take a chance of an adverse ruling by a jury who may have already formed prejudicial opinions about high profile clergymen based on the likes of Jim Bakker and Jimmy Swaggert.

A much different result might have occurred if the Second Mile Campaign had been newly incorporated and separate and distinct from Blair's congregation and the individuals who wanted to see Peterson's dream succeed. Simple, everyday legal choices can mushroom into a mega-lawsuit that can wipe out all but the largest of churches and organizations. Calvary Temple could withstand a $1 million blow—barely. Can your ministry?

The next section is designed to give the basic legal and business principles to prevent such costly mistakes.

LEGAL STRATEGIES AND PRINCIPLES

◆ We must be very careful that our confidence in God does not come across as an untouchable arrogance in legal challenges.

◆ Developing a peripheral vision for legal dangers in our midst will be increasingly important.

◆ Recognizing mistakes and being willing to admit when we might be wrong will be needed to demonstrate our humanity and thereby minimize the consequences of unfortunate actions.

◆ Simple, day-to-day legal decisions and non-decisions can easily mushroom into a mega-lawsuit and wipe out nearly any church or ministry.

PART THREE

Guides Through the Storm: Lawyers and the Law

CHAPTER SEVEN

The Legal Playing Field

Since pastors, churches, and those in other organized Christian ministries increasingly are going to be called upon to play the legal game, just what are the rules governing this new playing field? Since you might find yourself, your minister, or your beloved evangelistic mission being summoned to court, or otherwise unable to escape the world of legal negotiations, lawyers, and "the law," just how does this system work? When, where, and how does it not work?

First, let's try to answer the surprisingly difficult question, "What is the law?" I say surprisingly because it would seem at first glance that determining what is required by the law and what is prohibited by the law should be relatively easy. Why can't the lawyer, or any lay person, for that matter, just look it up in a law book and find the answer? How can lawyers get away with charging $100 to $300 per hour to give people their opinion of what the law says can or cannot be done? Wouldn't it make more sense (and be far less expensive) to put "the law" into a set of books that all people could access to answer their own legal questions and resolve their own legal disputes?

Frustrated clients regularly ask all lawyers these questions, either directly or indirectly. More often it's indirectly communicated by body language that says, "Okay, here we go again, another big bill for you folks to research my problem." Everyone, *even lawyers, judges, and legislators*, is puzzled about why the law has become so complex. The goal of this chapter then is to alleviate future frustrations and to help you operate on a more equal footing with your current or future lawyer. Let's now attempt to answer these widely held questions.

THE ORIGIN OF LAW

In the United States, laws come from two basic sources. One source is *statutes* passed by our legislatures at the federal level (Congress) and at the state level (state legislatures). Akin to statutes are *regulations* promulgated by administrative agencies. Essentially, state and federal governments have delegated the power to make certain laws to administrative agencies, which were created to develop expertise concerning a certain area of government. The most widely recognized agency is probably the Internal Revenue Service. Congress has given the IRS authority to administer the Internal Revenue Code (a statute passed by Congress) and, in the process, to create regulations that carry out, in detail, the purposes of that statute and the agency. These regulations are much like statutes in that they are written and implemented by "agency" lawmakers (bureaucrats) as opposed to elected politicians.

The second basic source of the law is *judicial decisions* rendered by state and federal courts of appeal. These decisions, also commonly called "opinions," are the results of actual lawsuits or controversies between people and/or organizations and businesses. A real-life dispute between real people was determined by a trial or other adversarial means within the litigation system. The loser then felt strongly that an erroneous application of a statute or prior judicial opinion had occurred, thus an appeal to a higher court was made. (In fact, losers in court often have two chances at an appeal when they believe an error in the application of the law has occurred. In most states there are two levels of appellate courts—the state court of appeals and the state supreme court. Similarly, the loser in a federal court case can attempt an appeal to the U.S. Circuit Court of Appeals and thereafter the U.S. Supreme Court.) We can count on the final decision of that appellate court or the yet higher supreme court, interpreting and applying a statute or other legal principle, as being "the law."

How then does this affect you, your church, and your ministry? First, the legislatures pronounce what the law in a given area shall be, while the judges and the courts interpret those pronouncements (statutes) by the legislature and apply them to specific disputes. The legislature presumably voices the wishes and wisdom of the citizens who elected it, while the judiciary exists to adjudicate, judge, or referee actual legal controversies and, in applying the statutes, will interpret general (and even ambiguous) language for specific application. Judges can also decide what "the law" is when no statute on a point of law nor a prior appeals court decision exists to give guidance in the lawsuit being adjudicated.

LEGAL PRECEDENTS

Before going further, I must comment briefly on the legal system's strong tradition that says judges must follow the judgment of prior decisions of higher courts. This is called following legal precedents. Its purpose is to create uniformity and certainty in legal decision making from case to case and year to year. In other words, the system places great value on making it possible for people and organizations *today* to make important decisions based on current court holdings knowing that *tomorrow* judges will—in fact, must—make their decisions in a consistent manner. What is permissible today will be permissible tomorrow under the same circumstances. At least that is the goal of a system based on legal precedents. Presumably, judges will not decide a dispute in a contradictory, arbitrary, or capricious fashion. When there has been a clear, previous declaration of what is the law, every judge at the same level or in a lower court is bound by duty to follow that declaration.

Legal precedents have limitations. Sometimes these limits are minor, sometimes monumental. As mentioned earlier, each of the fifty states has a tiered court system with "trial" courts at the bottom and one or more appeals courts above. The highest in nearly all states is called the state "supreme court." So when the State Supreme Court of Colorado declares XYZ to be the law in Colorado, every court in Colorado must follow XYZ. But one all-important limitation is that none of the state courts or state judges in the other forty-nine states are bound by, or even interested in, what your state laws have to say.

The Florida courts, in applying what they believe is or should be the law in Florida, are not in any way bound to follow XYZ. Neither are Maine, Washington, California, . . . nor even are Colorado's next door neighbors bound or particularly interested. Each state is sovereign in the determination and application of that particular state's laws.

Cases of First Impression

Now, to buffer slightly this example, other states occasionally look to a few larger states when new, previously unconfronted issues are presented. These are called "*cases of first impression.*" Other states often look to California, New York, and Illinois because of their larger, more complex populations and the fact that their law has become more developed and fine-tuned as a result. But even in this situation, no requirement says that one state must follow step with any other on state law questions.

This affects you in many ways. In the newly developing areas of religious litigation, you cannot jump to the conclusion that because XYZ has been held to be the law in Colorado, it is the law in your state as well. People often hear through the media that someone just won a verdict against a church or pastor in another jurisdiction on some very unusual theory of law. That new, unusual legal theory may be part of a trend, or it may be an isolated aberration. In either case, you need to remember to seek capable legal advice on whether your state recognizes or is headed toward recognizing anything similar to XYZ. If not, no worry, so long as you continue in your normal activities.

In national organizations where operations span many states, the response is no different, except for those programs and staff that conduct business in the errant state. On many issues facing multi-state organizations, even more care and shrewdness is called for, because divergent state laws make it difficult to adopt uniform policies that will not create legal exposure in every state.

Trial Judges and Juries *Don't* Make Law

Before we leave the area of statutes and appellate court decisions, let me address another misconception easily created by what people read in the papers, hear on the news, and even absorb from the religious periodicals. Frequently, Christians become either alarmed or comforted by some new jury verdict or trial judge decision. (Surprising to many people, most civil lawsuits are tried before a judge *without* a jury.)

As briefly mentioned, *only* appellate court decisions can make law or have precedent-setting value. The results of trials, whether by jury or judge, do not tell much other than what that group of six to twelve jurors or single judge thought about the facts of that particular case. Juries solely decide facts disputes, such as whether the stop light was red or green at the time of the accident when credible witnesses on one side say it was red and witnesses on the other side testify that it was green. The law needs someone to decide those kinds of issues as well as the ultimate question of who wins and loses. But what the law is or should be as determined by a trial court judge has no real bearing on future cases with similar, or even identical, factual circumstances.

APPEALS HAVE THEIR PLACE

Another interesting aspect of a number of these headline jury cases occurs when an appeal overturns part or all of the decision several years later. It is common practice among trial lawyers to request a trial before a jury whenever conventional sympathies favor their client or strong emotions would typically run against their opponent. Since individuals participate in lawsuits so infrequently, juries are very prone to getting excited about one side or the other's position. In fact, they can even want and expect the lawyers to get them worked up over their lawsuit. Judges are there every day, day in and day out, for many years. They are quite unemotional and can be offended by certain attempts to hook their personal feelings.

Therefore, when a jury goes overboard with its emotions, or even its biases, it is common for headlines to result and a successful appeal to be taken to bring common sense to bear upon the result. Of course, the successful appeal will take several years to complete and will likely produce few corresponding headlines to balance the previous public alarm. So let's keep these notorious cases in proper perspective. They do not make law and are not particularly instructive, except to teach that Christians should want to excel at shrewdness and stay away from the front pages.

In very general terms then, only statutes passed by lawmakers and *appellate* court decisions, for the most part, comprise what we call "the law." Seldom do these make the newspapers, and when they do, they are generally buried in the mid-section of your daily paper. For example, in a trial court in Minnesota it was recently argued that every church makes an "implied warranty" to its congregation that its pastors and staff are "fit for the particular purpose" for which they are employed.[1] This is an incredible stretch of prior legal theories and principles. Up to now, "implied warranties," particularly the warranty of "fitness for a particular purpose," have had their application solely in the commercial world of products and, in rare instances, when buying and selling services.

The implied warranty of fitness for a particular purpose is a feature of the Uniform Commercial Code (UCC) adopted in every state. An express warranty is one made affirmatively, clearly, and with the intent to make such a warranty about a product. For example, "this golf ball's cover is guaranteed not to slice or cut" is an express warranty, whereas the statement "this is a high-quality golf ball" may imply that "high quality" includes the characteristic that it will not cut or slice. It is not directly stated, but at least arguably intimates, suggests, or implies that the cover will at least last longer than an inferior or merely average ball. The implied warranty of fitness for a particular purpose is exactly like the general, objective implied warranty, except that it goes a step further and guarantees subjectively that the product or service will meet that customer's stated needs.

For example, a beginning golfer asks the golf pro who is giving her lessons to recommend a ball that would help her game. The pro's recommendation of a particular brand and model of a ball with nothing more said is an implied (indirect) guarantee that this ball will meet the specific, subjective requirements of that particular beginning golfer.

We now can see how unusual a trial court finding that a church can be sued upon its implied guarantee (warranty) that the person in the pulpit and available for pastoral counseling is properly trained and otherwise qualified (in other words, legally "fit") to meet the *particular subjective needs* of that church and congregation.

Now let's have a short bar exam review. Is a Minnesota judge's ruling, presumably on a request for dismissal by the church, *the law* in that state? No. Not yet, at least, because unless and until an appeal is taken and an appellate court in Minnesota upholds that trial judge, no binding precedent has been set. Another trial judge down the hall may laugh at such a suggestion and throw the same kind of lawsuit out the door. Unless and until an appellate court in Minnesota rules on this legal theory, no other trial judge in Minnesota is bound to follow such a rule of law. The other judges remain free to decide any similar case however they believe the law in Minnesota should be interpreted.

Is this ruling now the law in any other state? No. Will it be the law in any other state if the Minnesota Supreme Court were to uphold a lower court on that question? No. The only way such a new theory will apply in your state (or any other state) is for (1) your legislature to pass such a law, or (2) for one of your highest state appellate courts to adopt such a theory in a case on appeal in your state. Otherwise, you need not worry. But you should still learn to be shrewd. We know lightning strikes all over, and each minor secular victory against a church or pastor just adds more fuel to a rapidly growing fire.

Why is it so hard to find out what "the law" is? Of more practical benefit is an answer to the question, "Can I do this under the law?" or "Can they do this to us under the law?" When you seek advice from lawyers, why are their answers often so vague or oblique? With the background above, let me attempt to explain why even the best, most experienced lawyers still refuse to give concrete responses to these common questions.

UNCLEAR STATUTES

If there happens to be a statute on the books that is clearly applicable to your circumstances, then an obvious answer exists. But these situations are rare because prudent politicians recognize that great diversity exists in society and it is difficult to write a law that can equitably fit the myriad of likely events. Therefore, most statutes tend to be so general as to be of little immediate, clear-cut benefit.

A statutory example of an extremely general codified rule can be found in the Uniform Commercial Code adopted in some form in every state: "If the court, as a matter of law, finds the contract to have been unconscionable at the time it was made, the court may refuse to enforce the contract."[2] Hundreds, maybe thousands, of court cases around the United States have struggled with applying the term *unconscionable*. What shocks the conscience of one person may seem like everyday living to another. Biblical analogies are "Love your neighbor!" and "Thou shall not commit murder!" The first has caused religious authors to fill libraries and Christian bookstores with thousands of volumes seeking to clarify what this commandment means in various circumstances. Likewise, you do not need to go further than the abortion debate to see how what appears to be a specific prohibition against "murder" can lead to uncertainty in application.

Filling in the Gaps

Statutes, therefore, are important as firm general principles but still leave a lot of room for interpretation and clarification. This is what the legal profession calls "statutory construction," or "to construe a statute." What did the legislature mean by the words it used? Did it intend for this particular statute to apply to your particular circumstances? Since we cannot ask the legislature for answers as a practical matter, we need the courts to bring a statute alive that may appear to have some bearing on what is happening.

When lawmakers have pronounced no statute or rule to cover a particular situation, the courts are needed to fill in the gap (which can be very large in some places in the law) and conclude what should be "the law." Over time, all of these appellate cases build upon one another in each area where disputes, conflicts, and issues have arisen. This building effect has created a body of law that exists separate and apart from the statutes of the state and national legislatures.

Since the judges and courts, even appellate courts, have as their sole responsibility to resolve legal conflicts between the litigants before them, each judicial holding must be scrutinized on the particular facts and circumstances of that case facing the judge and/or court of appeals. Most judicial decisions are *facts-sensitive*. This means that any significant alteration in the factual circumstances may have caused the higher court to rule differently.

Considering the Facts

We will now look prospectively at what ministries can or cannot do, and where they may have future exposure to liability. As we look, keep in mind that every court case result could be different with a minor change or two in the crucial facts presented to that court.

For example, let's assume you read in the papers or heard at a party that a local youth worker and the church she attended were found by a judge not to be responsible for injuries to a teenager at a church youth activity program. It was reported that the court found that the student had himself been the cause of his injuries because of his own carelessness. His negligence, rather than any lack of supervision by the youth worker, was the real reason he was harmed.

At first blush, based on what you hear, it might be easy to conclude that "the law" does not hold ministries accountable to protect teenagers from hurting themselves. Even if this reported court case was from the highest court of that state, drawing such a conclusion could not be further from the truth. You must investigate the facts surrounding the injury, the age of the teenager, and whether your youth program has unique circumstances that might produce a different result.

What if the teenager in the reported case was nineteen, but you are working with thirteen-year-olds? What if their activity was bowling and this kid purposely threw the bowling ball in the air over his head, but your activity is racing all-terrain motorcycles against the clock? I trust you will agree that changes in the facts, even minor changes (what if the kid was fifteen?), can lead to dramatically different results.

Being shrewd means being slow to get excited over reported courtroom victories until you hear all the facts and evaluate their similarities to what you are doing. You also must recognize that your ministry cannot become inordinately fearful from losses in court suffered by other ministries because you have every opportunity to control your facts and circumstances and minimize the chances of the same thing happening to you. Remember, same facts, same result; different facts, different result.

LEGAL STRATEGIES AND PRINCIPLES

◆ The two main sources of "the law" are *statutes* passed by the legislators and *judicial decisions* rendered by various appellate courts. In other words, the legislators pronounce what the law will be, and the higher level courts interpret the finer points while resolving a real-life dispute.

◆ A state statute or state legal precedent recognized as law in one state will have no effect in the other forty-nine states until formally adopted by them. Hence, a victory for churches in Texas will not necessarily give those of you in Ohio peace of mind.

◆ A victory or a loss in a trial has little or no bearing as a legal precedent for anyone apart from the parties to that lawsuit. Only the higher courts of appeal in any state can "make law" with their decisions and orders.

◆ Being legally shrewd means being slow to get excited over reported courtroom victories, as well as standing secure in times of others' losses because we can control our own circumstances.

CHAPTER EIGHT

"L.A. Law" Is Not the Law

Most people probably recognize that "L.A. Law," "Perry Mason," and the like are not representative of real-world legal battles. Still, there remains a lack of appreciation for how truly different these television portrayals are from what goes on in the world of American lawsuits.

The most important differences between television and the real world are timing and the black-and-white portrayals of justice. In movies and on television, we see a wrong being perpetrated, a contract broken, or a slander spoken in the beginning moments of the production. Within just an hour or two, we observe lawyers being retained, a lawsuit commenced, and a dramatic, entertaining trial before an attentive jury. Of course, the good guys win; the bad guys lose; and American justice is affirmed. Everything is pictured black and white, with very little gray.

Actually, every lawyer and judge in the United States wishes that was the reality in his or her daily life. Sadly though, no lawsuit even comes close to following these scripts. Any belief by those in ministry that lawsuits do, will only further entrench them in naive suppositions. Real-world lawsuits take forever to bring to conclusion at trial. Most settle out of court after months of tedious pretrial posturing that costs the clients a fortune. Resolutions are finally extracted at a time so late that few can remember how it all started in the first place.

The legal system moves excruciatingly slowly. The judicial system has made sincere efforts in the last decade to streamline the process to bring cases to trial. In spite of this, *it is still the norm to wait anywhere from two to six years for an available trial opening in most urban courtrooms.* Cases brought in smaller communities and rural areas will likely present much quicker scheduling of trials, as will more petty cases in urban courtrooms, with dollar amounts at risk in the $5,000 or less range. These cases are handled more summarily in most states.

Interestingly, both sides of any given lawsuit are usually shocked and deeply discouraged when their respective lawyers advise them that it may be several years before their case can be heard in a courtroom. At the outset of every dispute, both sides are deep in the middle of their controversy and are highly anxious to have someone in legal authority and power agree with their position and vindicate their claims.

While it may seem strange under current circumstances, a long-held American legal maxim declares that "justice delayed is justice denied." This maxim is often cited to judges by lawyers resisting further delays. Nonetheless, the process has turned from this truism and has rejected the instinctive enthusiasm of every litigant by overburdening itself with too much "process" and far too little "result." In this sense the "means" have crushed the "ends." As you can well imagine, it is anticlimactic and unsatisfying for litigants to present their dispute six years after the fact to a judge and/or jury. While money may still exchange hands as a result, few other aspects of "justice" are served.

How do these delays affect you as you develop shrewdness in what you do in ministry? Initially we can see these factors.

THE EFFECTS OF JUDICIAL BACKLOGS

Credibility Can't Wait for Trial

Ministries must recognize that most, if not all, of the emotions will be gone by the time their case is resolved or settled by compromise between the parties. Rehabilitating the image and reputation of a ministry and organization by a courtroom victory will come so late as to be useless. Other immediate means must be used with the ministry's constituents. Ministries must take *proactive steps to reestablish credibility outside the realm of litigation.* Courtroom victories that come years after damaging newspaper headlines and editorials will do no good.

Often pastors and Christian organizations make the same canned responses to litigation inquiries that secular businesses utilize. A typical one is, "This whole ordeal is a great injustice and we are confident that we will prevail once all the facts are presented at trial." In all probability, such escapes from directly addressing the problem giving rise to a lawsuit are made upon lawyers' advice and instruction. Following such legal advice to keep quiet is born out of strategies that often work well in secular competitive enterprises.

What most ministries and their lawyers who are faced with litigation are missing, in my opinion, is that the strategies of avoiding the press and playing a poker game leading to trial is exactly the opposite of what people expect from them. Of course, ministries must be careful. I'm not suggesting otherwise. But what may be the best legal strategy for handling the defense of a secular case headed for trial several years down the road may itself be the cause of lost confidence in the ministry from those who are ministered to by the ministry and those who make the ministry financially possible. In other words, the constituents may not wait around long enough to hear "our side of things" at a trial. Worse yet, if a "quiet" settlement is reached out of court on the eve of trial (as often occurs), the ministry will have suffered years of "no comment" and nonrebuttals in the media and will have lost the opportunity in the long-awaited trial to regain the confidence of those who were emotionally involved years earlier.

In the business world, where the usefulness and desirability of specific products and services are the real focus, corporate integrity and honor rarely enter the minds of consumers. So settlements, or even courtroom losses, occurring years later do little harm to corporate reputations. Defense attorneys often refer to what they do as being on the "slow side of the case." Plaintiffs in all cases are most anxious to get to trial as quickly as possible, whereas the typical defense strategy is to accept delay.

For churches and ministries, however, their reputation and image in the community and with those with whom they work is critical. They cannot successfully do what they do and claim God's name in the process by trusting solely in a slow, arduous, secular legal system. Ministries must comment; they must publicly explain their side in detail to their people and to the community at large. Their constituents expect them to respond differently than the secular world when faced with legal confrontations, and rightfully so.

Boredom Strikes Deep

The second striking difference from the Hollywood version of lawsuits is that the typical real-life lawsuit is incredibly boring as it progresses and, therefore, is of little interest to anyone other than the principal characters at its conclusion. Since it all looks so interesting on television and film, people tend to believe the whole world will be watching with great interest as their legal drama unfolds. From the moment the painting contractor goes public with the accusation that he was not paid, that he was "stiffed" by the most prominent church in town, everyone wants to know what happened, the response of the church elders, and the pastor's point of view as the shepherd of the flock. But that high level of public interest will subside quickly. At this moment *the ministry's position must be articulated*—when the level of interest has peaked. Otherwise, the ministry's side will not be heard by those who need to hear it.

Who needs to hear will vary from case to case. This articulation *must* be done with advice of legal counsel and with consent of the ministry's insurance carrier, who is at risk financially and has a legitimate interest that nothing is said that would jeopardize defending the lawsuit. Nonetheless, I believe that ministries make a big mistake by not going toe to toe with their lawyers and insurers and not developing an affirmative detailed response to harmful accusations, one mutually acceptable both to the ministries' needs and the defense of the lawsuit.

It should be noted that nearly all defense lawyers and insurance companies will find it difficult to do what I suggest. Their reluctance is well-founded in many respects. Their job and interests are to defend any lawsuit to the fullest and to minimize any financial losses from the lawsuit to the greatest extent possible. Beyond those specific goals and duties, it will be most difficult to get them to do anything. For example, the defense lawyer's mindset will be, "If releasing information or responding to accusations outside the litigation will not help our courtroom defense of the lawsuit, don't do it." Every question you present to him or her will be screened by the question of whether it will help or hurt the lawsuit's defense. Sending explanatory letters to ministry supporters will not help win in court and somehow could present a risk of harm. The easy answer for the defense lawyer and the insurance representative is "no," when asked for permission to go public with your side of the story. Their kneejerk responses will need to be overcome in many cases to preserve the overall effectiveness of the ministry being sued.

The Anticlimactic Deposition

A deposition is an opportunity for each side's lawyer to question people who may testify at a future trial. The person being deposed must answer the lawyer's questions under oath, much like at trial. Because the deposition is under oath and is usually the opponent's first crack at questioning the adversary, the client in a lawsuit usually gets excited about the opponent's deposition, as if it were a mini trial. The big difference is that these depositions happen privately in a lawyer's conference room with usually only a handful of people present. The questions and answers are transposed into a written deposition transcript by a shorthand court reporter. The transcript usually gets tossed into the lawyer's files and used only for trial preparation. Public use of a transcript is rare.

In fifteen years in the legal profession, I have never attended a deposition that was other than anticlimactic for the clients involved. Lawyers notoriously allow little to be said by their clients about the matter in dispute. Ministry leaders, on the other hand, have an obviously high expectation level about the depositions of opponents, which are often dashed by these deposition realities. Depositions also become the first opportunity to voice a portion or all of one's own story. When they happen at lengthy intervals of time after the initial accusations have been made, they come off so flat, unemotional, and boring that it is common for litigants to wonder why and how they got where they are.

When the facts are finally heard, there's no one there to listen except the attorneys involved. When winning and losing is not at stake, it is hard to get a ministry's constituents to care at all about the testimony heard at a preliminary deposition. So to the extent ministries recognize a need to have others hear the true story, they must find other appropriate and effective means to do so at the beginning of the furor while public interest is at a peak. Expecting an opponent's revealing deposition to satisfy people's concerns is a great error. Ministries must recognize that the long, tedious task of litigation will dull the sensitivities of even the most tenacious observer. Affirmative strategies to reveal a ministry's side of the story must be developed early in the process and applied regularly over the course of any lawsuit.

The Lonely Courtroom

The typical civil trial is won before an empty courtroom. Few friends of the parties are there, if any. Even the witnesses rush back to work. The press, which showed great interest four years earlier, is off covering the latest "scandal." A few strangers may linger in the back of the courtroom. They are probably there with their lawyers waiting to get a few minutes with the judge to resolve a minor problem or procedural dispute. No cheers or applause ensue for the winner. The long-awaited moment of victory is dashed by the opposing attorney's pronouncement that a lengthy appeal will be taken. It's a much different ending than seen on television, but an everyday real-life ending across the United States. If an empty verdict in your favor years later is not what you have in mind, act swiftly, positively, and shrewdly at the beginning of legal problems to manage public opinion. There's much more to litigation than just winning in court.

The Checkbook Factor

The final distinguishing feature of real-life legal fights is the massive legal expense that can arise in even a fairly routine lawsuit that goes only slightly off course. It is probably not news to you that lawyers are expensive. This fact is widely reported and the subject matter of many lawyer-bashing jokes.

More specifically, the *National Law Journal* recently reported that partners in larger law firms in Los Angeles charge anywhere from $200 per hour up to $400 per hour. In Chicago the range is $155 to $350 per hour, and in Atlanta $165 to $330 per hour.[1] While hourly rates like these are dramatic indicators, they really don't tell the bottom line. What will the defense of an uninsured lawsuit cost your organization? Even if you win, what will the total financial costs be in opposing an unwanted lawsuit? When the lawyer's high hourly rates are multiplied against the hours he will spend, what will that figure become? And what will the other defense costs look like apart from your lawyer's fees?

The overall, total costs of litigation are normally unreported because they are not disclosed by lawyer and client to the public. Since the point of the total costs of finding oneself in court is where the rubber meets the road for any person or ministry, let's see what a fairly routine case can cost, regardless of the amount of damages that may or may not be awarded by the court.

STRANGER THAN FICTION: THE CASE OF PASTOR DOE

In a recent case that went to trial, a small Christian nonprofit organization, led by a man we'll fictionally call "Pastor Doe," was sued by its principal benefactor. The suit concerned the question of whether monies loaned were due for repayment. Further, the benefactor seized all of the organization's office equipment, computers, and so forth in an attempt to satisfy the loan that was believed to be in jeopardy of repayment. Pastor Doe and his ministry claimed that the seizure was improper. The loan balance was approximately $200,000, and the organization's equipment, furniture, materials, and supplies were appraised at a value of approximately $400,000.

When Pastor Doe retained a lawyer to defend his ministry against this challenge, he and all of his staff had been physically locked out of the organization's offices, prevented from utilizing or gaining access to their equipment, and kept away from much-needed files and materials. Even their mail and check payments for services were intercepted at the outset of this serious problem.

On "L.A. Law," we would see the lawyer hired, and after a few commercials, we'd see the closing fifteen minutes of an exciting courtroom trial. This is not even close to the real-world picture of what happened to Pastor Doe.

The Realities of Litigation

Six months after being displaced from its offices and equipment, the ministry was given an available time slot for a half-day hearing on whether it should get back all of its operating equipment and files pending a final decision at trial scheduled one year further down the road. During these six months, the ministry operated out of staff homes and church-donated facilities in a gallant effort to stay alive. Legal fees for the ministry's lawyer and legal research reached the $5,000 range by this first hearing. The judge agreed with the Christian organization and granted the ministry's "replevin" (restoration) request to get back its assets pending trial. But the judge placed a condition on the replevin.

The ministry was required to post a $100,000 bond. Since this small organization did not have cash in such sums, the ministry asked the judge to allow it to use a portion of its business assets as a property bond. The other side opposed. Another hearing with the judge was required, and expert appraisers were hired at hourly rates nearly equal to the lawyer's. The judge accepted the property bond, but lawyer's fees and expert appraiser's charges brought the ministry's defense expenses to around $10,000.

Between these court appearances and the trial date, certain trial preparation efforts had to take place. Because the ministry lacked funds and was forced to give every spare penny toward the defense of the case, the ministry decided to do only nominal investigation for trial preparation on its behalf. But no controls existed to stop the opponent from presenting lengthy, detailed written questions (interrogatories) that the ministry had to respond to under oath as required by court rules. Likewise, oral questioning of possible adversary witnesses at a deposition before a court reporter were taken. In this case, Pastor Doe's deposition alone spanned two days. The lawyer's time is added to the charges to obtain a copy of the deposition transcript from the reporter, at more than two dollars per page for a document that can be several hundred pages in many cases. Questions and answers continued hour after hour. One day-long deposition alone can easily cost a client $1,500 to $2,000.

A full year later—after depositions, legal research, and general trial preparation—the organization's cost-conscious defense bill reached the $20,000 to $25,000 range. The heavy crunch of the trial itself and its related expenses were yet to come.

The parties and the judge agreed that a five-day trial would be needed to hear testimony from nearly twenty-five individuals and to introduce and consider nearly one hundred documents. For the ministry's lawyer to prepare for the trial, along with each of its fifteen witnesses, almost seven twelve-hour days were required before the trial started on a Monday. The lawyer, Pastor Doe, and several key staff dedicated themselves almost exclusively to the trial for two weekends and the work week immediately preceding the five-day (Monday-Friday) trial. Painstaking hours were required to review and re-review every letter, meeting, phone call, or hiccup that may have been pertinent to what transpired between the benefactor and the ministry staff. Virtually no ministry business occurred during the week preceding and the actual week of the trial.

These two weeks of lawyer time cost $15,000. The fees for the appraisal expert who was needed again at trial as a witness to explain the value and condition of the equipment exceeded $1,000. Since five witnesses for the ministry resided out of state and had busy schedules, Pastor Doe was forced to purchase airline tickets and short-term hotel accommodations. Cost-saving measures such as Saturday layovers and thirty-day nonrefundable airline tickets were not an option, because the ministry felt that a last-minute settlement was possible between the parties. The airline tickets alone exceeded $3,000. Other related expenses brought the cost of these out-of-state witnesses to nearly $5,000.

At the final "exciting" and "dramatic" moment of this made-for-television trial, the Christian ministry had incurred approximately $45,000 in real costs for lawyers, experts, research, and travel expenses in fighting for its very life as an organization. As a defendant who did not start the lawsuit in the first place, no real alternative ultimately existed to defending a case like this. Settlement was pursued heavily with no success. Writing a check for a couple hundred thousand dollars was not fiscally possible, even if considered to be an option. Nearly one year after the trial, these litigants still waited for the judge's ruling on who won and who lost. While justice may still be reached, it will not have been delivered with certainty and timeliness at a reasonable cost.

When a loaded gun is aimed at you by others, expensive defensive measures are the only alternative to bankruptcy and the end of a viable ministry. Putting up a defense is the only choice when it's too late to become shrewd. Obviously, the best defense is to work especially hard to never get in that kind of position in the first place.

A proactive offense is absolutely the best defense. Legal strength and shrewdness will ward off those who would otherwise see a ministry as unprepared for the weight of a legal challenge. Remember, we live in a culture where hungry lions are on the prowl for the legally weak but possibly wealthy ministry. The strong, healthy, and prepared ministry will be left alone for easier prey.

Since a ministry can rarely bankroll a $50,000 defense such as this over an eighteen-month period and survive, it becomes imperative that ministries protect themselves with the easy-to-use and readily available shield of shrewdness.

PERSUASION: THE NAME OF THE LITIGATION GAME

The final element of real-world lawsuits often overlooked by the uninitiated is the fact that it takes convincing, persuasive *evidence* to defend a lawsuit successfully. In the movies, the "smoking gun" is always found. The essential star witness always appears at the last moment. The "good guys" always seem to have just what it takes to convince the jury to believe their version of the truth. Unfortunately, everyday life does not go so smoothly for all the good guys.

Most cases are settled prior to a trial, and substantial sums of money paid out, simply because the organization being sued could not produce the people or documents needed to substantiate its point of view. For example, I recently defended a minister in a lawsuit that was nearing trial. I became quite exasperated by his inherent inability to appreciate the fact that the judge in the case just might not believe everything he had to say, especially when his testimony was going to be directly controverted by several credible witnesses for the opposition.

An important issue in the case centered on the minister signing a contract on behalf of his Christian ministry. He claimed in court to have been told by his adversary that further aspects to the contractual relationship would later be negotiated. When the other side refused to negotiate these other aspects of the relationship, my client refused to perform the contract, and the lawsuit against him and his organization followed. The party suing him flatly denied that any other terms were mentioned.

Throughout the developmental stages of the lawsuit, the minister consistently maintained that when the contract was presented to him and signed, no one was present other than himself and the party suing him. What was said, or not said, at the meeting to finalize the contract was a matter solely within the personal knowledge of the two of them. Hence, I thought we had what many lawyers refer to as a "lying contest" on our hands—the minister's word against that of the plaintiff; the defendant's memory versus that of one other person.

Then, much to my alarm, the opposing lawyer in the lawsuit told me over the phone that a third person was in the office at the time of the signing. This new witness happened to be an independent professional accountant, who on the surface appeared to be impartial and trustworthy. But the CPA agreed with our *opponent's* version that nothing beyond the written contract was discussed at the time of the signing.

I was concerned. It was now two against one in the memory game, and judges and juries always are impressed with testimony backed by others. I immediately called my client to share this new development. I was uncomfortable about telling him what had transpired because I assumed he would be embarrassed by this stronger challenge to his integrity and capacity to recall critical events.

I felt this way, I guess, because I'm a bit old-fashioned and respect a minister's position. I also feared his reaction. After being in identical situations dozens of times before when representing business clients in litigation, I've found they immediately appreciate the ramifications of the "two-against-one" dynamic. Business clients also immediately go into a lengthy, heated explanation and detailed defense of their personal integrity.

My ministry client had a much different reaction—not exactly what I'd feared. His response was simple and unemotional. "No problem," he said. I countered with a curious, "Why do you say that?" He replied, "Because it didn't happen that way." Nothing more to be said. No further explanations. Not a hint of concern. Just, "It didn't happen that way."

He *knew* what the truth was and never considered for a moment that *anyone*, much less a judge or jury, might believe anything else. And why not believe anything else? Because "it didn't happen that way." All trusting? Maybe. Naive? Maybe. Arrogant?

My minister friend was not accustomed to appreciating that the judge and jury are the *only* litmus paper in a lawsuit. In court, you play to one audience, the judge and jury—*they* must be convinced; *they* must be persuaded. And they are persuaded only by what they are allowed to hear and see during the trial. In harsh terms, if you can't prove it, it didn't happen. Proof is everything in a lawsuit.

A witness who tells the truth may not be believed due to his nervousness in testifying, his station in life, or a myriad of other factors concerning the human experience. Important, even critical, documents may never find their way into court because their whereabouts are unknown within a careless, haphazard filing system. Jurors often cannot believe why such an important piece of paper cannot be found. They find it easier to conclude that the paper never existed in the first place. Hindsight in the courtroom is twenty-twenty, just as it is everywhere else.

Being shrewd means being able to back up what you say with proof—convincing, persuasive proof whenever challenged on important issues. Since every decision or action taken has significant consequences if misconstrued later, ministries need constantly to ask the question, "How will we explain today's actions to a group of totally disinterested people a few years from now?" Trustworthy witnesses and a favorable paper trail are the only convincing evidence of how events actually happen.

SUMMARY

Let's review, then, the stark contrasts between "L.A. Law" and the real-life pain of a lawsuit—something that actually happens to many ministries today if they fail to take precautions.

On "L.A. Law," we might see:

- An accusation made.
- An attorney hired.
- A quick summary of the evidence in the law firm boardroom.
- A love scene.
- A dramatic confrontation between the opposing parties.
- A spectacular deposition with a critical witness for the bad guys.
- Ten or fifteen minutes of tense courtroom theatrics.
- A surprise witness for good guys.

- Another love scene.
- A reading of the verdict by a jury foreman with a furrowed brow.
- The judge dramatically declares the good guys the winners.
- Another love scene . . . in celebration, of course.

In real life, we'll probably experience:

- A hurtful accusation made and critical ministry plans delayed.
- An attorney concerned that this could cost the organization up to $100,000 in legal costs alone.
- Press reports about the ministry "allegedly wronging someone."
- Angry letters from donors and constituents who threaten to cut off funds if the ministry is proved to be in the wrong.
- Pressure from the insurance company to keep the lid on public response.
- A six-month delay for the second "hearing."
- A constant nagging possibility that the ministry could lose (which we deny even to ourselves).
- A critical document that can't be found.
- A witness hesitant to cooperate.
- The third hearing delay.
- Vigorous opposition and more accusations from the opposition.
- After a year-and-a-half of delays, depositions taken.
- Another delay due to objections by opposing attorneys.
- After three-and-a-half years, a painful trial before an empty courtroom.
- A phone call from two of the ministry's remaining constituents to say they are praying for a judgment in the ministry's favor.

Then, either:

- A last-minute compromise and settlement that could have occurred three years ago if it hadn't taken so long to find that critical document, or

◆ A judgment in the opponent's favor that costs another $300,000 (not counting legal fees) and cripples the ministry for another five years—or kills it altogether.

This is not a happy picture.

LEGAL STRATEGIES AND PRINCIPLES

◆ Real-world lawsuits take many years to bring to trial. Most cases settle after months, or years, of tedious, expensive pretrial posturing. Justice delayed may well be justice denied.

◆ Ministries must take immediate, proactive steps toward reestablishing credibility outside the courtroom if a lawsuit strikes. Trusting the legal system to provide vindication when wrongly accused will likely leave us deeply disappointed. Ministries must realize that the "no comment" approach in a lawsuit may hurt far more than it helps.

◆ When your day in court finally comes, there may be no one to listen. Your ministry constituents need to hear your side early in the process. In the likely event that your trial takes two or three years to come to court, you'll need that early advantage of publicity to make an impression on supporters and constituents.

◆ Everything you hear about how expensive lawyers and lawsuits can be is absolutely true. You may win a battle in the courtroom but still lose the war, because of the financial drain from defending a lawsuit.

◆ The essence of the legal game is proof and persuasion. How today's actions may be perceived by a judge or jury in the future cannot be certain. We must be able to demonstrate the rightness of our policies and conduct with persuasive evidence.

CHAPTER NINE

Lawyers:
Friend or Foe?

At first, the question of whether lawyers are friend or foe seems absurd, surely only rhetorical. Of course, we all know they are a foe—to be avoided at all costs. There is also a widespread impression that even your own lawyer is not to be fully trusted. At the very least, people are at the unfettered whims of lawyers when it comes to paying their ridiculously high bills.

Such reactions and responses to whether lawyers are our friends are also the same for those in purely secular pursuits. As a group, lawyers are not high on most people's party list. Culturally, the profession in the United States has passively witnessed the creation of the stereotype of lawyers being cold, unfeeling, argumentative, unsympathetic, ruthless, aggressive, combative, and greedy. The most commonly used synonym for lawyers is *sharks*. And in many cases the metaphor fits, unfortunately.

But rather than continue to commiserate, complain, and whine about all the evils in the legal profession, Christians must become shrewd by forming their own army of warriors to fight the legal battles that lay ahead. As secular business learned long ago, the law (like the IRS) is now a *necessary partner* in all that Christian ministries do. It can be a partner that contributes to the successes of a ministry or one that holds it back and wastes away precious resources. There is no third choice.

Legal traps for the unwary will continue to grow in number and in severity of the risks presented. It only makes sense to begin to seek and enlist the very best warriors you can find. If you act shrewdly, your lawyer will be one whose goals align with yours. If not, then at least he or she will be a true professional who has learned from experience, is trustworthy, and has demonstrated consistent integrity in the practice of law. This person must be counted on to set aside any personal agenda to give complete allegiance to the client as the lawyer's oath compels him to do. These kinds of lawyers *are* still out there. In fact, large numbers of highly ethical lawyers exist in every community but are not approached, or are simply overlooked, because people give too much credence to the stereotype that all lawyers are sharks.

God would not be very trustworthy if He were to allow these present dangers to arise in front of ministries without at the same time equipping these ministries with capable legal counsel to meet these serious challenges. So who are these lawyers that everyone seems to detest so much? What is their education like? Do lawyers specialize like doctors do? Are there any ethical duties they owe to you, the client, that you should know about? How do lawyers handle their legal billings and fees? How do you hire a lawyer for the first time?

LAWYERS: A PORTRAIT

Lawyers are a very diverse group of professionals. Although the "shark" jokes portray lawyers as all being alike, nothing could be further from the truth. To work with lawyers, and against lawyers, more shrewdly and more comfortably, it is helpful to know some of the following simple facts about the profession. I hope some erroneous myths can be put aside.

Age
Lawyers are getting younger. Not only do they keep making more money, but they also seem to have found a way to fight off middle age. Seriously, lawyers as a group on average have become younger. For example, in 1960 just under 25 percent of all American lawyers were under the age of thirty-five.[1] In 1980 the percentage of lawyers

under thirty-five years old grew to about 36 percent due to the rapid expansion in the profession fueled by new law school graduates.[2] The chances then are one in three that the lawyers who you will retain (or already have retained) and who will handle your organization's legal matters are under the age of thirty-five. This holds true for your adversaries as well.

Actually, "young" lawyers, commonly called young "associates" in law firms, can be an extremely valuable asset. A common, not so facetious, comment within firms is that when you need to know what the law is, go find the youngest associate in the place. The logic is obvious. Young lawyers are closest to their law school education and presumably have forgotten the least. Additionally, their education, being more recent, included the most applicable state-of-the-art legal trends and developments. So, if having quick access to the current state of the law is important, a young lawyer can be most beneficial.

On the other hand, younger lawyers usually have not learned how to *use* the law, which comes from professional experience. So many times a judgment call is the all-important thread holding together a strategic legal course of action. Applying what the law says, or has omitted saying, to real-world dreams and dilemmas is most often the key role of good legal advice. Wise counsel often only comes from experience in the trenches.

Depending on the type of legal work needed, a choice between youth and age may be appropriate. If your organization is large enough, you may be fortunate to be able to have access to the young, the old, and the in-between. For others, selecting a law firm of several or more lawyers that includes a diversity of resources is probably the best option.

Gender

The number of women lawyers in the United States has grown dramatically in the last twenty years. In 1970 only about 5 percent of all lawyers were female. In 1980 the percentage had tripled to 16 percent. By 1986 the number of women attending law school had grown to more than 40 percent. Essentially, in 1992, the legal profession is close to becoming an arena almost equally shared by men and women.[3] While women still do not come close to parity in other professional areas such as partnership status, professorships, judgeships, and salaries, their sheer numbers in this profession are noteworthy.

When other minorities are added to the statistical analysis, the once white male domination of law wilts further. In California a bar-sponsored study presented in September 1991 showed that 51 percent of all California lawyers practicing five years or less were women and minorities.[4] People must now learn how to analyze the skills of lawyers by nonsexist and nonracial standards. An attorney's ability to interpret the law and give counsel on legal strategy does not depend on gender, race, creed, or color. Furthermore, there are situations in which it is particularly shrewd to acknowledge the special tactical roles certain lawyers can play in the real world of litigation.

An excellent example of a tactical role that women lawyers can play is from the previously discussed case against Bishop Frey and the Episcopal Diocese. In the jury trial that lasted three weeks, the plaintiff was a woman claiming sexual abuse by a male priest of the Episcopal church. The alleged victim was represented by a female lawyer. Bishop Frey, the Episcopal church, and their insurance company presumably could have chosen their defense lawyer from several hundred excellent trial lawyers, including many women. The choice was a male lawyer.

The jury in the Bishop Frey case included four women out of six jurors, and they came back with a unanimous verdict awarding nearly $1.2 million in damages to the female plaintiff. The question that should be asked is whether the outcome would have been any different had the bishop and the Episcopal church been represented by a woman lawyer. The subtleties of a lawsuit for sexual misconduct with women on one side against men on the other might have been mitigated. One attorney suggested that she found it surprising that the church did not retain a woman lawyer to diffuse such overtones. The plaintiff's counsel's job in trying the case before the jury would have been much more difficult with a female lawyer opposing her, in my opinion. The case might have taken on a whole different tenor since the accusations of sexual misconduct by a priest were reportedly defended with the theory that the woman seduced the priest, not vice versa. In the 1990s and into the next century, the sex of a person's trial lawyer will still be a factor in legal strategy. Shrewdness dictates that you at least consider the same factors that your opponents will analyze in their efforts against you.

Numbers

Lawyers are everywhere. The increase in the numbers of lawyers is absolutely phenomenal. In 1960 there were 285,933 lawyers in the United States, which means there was one lawyer for every 632 people. By 1980 the number doubled to 542,205.[5] In 1988 the U.S. had approximately 622,000 lawyers, which is about one lawyer for every 377 people. The scary thought, however, is that these growing numbers are not projected to cease in the near future. Projections show that there will be *810,000* lawyers in the U.S. by the year 2000.[6] These projections may also be conservative because the American Bar Association (ABA) itself estimated in July 1991 that there were already 777,119 lawyers in the U.S.[7]

The ABA and its membership are not alarmed by these dramatic increases. The ABA boasted a membership in 1991 of 368,976 lawyers (nearly one-half of the total) and is a powerful organization, politically and otherwise.[8] At the annual meeting of ABA's leadership in Atlanta on August 13, 1991, Vice President Dan Quayle gave an address that was clearly meant as a challenge to the profession to control the legal explosion in America. Quayle queried, "Does America really need 70 percent of the world's lawyers? . . . Is it healthy for our economy to have 18 million *new* lawsuits coursing through the system annually? Is it right that people with disputes come up against staggering expense and delay?"[9]

Fair questions to be asked? Just the kind of honest inquiry we'd expect should be a topic of discussion at a conference of the nation's legal leadership. Point well taken? No, not at all.

Quayle's call for reforms by lawyers did not receive a warm reception. This was probably to be expected. What was not expected by the vice president, himself a lawyer, was the openly terse, immediate response from no less than ABA President John Curtin, who reportedly replied in part that Vice President Quayle should focus on "real problems and not be distracted by illusory ones."[10] The vice president had been greeted politely by the 600-member delegation and received a "smattering" of applause at the end of his remarks. In contrast, the ABA president's sharp words drew a "loud and sustained applause," according to the *American Bar Journal* report "impartially" entitled "Quayle Raps Lawyers."[11]

This isolated, under-reported exchange leaves only a couple of conclusions to draw. First, the majority of "mainstream" lawyers (at least those represented by ABA President Curtin) either are still not aware that the legal system is a mess, or simply do not care. Second, lawyers themselves and their institutions will not be leaders in reform. At best, they will be unwilling stragglers forced to go with the flow. Restrictions on the growth and self-perpetuating power of the legal profession will have to come from outside pressures.

Happy or Sad? Glad or Mad?

If you, and everyone else in the United States, are unhappy with the state of the legal system, should it be any surprise that lawyers too are unhappy? For a variety of reasons, lawyers as a group are not very happy being lawyers. The salary and influence ultimately don't provide satisfaction and well-being. Most people in Christian ministry probably would have suspected that would be the case.

A recent survey of lawyers in North Carolina unearthed some revealing patterns of unhappiness in the North Carolina bar. In a report, 23 percent of North Carolina lawyers said they would not even become a lawyer if they had it to do over again. Twenty-four percent of those polled reported symptoms of depression, such as loss of appetite and trouble sleeping. Another 25 percent reported symptoms of anxiety—namely, hands trembling, heart racing, and faintness. Finally, 22 percent reported having ulcers, coronary artery disease, or other stress-related diseases.[12]

I do not intend even in the slightest to insult the state of North Carolina. But I think it is safe to say that the professional pressures and other negative attributes of being a lawyer in North Carolina do not, on the whole, rise to the same level that occur in large metropolitan centers like New York, Philadelphia, Boston, Chicago, Atlanta, San Francisco, and Los Angeles. If one out of four lawyers in North Carolina is experiencing such unhappiness, what might a survey in one of our hustle-bustle urban centers conclude? If the practice of law is killing the attorneys in North Carolina, Manhattan must be the land of the walking dead.

If so many lawyers are unhappy, stressed out, and feeling beat up, how can you be shrewd with and against such people? Maybe it's a kind word or a simple, sincere thank you. Maybe it's asking how the weekend went. Human kindness and genuine Christian graciousness, even to your adversaries, could do a lot to diffuse so much of the hostility surrounding the adversarial nature of legal negotiations. Due to the law school indoctrination process that we will look at in the next chapter, lawyers, by and large, have become combative and comfortable in aggressive, threatening situations. It is so easy to become immune to it all.

A certain amount of emotional denial is required concerning the levels of hostility lawyers live with regularly in their job. Supposedly lawyers are the client's guardian—many people would say "hired gun." Hence, lawyers are always to be on the lookout for those who would harm their client. Naturally, this high level of instinctive protectionism overlaps with protecting one's own interests. A growling, angry bulldog is synonymous with strength and security. Mack Trucks bases its entire corporate image on its bulldog trademark. Similarly, lawyers have consciously and unconsciously seen themselves as the angry bulldog protecting their clients and themselves.

LEGAL STRATEGIES AND PRINCIPLES

◆ The law, and lawyers, can be partners that contribute to our ministry's success, or ones that hold us back and waste precious resources.

◆ God would not let us face these mounting legal dangers without providing us with capable legal counsel to help us meet such challenges. But we must do our part and find that appropriate attorney.

◆ Lawyers as a group are becoming younger and more ethnically diverse. The profession includes rapidly increasing numbers of females. Perpetuating older stereotypes concerning the "successful" lawyer may be quite harmful to our own cause as we work with, and against, lawyers.

◆ Lawyers are everywhere, and their numbers are still increasing at a record pace, in spite of the public outcry that "Enough is enough!" Too many lawyers can result only in too many legal controversies, with no end in sight.

CHAPTER TEN

Professor Kingsfield Revisited: Lawyers' Education and Ethics

Many people will remember the movie *The Paper Chase* and its most notable character, Professor Kingsfield. The starring role of Kingsfield was played by actor John Houseman, also known for his Smith Barney advertisements. ("We make money the old-fashioned way. We earn it.") These ads further enriched his Kingsfield image. Houseman became synonymous with the fictitious character Kingsfield in the "Paper Chase" television series that lasted a handful of seasons.

If these images conjure in your mind the Kingsfield classroom scenes from the movie, you probably have a pretty good sense of a lawyer's law school training—highly intense, highly competitive, a true sense of being tempered by fire.

THE UNIQUE ASPECTS OF LAW SCHOOL EDUCATION

The academic and scholarly aspects of a law school education are generally no more demanding intellectually than other professional graduate school programs. Clearly, becoming a doctor, psychologist, or church pastor requires equal or greater intellectual capacities. Where the lawyer's education is markedly different, and what accounts for many lawyers being the way they are, is the emotional and psychological conditioning that law schools intentionally inflict.

Probably every law school professor uses the "Paper Chase" phrase, "We are not just teaching you the law, but how to *think like a lawyer*." These professors mean it in the literal sense. The educational process in most law schools has been designed to alter one's previous way of looking at the world. If the law school has done its job as it's generally envisioned, its graduates will no longer accept anything at face value. They will no longer place trust in another person until that person has proven to be worthy of trust. Finally, the well-educated lawyer will analyze and challenge to death every principle, concept, and theory life has to offer. When no theory, system, or person can be accepted just as they are, can you imagine what kind of individuals these law schools produce? Argumentative, competitive, caustic, unprincipled, cool, aloof, unattached, . . . and shark-like. Sound familiar? Sounds like all the lawyer-bashing jokes.

How do law schools accomplish this task in three short years? They don't complete the task, they just do everything to purge as many normal thought processes as possible and replace them with the "think like a lawyer" fundamentals. After graduation, the profession itself takes over and completes the task in about five more years when the average lawyer has finally proved herself or himself to be partnership material.

Law school accomplishes its primary task in three simple ways. Those who remember Kingsfield will know what I mean.

The Socratic Method
First, most law schools still use the classroom teaching style known as the "Socratic" method. The professors rarely lecture as in undergraduate school and in other types of graduate schools. Rather, a principle of the law is presented in a series of hypothetical fact patterns posed by the professor, who then asks questions of individual students intended to help the students find their own answers. Students are grilled by the professor while standing alone before seventy-five to one hundred fellow students. In the first few months of the first year, every student feels sympathy for those souls who are selected and run through the fire. It is a system of teaching that operates heavily on students' feelings of fear, embarrassment, shame, and cruelty.

Oddly, by the end of the three years, the process has acclimated the student to be able to witness a friend go through a shaming series of questions without any personal feelings of sympathy or empathy. Such questioning no longer stirs feelings of anger toward this "cold-hearted" professor. The graduate is now trained to coolly, calmly, and unregretfully make an opposing witness look like a complete fool in the courtroom or at the bargaining table. No wonder society perceives lawyers as cold, calculating, and soulless.

Cutthroat Individual Competition

The second unique aspect of the law school education is the extremely high level of competition among the students from beginning to end. This competition is created by a standard ranking system of students used by most schools. From the first set of semester grades to gradua-tion ceremonies three years later, every student in his or her class is ranked on grade point averages from top to bottom. There's no guessing or speculation where a student stands in class. If a student is last in his class of 237 students, his semester or quarterly grade card will show, "Rank: 237 of 237." Obviously, this is an inherently competitive approach to grade point averages.

Students are continually reminded of the fact that they will be asked by prospective employers throughout the balance of their career, "What was your class rank?" This makes the competition very meaningful. It is no consolation for anyone to hear the say-ing, "Half of all lawyers graduated in the bottom half of their class." Everyone entering law school has been accustomed to experiencing high levels of academic success, and not one finds it palatable to see a low class rank on a computer grade card each quarter or semester.

The students' response to this incessant ranking of individual against individual, which will determine whether they are invited to be on Law Review at their school and will be a major factor in the quality of jobs for which their résumé will qualify, is good old-fashioned, cutthroat competition. It is every man and woman for themselves. By helping others, students only dilute their progress up the mathematical G.P.A. ladder. At graduation, students have a strong indoctrination that practicing law is by no means a cooperative effort in finding justice. It is not a joint effort of reaching agreements. Rather, it is all about winning and gaining a leg up on the other guy. It is about reaching agreements with adversaries by creating illusions of superior strength. Being a lawyer is not a team sport.

The Extremities of Logic and Argument

There is a third aspect of legal education that makes American lawyers what they are today. The examination process teaches law students that it is more important to demonstrate the logic and analytical skills used to reach a conclusion than to have a correct conclusion. Essentially, the methods and means leading to an answer are much more valued in law school than is the answer at the end.

For good reason, lawyers do need to be trained to argue both sides of an issue, in spite of all the jokes about lawyers being able to talk out of both sides of their mouths. Obviously, in every dispute the two clients have differing points of view on the same subject. Each position is entitled to be presented and argued vigorously by each side's lawyer. That's the essence of the American justice system, with which few people quarrel.

But law schools have taken the analysis and debate skills and placed them equal to, and in some cases above, the goals of finding the truth and rendering justice. Modern-day American lawyers need to be reminded, sometimes constantly, of the client's goals and wishes. It is too easy for them to slip into their routine of analysis and argument, and forget altogether how the problem was started and what result the client hoped to obtain.

I believe I was trained well in the system's methods. I wish I had a dollar for every time my wife has had to remind me that I am again arguing for the sole sake of arguing. The process of debating an issue can become invigorating in and of itself to a law school-trained individual. And believe me, it is extremely difficult to let go of this.

As a Christian in ministry employing attorneys, you need to constantly remember that the lawyer represents you. You have retained him or her to work on your behalf. Therefore, it is your goals and desires that must be pursued and respected. You need actively to remind your attorney that notwithstanding his or her personal enjoyment of being in competition with a fellow attorney, you want your goals pursued at all times in a manner fitting to your ministry and its reputation in the community.

LAWYERS' SPECIALTIES
(OTHER THAN MAKING MONEY)

Lawyers are commonly asked, "What is your specialty?" or, "What type of law do you practice?" These are relevant questions for most people conversationally and for those actually in the market to hire a lawyer. "Are you a corporate lawyer, tax lawyer, trial lawyer, or real estate lawyer?"

While very few lawyers truly "specialize" in a formal way like doctors, the essence sought by these questions should never be overlooked. I often see Christians new to legal matters ready to hire a lawyer solely because he or she is a Christian. You always need to remember that you retain lawyers for their skill in dealing with particular issues and problems. Matching the lawyer's expertise to your specific need is just as important (probably more so in most cases) as his or her beliefs or brand of theology.

The comparison of lawyers' specialties to doctors' specialties is analogous but not all that helpful. Most physicians specialize in one area of medicine that begins in their residency training at the beginning of their career. A conscious choice is made at the completion f medical school to become a pediatrician, an anesthesiologist, a gynecologist, a podiatrist, and so forth, and each doctor's residency training is focused on that field.

Lawyers' practices and areas of expertise occur rather differently. To begin with, all law school curriculums are pretty much the same. The required courses for every law student are generally the same from school to school. A few elective classes are permitted, but most students choose electives that follow the common themes of the required courses.

The bar exams for licensing as a lawyer in all fifty states are quite uniform from state to state. The method of testing may differ, but the content is the same. Any student graduating from any of the 175 or so law schools approved by the American Bar Association may sit for the bar exam in any state. Each state's test is the same for every applicant. In other words, there is no special bar exam or unique portion of a bar exam for those wanting to become a real estate lawyer as compared to those desiring to practice corporate law or family law. At the beginning of every lawyer's career, he or she has passed a state bar exam for licensing that tests on a broad spectrum of foundational legal principles and concepts. No specialization takes place at the bar-exam level.

Some states have implemented formal certified specialization programs. If you or your organization is seeking to hire a lawyer in one of these states, it would be helpful to investigate whether the certification program covers the area of law in which your needs arise. For example, if your organization has been sued and you are searching for a competent attorney to handle your defense, it would be helpful if your particular state does, in fact, certify trial lawyers as specialists. If it does, you could ask in your hiring interview whether the lawyer you are considering is currently certified as a trial specialist, for how long, and so forth. As of August 1990, the American Bar Association reported that only fifteen states had any form of a lawyer certification program for specific areas of legal specialization.[1] These fifteen states are:

Alabama	Minnesota
Arizona	New Jersey
Arkansas	New Mexico
California	North Carolina
Connecticut	South Carolina
Florida	Texas
Georgia	Utah
Louisiana	

Lawyer certification programs in these states can range from Louisiana, which only certifies qualifying tax lawyers as "specialists," to California, which provides specialist certification in six areas: criminal law; family law; immigration and nationality law; probate, estate planning, and trust law; taxation law; and worker's compensation law. Connecticut goes further with twenty-five separate areas of certified specialty.[2]

Certification requirements vary from state to state, but each has formal requirements of education and training beyond law school, testing, or both. In some trial specialist certificates, the lawyer must have previously conducted a minimum number of trials before becoming certified as a trial specialist.

State programs for specialty certification will not guarantee that your choice of a lawyer in a specialist field will necessarily win your case for you. What they contribute most is to help you avoid hiring someone who is a novice on your kind of problem. You'll attain a greater level of expertise when hiring a true certified specialist in those states with such programs. Even if your state is not among the fifteen listed, you should still make an inquiry of your state's bar association because certification of legal specialties is on the upswing. Clients want it, and most lawyers prefer it. Only those fearing the requirements voice opposition. The future should see more states implementing programs and expanding those already in place.

Knowing If You Need a Specialist

With almost every question in the law, the most often heard answer to the question of whether you need a legal specialist is, "It depends." Whether a true specialist is needed *depends* on the problem's complexity and the magnitude of the risks involved. You may not need a trial specialist on a $750 lawsuit. On the other hand, a $750,000 lawsuit concerning sophisticated land use questions probably should only be handled by a specialist or team of specialists (e.g., a trial lawyer and a real estate lawyer) if specialization exists in your jurisdiction.

Your church or organization may serve itself best by developing an ongoing relationship with a business law generalist, just as the corporate business community has done for decades. In business, these business lawyers are referred to as "corporate general counsel" and are the first place the client turns with any sort of legal problem or issue. A long-term loyal relationship of mutual trust and respect can develop with one lawyer who can play a dual role for your ministry.

A general counsel lawyer can handle routine day-to-day matters, but more importantly, can act as your liaison to retaining legal specialists if and when unique, esoteric legal matters arise. The general counsel can be of great value in the location and selection of a competent specialist. The general counsel can then monitor the matter with undivided allegiance to your interests. General counsel can also save significant amounts in legal fees charged by these specialists, as the general counsel is in a much better position to evaluate options and keep fees in line with estimates. Developing a long-term relationship with a business law generalist can become the most effective way to function shrewdly in this new era.

If a general counsel is not on board and your state does not certify specialists in your legal problem area, how do you select a capable lawyer? Adhering to the following suggestions should get you on your way toward finding capable, trustworthy legal counsel.

First, actively seek referrals from your peers. If you are in church leadership and are seeking a lawyer for the church, try calling other churches in your community for a reference to a good lawyer. Again, try not to let denominational and theological differences deter you. Normally, being a Methodist, Presbyterian, or Baptist won't alter a real estate lawyer's opinions on a legal zoning question. While there probably won't be any "church law" specialists in your town, the mere fact that a lawyer or firm has one or more church clients will necessarily give it some advantages due to prior experiences, certification issues notwithstanding. If church referrals are not helpful, contact Christian businesspeople in your congregation as well as nonprofit organization leaders in your community. Again, a reference from someone you know and trust will more than likely yield a more qualified referral than will a bar association referral program or other impersonal ways to get in touch with lawyers. More detail on selecting and hiring a lawyer is provided in the next chapter.

LAWYERS' ETHICS (YES, THEY HAVE THEM)

The jokes about lawyers not having any more of an ethical code than a sleazy con artist are really off the mark when measuring the average lawyer. Most lawyers take their ethics seriously, even if it stems solely from a fear of losing their license. Sometimes, though, the code of professional legal ethics itself creates the impression that most lawyers were at the end of the line when moral fortitude was being allocated.

Most (not all) of the public's impressions of lawyers' ethics are captured in another extremely common question asked of every lawyer at social gatherings: "How can a lawyer defend someone that he knows is guilty?" At a less conscious level, I suspect, many people wonder how lawyers can, for example, be an advocate for Exxon in connection with the terrible Valdez oil spill. Or, how can a lawyer of conscience bring a lawsuit on behalf of a group of church members against its pastor for breach of trust concerning the location of the church sanctuary?

An obvious and easy answer to some of these tough ethical points is money. Surely greed can be a big motivator. Ego and public reputation can also be motivators in some unpalatable cases. But to provide some balance and complexity to these issues, let me reveal some of the ethical mandates on lawyers that also have some bearing.

Lawyer's Oath

Every lawyer at the time of being licensed as an attorney, also called being admitted to the bar, *takes a solemn personal oath referred to as the "Lawyer's Oath."* This oath is analogous to the doctors' Hippocratic Oath. The lawyer's oath required of me in Colorado states:

> I DO SOLEMNLY SWEAR by the Everliving God: that,
> I will support the Constitution of the United States and the
>   Constitution of the State of Colorado;
> I will maintain the respect due to Courts of Justice and judi-
>   cial officers;
> I will not counsel or maintain any suit or proceeding which
>   shall appear to me to be without merit or to be unjust;
>   I will not assert any defense except such as I honestly
>   believe to be debatable under the law of the land;
> I will employ for the purpose of maintaining the causes
>   confided to me such means only as are consistent
>   with truth and honor; I will never seek to mislead the
>   Judge or jury by any misstatement or false statement of
>   fact or law;
> I will maintain the confidence and preserve inviolate the
>   secrets of my client; I will accept no compensation in
>   connection with my client's business except from my
>   client or with my client's knowledge and approval;
> I will abstain from all offensive conduct; I will not advance
>   any fact prejudicial to the honor or reputation of a party

or witness, unless required by the justice of the cause
with which I am charged;

I will never reject, from any consideration personal to myself,
the cause of the defenseless or oppressed, nor will I delay
any person's cause for greed or malice.

I will at all times faithfully and diligently adhere to the Code
of Professional Responsibility.

You will note that the oath requires lawyers in Colorado not to
refuse employment of a client solely because of the unpopularity of
the client or his cause. In other words, it would actually be unethical of
me to refuse representation to a Charles Manson, a Saddam Hussein,
or a minister accused of sexually molesting children in the Sunday
school, solely because of the unpopularity and unpleasantness of the
person or the circumstances.

In a strange way, then, one could argue that it is the truly ethical
lawyer who accepts unpopular employment opportunities of the type
many Christians find objectionable. It is remotely possible that the
lawyers defending the guilty do so out of allegiance to the oath given.
We should be slow to assume, therefore, that the lawyer is always cut
out of the same cloth as the client.

Lawyer's Code of Ethics

In addition to the lawyer's oath, which is fairly general in nature,
every state has some form of *ethics code* for lawyers. This code
lays out the very detailed duties and obligations placed on each
lawyer practicing law in that state. These detailed rules of ethics
are mandatory in most respects and are not mere suggestions or
lofty goals to seek. In addition to the not-so-surprising general
rules prohibiting lawyer dishonesty, fraud, and deceit, there are
a number of specific mandates that may give a new perspective
on the role of lawyers.

Zealous representation. "A lawyer should represent a client
zealously within the bounds of the law"[3] (emphasis added). This
rule is the most applicable to lawyers who represent a person who
appears to be guilty or those lawyers who appear to maintain an
unjust position or cause. The rule requires all lawyers to give 100
percent of their effort and ability to the cause and position of their

client so long as the law is not knowingly being violated by the lawyers.

This rule—particularly the aspect of what is "within the bounds of the law"—is the subject of great ongoing differences of opinion among judges and lawyers. But the fundamental principle of going all out for your client and not allowing yourself as lawyer to play the role of judge or jury is what everyone wants of his or her lawyer. So we should not be shocked or disgusted when we witness a lawyer representing his or her client in a zealous fashion with complete conviction and concentration on the task. The attorney is merely living up to this ethical rule placed on all lawyers. It is said that the duty a lawyer owes to his client and the duty owed to the American legal system are the same: to represent the client zealously within the bounds of the law.

Other ethical rules that are less widely known, but pertinent to your employment of lawyers, focus specifically on the private relationship between the client and the lawyer. Every client should realize that these exist and understand their application.

Reasonable fees. "A lawyer shall charge a reasonable fee."[4] Now you may be thinking, *Sure, Lansing!* Not many lawyers willingly promote the fact that the ethical rules governing their license to practice law prohibit a clearly excessive fee. Sadly, far too many lawyers and law firms believe that a fair, reasonable bill is whatever the client can be induced to pay. You should check with your local bar association for your state's particular definition of reasonable fees. More detail on legal fees and the ethics of lawyers' bills will be covered in the next chapter.

Confidentiality. "A lawyer should preserve the confidences and secrets of the client."[5] This ethical rule is one that will not need a reminder from client to lawyer under normal circumstances. But it may nonetheless be advisable for you as a pastor or ministry staff to advise your lawyer and ask the lawyer to relay to the firm's secretaries who will be handling sensitive documents exactly what you deem to be a confidence or secret. The typical rule in this area defines a "secret" as any information arising in the professional relationship that *the client has requested be held inviolate* or the disclosure of which would be embarrassing or detrimental to the client. The client's requests in these regards must be honored.

I suggest that you do not assume that all your legal matters will be held in confidence in all respects due to the very nature of the practice of law. Lawyers and law firms are in the business of lawsuits and legal problems. Conversations, professional and otherwise, with lawyers and their staffs naturally gravitate to cases and unusual projects. Your case or project as a church or other ministry will likely be considered unique and *newsworthy* simply because you *are* a pastor, a church, or a Christian organization needing a lawyer. Day-to-day business clients are not noteworthy, but until the past few years, representing a church in litigation has been out of the ordinary in most firms.

For example, the fact that your church or organization has been sued is not in and of itself a "confidence" of a client because it is a matter of public record at the courthouse. Anyone can gain access to the court's file and its contents. But what if you want the whole situation to be kept as secret as possible? Being sued could alone be detrimental, even if it concerned a simple real estate boundary dispute with a neighboring property owner. A simple, yet sincere, request to keep the lawsuit and its subject matter secret by the lawyer and his firm's staff would be prudent. All of us can use a reminder of our responsibilities in our work from time to time.

Conflicts of interest. "A lawyer should not represent multiple clients with differing interests."[6] Lawyers are generally not permitted to represent clients in the same matter or lawsuit if the clients have opposing or even different needs and goals. Only after a full explanation of the conflicts of interest between the clients and after receiving their consent should a lawyer attempt to represent, zealously, two or more divergent clients.

This issue arises most frequently in church litigation when someone has sued the church (or other Christian organization) as well as the pastor, staff, or elders as individual persons. A recent case illustrates this type of conflict of interest quite well.

A pastor and his church were sued along with a diverse group of church committee members. Initially, the pastor and his staff asked one lawyer to represent all the defendants, including each of the committee members. It made sense financially to have one lawyer rather than several involved in the case, and everyone believed the plaintiff's claims to be without merit. No disclosure of the possible conflicts of interest that could arise on the defense side was ever made.

Everything went well in the initial months of pretrial posturing. Church funds were used for defense costs, and the committee
members felt comfortable. Then things began to change. The opposition requested and scheduled depositions of the committee members.
More frequent phone calls and meetings with the lawyer began to
occur. The whole ordeal became a substantial inconvenience. The
committee members began to ask why the case couldn't be settled to
avoid further inconveniences and possible risks of losing the trial.

The pastor and church staff were far less concerned with inconvenience than they were with clearing the church's name. They
wanted a trial victory to demonstrate to everyone that they were in the
right. Soon it became apparent that the lawyer could not go forward
trying to represent two now diverse groups. The committee members
wanted the matter over as soon as possible, while the staff wanted
to fight to the bitter end. The whole group began unified against the
plaintiff's allegations, and its unity on that level never changed. What
changed were the levels of commitment to the lawsuit.

At a very late date, the committee members retained new counsel, and within a matter of weeks they had worked out a non-monetary
settlement with the opposition. The settlement allowed them to get
out of the lawsuit that continued on for two more years against the
pastor, his staff, and the church organization. A less discerning group
of committee members might have been stuck in the case and suffered
through another two years of unnecessary hassles and worry. In such
situations, the client should ask the lawyer how he expects to handle
divergent interests in case the attorney might have overlooked his ethical
duties in the enthusiasm of being hired for an interesting new case.

The duty to inform. "A lawyer has a duty to inform the client."[7]
Many a lawyer and client begin to drift apart over this issue. Lack
of communication by the lawyer to the client on important developments for which the lawyer was hired is the foremost cause of client
mistrust. As a client, you are entitled to know about the progress of
your case and what exactly the lawyer and his opposition are doing.
If you feel you are being left out in the cold, speak up. You have every
right to receive an appropriate explanation on a regular basis of what
is happening.

This includes the very sensitive subject of legal fees, which will be addressed in the next chapter. Just as you would ask your plumber or electrician for an estimate of his charges (and how the estimate was determined) and would readily question him if the estimate were exceeded significantly, so you should likewise inquire on the subject of your lawyer's fees and billings. If you cannot afford the way the billings are going, let that fact be known.

Any reluctance in the 1990s to question a professional concerning his or her fees is unfounded. If you think the lawyer will be offended or find it crass that you are probing about his fees, you need not worry. Believe me, it has become the norm rather than the exception for clients to be quite up front in asking about fees and questioning bills. Lawyers, like everyone, find it uncomfortable talking about their personal value in the marketplace. Nonetheless, it is common practice for frank discussions to occur about fees. After all, the *lawyer* has an affirmative duty to do so under every state professional ethics code. If you detect a serious unwillingness to discuss fees in detail or a resistance to keep you informed on the legal developments in your case, you should probably consider a new lawyer, one who is willing to serve you in a professional and ethical way.

SUMMARY

Remember, lawyers work for *you*. They are acting on *your* behalf. Understanding their education and the ethical codes that govern their legal conduct in every state will put you and your ministry ahead in the event of a lawsuit or the threat of one.

LEGAL STRATEGIES AND PRINCIPLES

◆Lawyers are trained in a highly competitive atmosphere designed to teach them to think professionally and logically "like a lawyer."

◆Lawyers are trained to remain emotionally and psychologically aloof so that they can represent their clients in the best manner possible without being caught up in the emotions of a case.

◆Law schools train lawyers by utilizing three primary means:

1. The crucible of the Socratic method.
2. The encouragement of extreme levels of academic competition.
3. The "examination premise," which focuses on correct logical and analytical skills rather than correct conclusions.

◆Lawyers must be prepared to represent either side of a legal dispute.

◆Some lawyers do specialize, but every ministry should at least consider a relationship with a general counsel.

◆General counsel can guide a ministry to specialists when needed.

◆Lawyers have ethical codes of conduct of which you should be aware:

1. Lawyers must take a lawyer's oath (similar to doctors' Hippocratic Oath).
2. Lawyers are duty-bound to represent every client zealously within the bounds of the law (which explains why some represent persons who appear guilty or even take on what appear to be unjust causes or positions).
3. Lawyers must charge reasonable fees.
4. Lawyers must preserve confidences and secrets of clients.
5. Lawyers must not represent multiple clients with important differing interests.
6. Lawyers are duty-bound to keep their clients informed of the progress of their case and of the nature of their legal fees.

CHAPTER ELEVEN

Ten Commandments for Working with Lawyers, Part I

Lawyers' fees are often considered to be unreasonable. This is partly due to the fact that many lawyers' fees *are* unreasonable. It also tends to irk people that lawyers singlehandedly can wreak so much havoc in other people's lives and make so much money for themselves while doing it. Much of this criticism is warranted, and many law firms are unable to recognize the legal fee ruts that they have created for their clients. Many don't want to see; others just can't.

However, times are changing rapidly for lawyers and their exorbitant rates. Throughout the business community, the purchasers of legal services have had enough and are rapidly taking action. For once, law firms are being held truly accountable for their fees and the quantity of work they perform on routine matters.

Before addressing the key "commandments" for working with lawyers and controlling your organization's legal expenses, let's take a look at the ethical foundation for legal fees of which most clients are not aware. Many lawyers don't care to discuss these ethical rules governing their fees. I trust the reason for their inhibition is obvious.

WHAT IS A REASONABLE FEE?

Part of the ethical code governing lawyers in every state is a clear, unequivocal requirement for lawyers' fees to be fair and reasonable.

Remember this at all times as you consider legal expenses and any lawyer's bills to you for services: A lawyer has an ethical duty, as a condition of his or her professional license, to *charge* a fee that is not excessive. This should be your rule too. No client should *pay* an unfair, unreasonable, or clearly excessive bill from a law firm. Most state ethics codes will list the following guidelines for the reasonableness of a lawyer's bill:

1. The time and labor required
2. The novelty and difficulty of the legal questions involved
3. The amount of money at risk
4. The results obtained
5. The time limitations imposed by the client or by other circumstances beyond the lawyer's control
6. The nature and length of the relationship with the client
7. The experience, reputation, and unique abilities of the lawyer performing services
8. Whether the fee was fixed or contingent
9. The fee customarily charged in the locality for similar services.

If you have ever worked with lawyers and have had the opportunity to discuss a disputed ridiculously high bill with a lawyer, you will recall how the discussion went. If you have not, here is what you may expect to hear. First, "We spent X number of hours, and we charge $X per hour." Then, "It was a very difficult, complex project" (though it was considered routine and straightforward at the time of hiring the lawyer in the first place). Rarely is there any mention of these factors, although the "what is a customary fee" guideline may also have been mentioned. The customary fee can be a somewhat misguided factor, especially if most other lawyers are "customarily" charging excessive fees.

The circuity of the fee-charging argument needs to be broken. If a lawyer insists on the bill-by-the-hour format, then why don't clients get billed only for the ten minutes it takes to change the names in a routine will that is in memory storage in the word processor? In this instance, billing by the hour nets the lawyer less than fifty dollars for a fifteen-page will, and that's just not fair and reasonable to the lawyer.

As shrewd purchasers of professional services, those in ministry need to always keep in mind that a truly reasonable fee is one that is so to both the lawyer *and the client*. What is reasonable for the lawyer to sustain a professional image and lifestyle is not at all what may be reasonable for your organization.

But there's more to dealing with lawyers than simply knowing that they are ethically bound to charge reasonable fees. For the rest of this chapter and the next, we will look at ten more important guidelines for working with lawyers, guidelines that will aid your ministry in maintaining a helpful relationship with your attorney and keep those legal fees in check. We'll call these the "Ten Commandments for Working with Lawyers."

FIRST COMMANDMENT: CHOOSE THE RIGHT LAWYER

Christians in ministry typically make two very dangerous mistakes when it comes to the use of lawyers. One, they often don't confer with a lawyer at all because of a fear of what it will cost. The reputation that legal services can be very expensive scares many away from exploring preventive legal measures. Obviously, a realistic legal fee budget must exist and then be used. Legal protection is now as important to what people do as electricity, heat, and telephone service. Flying by the seat of your pants legally is not a wise option.

The second, and equally significant, mistake to save money is the use of a lawyer who is a good friend or belongs to the church or is an active member of the parachurch ministry. Out of a desire to minimize expenses and also from a general unfamiliarity with lawyers in the first place, churches regularly look to the lawyer in their congregation for a favor. Most often there is an unspoken, unclear expectation that the lawyer's advice and related services will be rendered for free. This is not just an expectation held by the ministry staff member but is usually the expectation of the lawyer, who sincerely wants to help out his church or favorite ministry. Sounds like a marriage made in heaven. No wonder this is the single most common basis of a relationship of ministry and lawyer. But is it the best situation for you, the client? Or, for that matter, for the lawyer?

My concern is this. The lawyer has been selected solely for convenience and money savings. Rarely in these situations is the lawyer selected because he or she has the professional qualifications needed at that time. More often than not, for example, churches end up asking corporate law experts questions about real estate law and tax lawyers questions about appropriate levels of insurance and policy coverages.

The lawyers involved are often as much to blame. If a church asks for help or advice outside the lawyer's area of practice, he should decline to get involved and refer the client to a suitable specialist if any issues beyond the most straightforward are involved. But the lawyer may be eager to serve his church or does not know how to say no. The lawyers in churches and involved in ministries are not likely to be of the shark variety. Most work hard at living out their Christian beliefs at work. Nonetheless, there's a fear that if they say, "No, that's out of my area," they will be perceived as avoiding a nonpaying or low-paying engagement. A variety of unstated, ambiguous misapprehensions on both sides can easily lead to a Christian lawyer getting in over his head with his own church or ministry. If the project becomes much more involved than anyone ever expected, the lawyer now feels like he's out on a limb with no way to turn back.

Next, the lawyer's human nature can easily begin to cause frustration and a feeling of "how did I get roped into this deal?" since many hours are spent without compensation or any hope of remuneration. Other feelings follow, "When will this be over?" and, "I'll never do this again!" This is not how I want my doctor to feel as he begins surgery. Ministries must then question whether the gratuitous help from lawyer constituents is really in any ministry's best interest. Ministries must budget for and be prepared to pay *reasonable* fees to the lawyers and other professionals serving their needs.

The quality of legal protection will surely increase dramatically with a realistic legal budget and routine use of lawyers. With a budget in place, you can seek out particular lawyers with the experience and special training needed for each project. Common sense says you need to ask real estate questions to real estate lawyers, tax questions to tax lawyers, and so forth. This is not feasible without committing resources that will allow you to pay for quality counsel. With funds budgeted for legal protection, you can operate from a position of strength and confidence. You may also be surprised to find that quality legal advice may be had without actually spending the funds allocated after all.

The lawyer most suited to give free legal work is the lawyer being asked to do work *within* his primary area of practice. Because the work is familiar and can be rendered with confidence of its quality (in other words, "without reinventing the wheel"), an expert lawyer may be surprisingly open to help out a church or parachurch organization. This is true because it costs less than doing free work *outside* the lawyer's expertise. Aren't we all more generous with what comes easily to us? Therefore, if a low-fee legal service is required or desired, try doing the opposite of conventional thinking ("get a cheap lawyer"). Instead, seek the most qualified expert in that area of law. You may be surprised that you are able to receive the best in quality and price by simply being prepared and willing to discuss your budget openly.

SECOND COMMANDMENT:
ASK QUESTIONS BEFORE YOU HIRE A LAWYER

All lawyers are not created equal. Some are better educated and have had more experience. Some have had better experience. Some have wisdom and shrewdness. To make an informed choice of a lawyer or law firm, you should ask a lot of questions of a number of people. *You* should also be pleased with the answers. As a lawyer and as a Christian, I am frequently told by new clients that they chose me because they heard I was a Christian lawyer. If everything else were equal, I could agree with a Christian selecting a lawyer because of his faith and brand of theology. But rarely are all things equal that need to be considered.

The following inquiries are the type that you should make of your ministry (perhaps at the board level), the prospective lawyer, and his or her client references. While some of these questions may strike some people as "tacky" to ask of a professional, they are nonetheless proper and increasingly commonplace. In fact, a number of these questions and more can be found in this 1988 publication: *101 Ways to Cut Legal Fees and Manage Your Lawyer*, by the National Chamber Litigation Center, a nonprofit public policy arm of the U.S. Chamber of Commerce, which solely represents business interests.[1] Since businesses are scrutinizing lawyers and law firms, those in ministry should not fear being offensive by making the same inquiries. The professional lawyer has become used to these kinds of questions. If you detect a level of discomfort at such dialogue, you're probably talking to the wrong lawyer anyway.

Before handing over your ministry's legal matters or requesting professional advice, please explore the following areas in detail.

Questions to Ask Yourself

1. What exactly are our organization's legal needs right now and in the future?
2. Do we need a one-time service or are we looking for a long-term relationship with a lawyer or firm that can serve us as a "general counsel"?
3. At this time, or for this project, do we need a single lawyer or small (three to ten lawyers) specialty law firm? Or, would we benefit from a large law firm (ten to one hundred lawyers) that offers a broad selection of services and significant resources?
4. Do we desire personalized attention and/or customized work, or will "any competent lawyer" do?
5. Is our current legal problem one that has a spiritual/religious dimension (e.g., the legality of excluding practicing homosexuals from our work force)? Or, is our legal issue needing assistance truly secular in nature (e.g., legal review of a contract to buy land to be used for a camping program)?

Questions to Ask the Lawyer over the Phone

1. Do you charge for an introductory one-hour conference (thirty minutes is never enough time) to discuss employing you as a lawyer? If so, how much, and will this amount be credited toward the overall cost of completing the project?
2. Do you or your firm have any *professional* conflicts of interest? Do you represent any of our "adversaries" specifically or generally? For example, do you do work

for the other party to the contract you will review? Have you ever done work for the people threatening to sue us? Have you ever taken an opposite legal position to ours in a court or other governmental proceeding for a client?

3. Do you or your firm have any *personal* conflicts of interest? For example, have you taken any positions for clients that are obviously opposite to beliefs and tenets we maintain in our ministry? Do you represent clients whose business activities are objectionable to our organization? (For example, it may not be good for a long-term, or even short-term, relationship to learn that one of your law firm's other clients is an entrepreneur who owns a number of topless night clubs in your community.)

4. Do you currently have the time in your schedule to take on this project? (Lawyers are often guilty of an inability to say, "I'm too busy," for fear of losing an existing or new client. So don't take a simple, "Sure, no problem" as necessarily being the complete picture of the lawyer's time commitments.)

Questions to Ask the Lawyer at the "Interview" Conference

1. What kinds of clients do you represent?
2. Do you have clients of comparable size and in the religious or nonprofit areas?
3. In addition to client matters, what other experience do you have that would be relevant to representing our church or ministry?
4. Are there any areas of law in which you have expertise? Are you a certified specialist in this state? In what areas of law do other lawyers in your firm have special expertise?
5. Do you have any recent experience with cases like this? Could you give me some examples? What was the outcome? Might I have the names and telephone numbers of these clients and your permission to call them?

6. Why are you particularly qualified to handle this case or matter? What special background or expertise do you have that would be useful? (If the matter involves litigation: How many trials have you handled during the past five years?)

7. What are the various alternative ways in which our case or problem might be handled? Do you anticipate any special problems that might be encountered? If so, how will they be handled?

8. Will you be doing all the work? If not, will you introduce me to the other people who will be working on my case or problem? Will you provide the necessary supervision of work performed by others in the firm? Do you have the time to supervise all aspects of our case or problem?

9. How long do you estimate the matter will take? What variables would affect your estimate?

10. What are the alternative fee arrangements for handling our case or problem? What fee arrangement do you recommend? If you recommend that our case or problem be handled on an hourly basis, what are the hourly rates of the persons who will be involved? What fraction of an hour do you use in billing?

11. What is your billing procedure? Will your bills itemize the legal work done, including a description of the service, the date the service is rendered, the name of the person who rendered the service, and the charge for the service?

12. Will you provide a contract or engagement letter describing the fee and billing arrangements on which we have agreed?

13. How might I assist you in handling our case or problem? What steps can our ministry take or can we together take to maximize the chances that our matter will stay within our legal fee budget?

14. How much do you estimate the total fees will be? What variables can affect what the fees will be?

15. Have you and/or your firm ever had a malpractice claim or

professional grievance action of discipline made against you? If so, please elaborate.

THIRD COMMANDMENT: PREPARE AND REVISE FEE BUDGETS IN ADVANCE

As mentioned in the suggested initial interview questions, you and your lawyer should always keep in mind the overall legal fee estimate given and that budgeted. In litigation matters particularly, it is very easy to go off budget, and even forget that there was a budget until it is too late. Lawsuits can routinely span several years, and it can be a very painful experience to approach the trial date and learn you have spent more on fees than you are being sued for in the first place. Monthly billings, monthly reviews, and routine reassessment of legal fee budgets for substantial projects is a must for controlling resources. Cases can be settled or alternative courses of action can be taken on other legal projects before a crisis develops between you, your lawyer, and your organization.

The Charles Blair case described in chapter 6 is a classic example of when a detailed, up-to-date legal fee budget could have avoided tremendous turmoil. In the best analysis, spending $350,000 in lawyer fees and expenses is something to avoid in a $750,000 lawsuit.

A legal fee budget for all matters and issues for the year should be prepared in addition to mini budgets for each separate matter or court proceeding that may arise. Using prior years' figures can be helpful but may also be misleading. For the best quality of legal advice and service on a long-term, ministry-wide basis, it is best to begin budget discussions with a complete wish list of legal needs with your lawyer. After a complete, exhaustive compilation is prepared, you and the lawyer can prioritize how and where your available resources are to be used. Permitting the lawyer to participate in this process will help assure the following:

◆ The lawyer is equally committed to your priorities.
◆ The lawyer is not uninformed or misinformed when choices need to be made between competing needs for legal services.

♦ Your budget is founded in reality and is not out of balance favoring what you want versus what you can truly afford.

Lastly, comparative shopping, both before and after the purchase, is very helpful. Before a firm is hired, and a new project is commenced, the shrewd consumer of legal services will get a second or third opinion on legal fees. Be sure that an apples-to-apples comparison is made, and let the lawyers participate in establishing the variables.

For example, a lawyer may indicate that the fee will depend on how much legal research is needed. But don't let him off the hook with that. Ask him what legal research he foresees being needed now and what could happen later to change this adversely. Don't be afraid to pin him down. If he resists being specific, you may very well have the wrong lawyer. You wouldn't hire a painter by the hour who absolutely refused to give you any estimate of the number of hours involved. Don't hire a lawyer under similar circumstances. You're paying for the services and are entitled to know what it will likely cost without a ten-round struggle with your professional.

FOURTH COMMANDMENT: BE INVOLVED IN YOUR CASE AND ASSIST WHEN POSSIBLE

The surest way to be billed a shocking figure by your lawyer is to hand him or her your problems and walk away from any further participation. Even a fair and reasonable fee will astound you if you have no idea what legal hurdles were cleared. Furthermore, the client who communicates a disinterest in what his lawyer is accomplishing is the kind of client who will not receive any sympathy from the lawyer when invoices for services are reviewed. Often lawyers will "write down" a final bill once the firm's office manager or secretarial staff has prepared the bill from time records. To "write down" a bill is to lower the amount because the lawyer, in his conscience or from a less noble gut feeling, considers it too high in spite of what the time records indicate. At that subjective moment, the appreciative, caring, active client is probably going to be treated much more graciously than the client who has dropped his mess in the attorney's lap and gone off to more appealing endeavors. That latter kind of client will pay for every one of the 3,600 seconds found in a billable hour.

Offering to assist can potentially save you money. In certain cases, you might need to sift through mountains of paper, looking for needles in the haystack. Your assistance might save an expensive lawyer or paralegal from doing this tedious but necessary task. In other words, some work assignments that are part and parcel of what a lawyer does can be done by the client or one of the client's staff. Routinely asking where you can help out to keep costs down will accomplish at least one of two things: (1) You'll be in the right place at the right time to actually help and save money, or (2) your lawyer will be reminded again that staying within the legal fee budget is very important to you.

FIFTH COMMANDMENT:
DON'T TOLERATE PERSONALITY DISPUTES

One little-known but very expensive side effect to legal work is the ever-present need for attorneys to "out-lawyer" each other. This is true in lawsuits, but is also very prevalent in all areas of legal negotiations (i.e., contracts). Modesty, humility, and letting the other guy get the credit are not concepts taught in either law school or in the initial training years at any law firm.

To obtain and maintain clients, lawyers are repeatedly led to believe that they must create an image of being the strongest and smartest animal in the jungle. Lawyers believe that their clients may wish they'd hired the lawyer's adversary if it seems even remotely possible that the other lawyer had an ounce of greater intellect or skill. Professional and friendly one-upmanship is always present whenever two lawyers or two law firms come together in representing their respective clients. Some of this is conscious; some is inbred after years of playing the legal game.

The rare lawyer can keep his or her ego and professional image continually subservient to the client's needs and interests. In this regard, clients must be on their toes because even minor unspoken communications of superiority can quickly send their matter into the throes of an expensive lawyer-to-lawyer imbroglio. Not unlike a canine in a brutal dogfight, a lawyer's ability to take his attention off the battle with the opponent diminishes rapidly. When the dust finally settles, usually when a judge or senior partner in the firm calls the combatants back to reality, the clients have unnecessarily experienced an unproductive dog-eat-dog contest that got them nowhere.

How do such lawyer-versus-lawyer spitting contests start? They happen in a variety of subtle ways; some the client can stop in advance, and some may not be discovered until later. Essentially, you should keep on the lookout for any subtle, or not so subtle, comment from your attorney that he will not be giving due respect to the other side's lawyer. It might concern a prior case or negotiation, or it might be based solely on what your lawyer has heard from other lawyers. It might involve the opponent's law school rating, or the size or location of the lawyer's firm vis-a-vis the opponent. It might even be quite explicit, as when your lawyer advises that he plans to take some step solely to embarrass, irritate, or frustrate the other side and/or its lawyer (e.g., serving a subpoena on Christmas Eve or New Year's Day, or at home as opposed to an office). Anything that will tend to make the other lawyer look naive, foolish, slow, or embarrassed should be avoided if alternative measures are available.

You can count on these unnecessary tactics costing you substantial unnecessary legal fees. Here's how: The other lawyer is also well versed in how important appearances are and will set about to even the score. He will perform hours of contemplation and even legal research to find a way to get revenge. Sometimes getting even comes by causing the perpetrator to do otherwise unnecessary, tedious work. Revenge might also be had by causing delay for the one who is anxious for a speedy resolution. In any event, a counterpunch will be thrown in the negotiations or in the litigation process. Each counterpunch begets a response. Soon your lawyer and his adversary are in a cold war or an all-out *Top Gun* type skirmish. You might have no clue this is occurring until you receive the lawyer's bill. Sometimes even then what transpired is not apparent.

Handling Tussles Between Opposing Lawyers

There are ways to keep informed and avoid paying the price for a lawyer's school-yard fist fight. Here's what you can do:

Make your goals clear. At the initial meeting when you are retaining your lawyer, make it clear what *your* goals and objectives are in the contract negotiation or lawsuit that is upon you. One of those goals as a Christian organization should be for your lawyer (not just you and your staff) to at all times represent the ministry in a way consistent with your values. You should elaborate as much as necessary and politely ask the lawyer to commit to abiding by those goals as he does his job for you. So if your lawyer believes an action is necessary that might irritate or embarrass the opposing lawyer or his client (because every lawyer believes part of his job is to protect the client and create a feeling of intimidation in anyone considering "messing" with his client), ask him to contact you to discuss how it can best be handled.

Put an end to disputes. You should also advise your lawyer when you sense a personality dispute developing that you do not want to see it escalate. Make it clear that you do not appreciate nor will you tolerate having your organization's matters handled in any fashion less than with the highest levels of graciousness, dignity, and professionalism (in the traditional meaning).

Scrutinize your lawyer's work. You should question your lawyer in detail about why certain courses of action are being taken. Scrutinize your legal fee bills, and call your lawyer to inquire if you sense any problems. For example, ask your attorney why a lengthy letter to his opposing attorney was required instead of a quick phone call. Why are there so many "drafts and redrafts" of your agreement going back and forth? Can't the lawyers *talk* and agree on contract language without all the revised versions passing in the mail without so much as a phone call to propose alternative wording?

Get copies of letters. Request and insist that you receive copies of *all* letters sent to and from opposing counsel. You may see a personality dispute developing overtly through threats and unveiled innuendo. You may have to watch for the telltale signs by reading between the lines. For example, why does it take four letters between two lawyers simply to schedule a witness deposition? When you see things like this happening in the correspondence you receive, one of two undesirable things has happened: Either your lawyer is "churning your file" to unnecessarily increase your bill, in which case he should be fired; or your lawyer and his opponent are getting into one of those lawyer-to-lawyer tussles that will cost you thousands. When opposing lawyers cannot even speak over the phone to compare calendars, it is time to give your lawyer a wake-up call.

Basically, let your lawyer know that you expect him to remove from your case his or her personal feelings or problems with the other lawyer. When your matter is over, the two sides can write all the blistering letters and innuendos and threats they desire to one another—on their own time and postage.

LEGAL STRATEGIES AND PRINCIPLES

◆ State ethics codes require lawyers to follow reasonable guidelines in assessing fees.

◆ Fees must be reasonable for both lawyer and client.

◆ Ministries can follow guidelines to build helpful relationships with their lawyer and to regulate their legal fees. These guidelines are called "Ten Commandments for Working with Lawyers."

◆ First Commandment: Choose the right lawyer in the first place.

◆ Second Commandment: Ask questions and get answers you like before hiring a lawyer.

    1. Ask questions of your ministry to clarify your need.

    2. Conduct a phone interview with prospective lawyers.

    3. Schedule an in-person interview before making a final hiring decision.

◆ Third Commandment: Prepare and revise fee budgets with your lawyer.

◆ Fourth Commandment: Be involved in your case and assist when possible.

◆ Fifth Commandment: Don't tolerate personality disputes.

CHAPTER TWELVE

Ten Commandments for Working with Lawyers, Part II

We're continuing to look at the best ways to deal with lawyers in order to get the best service for your ministry or church. We're also trying to learn how to keep legal fees at a minimum without sacrificing quality service. In the last chapter we looked at the first five of "Ten Commandments for Working with Lawyers." Now let's look at the last five.

SIXTH COMMANDMENT: REVIEW INVOICES, ASK QUESTIONS, AND GET SECOND OPINIONS

Most clients at least read their lawyer's bills. After they pick themselves up off the floor, they write a check and mail it without ever really understanding what the lawyer did and why. To the layperson (and sometimes to lawyers themselves), most legal bills are just as unintelligible as contracts and legal briefs. This is at least partly understandable. After all, the law is technical and requires high levels of professional education and experience to use it to an advantage. But to decipher a legal bill, you, the client, should have a good understanding of what you are paying for. If it is your own money, it is important. If it is your organization's funds, you have a duty to your donors and members to use it wisely. Wisdom requires understanding, so ask questions.

Before you hire a lawyer, ask if the firm will allow you to call the lawyer and talk *for free* about each monthly bill. Ask for at least fifteen minutes per month. The conversation should be nonconfrontive, as between members of the same team. The lawyer should readily agree to ten to fifteen minutes, because it is his or her bill you are hoping to understand.

A monthly call like this will accomplish a lot. First, you will become more and more knowledgeable about how the law and lawyers function. Since your legal shrewdness is a career-long commitment, you will be building upon prior knowledge and the nature of your questions will change from month to month. Your sophistication level will increase and the need to use lawyers on routine questions may decline, thus saving money.

Second, your lawyer will be much more careful about your bill than others. Just knowing you will be calling to go over the contents of the bill and the nature and necessity of the work performed will make him or her feel more accountable to you. Letting a lawyer know you are a scrupulous purchaser of legal services will have a positive effect whenever that person marks a time sheet for you.

After talking about your bill, it is a good idea to get a second opinion from time to time about any work performed or sums billed that have a ring of peculiarity. It's always a good practice to have a lawyer friend to go to before you accept just anything, particularly if you don't have a "general counsel" relationship established. This is a perfect reason to talk to the lawyer who is a church member or the attorney who serves on a parachurch committee. As a favor, most lawyers would probably be happy to review a bill or answer a question. Since they cannot benefit by getting your business, they will very likely give an honest, objective answer. For example, ask, "Should it take four letters back and forth between two lawyers to schedule a deposition?"

SEVENTH COMMANDMENT: NEGOTIATE THE LEGAL FEE ARRANGEMENT BEST FOR YOU

While the bill-by-the-hour method of calculating fees is the most common form, several alternatives could save you money. The following are the most frequently used arrangements. In the 1990s we are seeing a steady trend away from the billable hour, so you should have some success if other forms of billing make more sense to you.

Billable Hours

As the name signifies, the lawyer, her associates, and paralegals or law clerks will keep track of time spent on your matters, and the firm will multiply its time by the applicable billing rate. Hourly rates for lawyers just out of law school are typically from sixty to ninety dollars per hour. More experienced lawyers will be higher, typically $100 to $250 per hour. The larger the city you are in, the higher the rates. The lawyer's number of years out of school and level of expertise in her field of law will often serve as the distinguishing factors on which rates are applied. Paralegals and law clerks (usually law school students) will usually be billed at rates below that of the young associate attorneys (i.e., thirty to sixty dollars per hour). Some firms now bill for secretarial time because modern computer word processing equipment permits the operator to keep track of the time spent typing and revising a particular document for a client. Since all "expenses" (mileage, photocopies, long-distance calls, filing fees, postage, FAX charges, and so forth) are billed separately, one begins to wonder just what the client is getting for the "lawyer's hour."

The main problems for clients with the use of the billable hour are: (1) There is no reason for the lawyer to be time efficient (in fact, the lawyer is often rewarded for being slow and ponderous), and (2) the client has a difficult (impossible?) time budgeting from month to month what the lawyer's bill will be.

If hourly billing is to be used, make sure you negotiate a fair hourly rate and establish which lawyer will be doing the work. Consider negotiating a much lower rate for hours over a certain number each month, so the lawyer is motivated to complete the work within the level that the firm's normal hourly rate is applied. Also consider negotiating an hourly fee "not to exceed" a certain amount of fees. This is similar to a fixed fee but allows the client to benefit if the estimate of time needed by the lawyer turns out to be too high.

If additional motivation for the lawyer is desired, consider negotiating a bonus for winning the case or reaching some other objective goal. With a set bonus, a lower hourly rate may be palatable to the lawyer. He knows if he is successful for the client, he will make it up with the bonus.

Fixed Fees

For routine tasks like reviewing or preparing a contract, the fixed (or flat) fee can be most advantageous. Discuss and agree upon a set figure to be paid for a specific task the lawyer will perform. The client can budget the established amount and avoid the shock of an unexpectedly high figure. With computerized word processing available in virtually every lawyer's office, a wide variety of legal forms and routine documents and instruments are at the lawyer's fingertips in seconds. Each lawyer has created, or tailored, his or her own versions of regularly used documents. Since few lengthy items are drafted from scratch, fixed fees are more feasible than ever before. In fact, the law firm that bills strictly by the hour is becoming an anachronism.

Contingent Fees

This term refers to the fee charged by lawyers who bring personal injury lawsuits for clients who could never afford the enormous fees involved in large lawsuits. Generally, a "percentage fee" is agreed upon, and whether the lawyer earns it and is paid is "contingent" on winning or settling the case and receiving the money from the adversary.

The contingent percentage fee is used primarily in lawsuits and almost exclusively by the plaintiff's lawyer, but there is no reason why a defendant's fee could not be made contingent on winning the defense of a lawsuit. For example, a defendant church could negotiate a contingent fee with its lawyer to pay one-third of every dollar below the amount the plaintiff asks for in the lawsuit. If the plaintiff sues for $100,000 and wins only $40,000, the defense lawyer would be paid one-third of the $60,000 saved, or $20,000. The more saved, the more the lawyer earns.

A contingent fee could also be used in other non-litigation areas. For example, a contingent fee could be used in the process of rezoning property to accommodate a new ministry use. The success of the lawyer's work in preparing rezoning materials could be measured by whether the rezoning is approved, how quickly, and whether the full scope of uses is achieved. Perhaps you would agree to pay a very low fee if the new zoning is denied by the applicable authorities, but a significantly higher fee if approved in all respects on schedule. Contingent fees can be a great way to get your lawyer both motivated and fully committed to his initial legal opinions about the merits of your case.

Monthly Retainer Fees

The old way of retaining a personal lawyer on a monthly basis is coming back into vogue. It's an alternative to the unpredictable billable hour system for those who have a regular need for legal advice and routine work to be performed. It works best for an organization with a large number of front-line staff who confront legal issues on a regular basis and need quick answers. They don't have the time to wait to funnel their inquiries through management to the organization's lawyer and wait for an answer to come back through the channels. In that case, management might normally require the staff to bring questions to them first primarily because of the budget fear created by allowing a large group of people direct access to a $150 per hour lawyer. But the monthly retainer can make such direct access affordable.

A set monthly fee is negotiated that will cover all phone calls for advice, routine contract reviews, and attendance at strategic staff or management meetings where legal topics will be discussed. An initial trial period of ninety days or six months is usually set to see if the amount of work performed by the lawyers corresponds to the monthly retainer being paid. If the workload is too high or too low, a negotiated adjustment is made either in the fee figure or the types of legal services covered.

The net result can provide maximum benefits to all. Lawyers are pleased because their cash flow is stabilized and a valued client is somewhat "locked in" to their services. Clients are pleased for several reasons:

1. They have a set figure to use in their budgeting.
2. The quality of their legal protection has increased because previously unasked questions and unreviewed contracts and letters are getting a lawyer's eye.
3. Management is freed from being the pipeline for evaluating and transmitting (often losing something in translation) legal inquiries and responses.
4. They are further freed from the fear of escalating, unpredictable legal costs.

Negotiation Hints

To many ministry leaders, the challenge to negotiate legal fees with the trusted lawyer, or with a stranger, may sound unpleasant. It may make you uncomfortable. But let me encourage you in two ways. First, to "negotiate" does not have to mean the type of give-and-take one may experience when buying a new or used car. It can be handled in a sincere, professional, good faith manner. After all, you are in ministry and have a solemn duty to God and your donors to use your resources wisely. Why not begin your next legal fee discussion with something like this: "As you know, our organization (church) is entirely committed to charitable goals. Our calling is to serve people, particularly people in need, and we feel compelled by scriptural mandates to maximize the ministry use of every single penny God places in our hands.

"Every place we can save a dollar on administrative expenditures means one more dollar used directly in meeting people's needs. We want you to know that we value highly your professional services and recognize that you and your firm are worth every bit that you normally charge your business clients, but we do need to talk with you about what options you might be able to make available to allow us to work with you and your firm within our tight budgetary limits. What can you suggest?"

Any ministry leader can revise and make a similar statement to any professional. If not, you may have the wrong person meeting with the lawyer to discuss fees and billing.

Notice that I included a recognition of a lawyer's high value and importance to the organization. Reducing fees is made easier for anyone so long as the person knows it is for financial reasons as opposed to an unwillingness by the client to adequately value the person and his or her services.

I also ended with a question to the lawyer. It's best to let the lawyer make the initial suggestion. He will then have future ownership in the fact that a reduced fee arrangement was instituted. So don't let the lawyer quickly throw the hot potato back in your lap with, "Well, what did you have in mind?" Your response could be, "We are not all that sure what kinds of options there are and wanted to hear about the various ways your firm has worked with clients in the past to accommodate a nonprofit organization's budget." With statements like this, you should be well on your way to a natural, open conversation about fees and what your organization can and cannot afford. Your "negotiations" can result in a fee agreement that will be mutually beneficial.

The second encouragement is that clients are negotiating fees with lawyers on an ever-increasing basis. For example, the U.S. Chamber of Commerce offers the business community a publication entitled *101 Ways to Cut Legal Fees and Manage Your Lawyer*.[1] Another publication receiving attention within the business sector is Mark McCormack's book, *What I Should Have Learned at Yale Law School: The Terrible Truth About Lawyers*.[2] While McCormack gives a salty perspective on certain realities within the legal profession, his book could be particularly helpful to someone interested in how the secular side thinks.

The trend toward clients driving bargains with their lawyers is clear. The *National Law Journal* reports that in-house legal departments are claiming major successes across the board in controlling fees for outside law firms. For example, some companies are putting out legal projects for competitive bidding. One request for proposals given to four law firms netted quotes ranging from $15,000 to $60,000.[3] One company received a 20 percent discount in hourly rates from its lawyers in exchange for a premium (bonus) if the case was won. One corporation even saw its legal expenditures drop a whopping 50 percent from prior years, solely as a result of requiring detailed monthly bills.

Detailed monthly bills (which most law firms now provide anyway) are widely recognized as being essential to understanding what your attorney is doing as well as keeping the lid on legal fees. The bill should show the date, amount of time, lawyer or paralegal involved, hourly rate, and a description of work performed. A novel requirement is to show "year to date" totals for each long-term legal project, along with the monthly bill. Both the lawyer and client can see right away when and if a project veers off the budget track. If detailed monthly bills are used, tighter controls can be imposed or the whole project scuttled before it is too late.

Obviously, those in Christian ministry can benefit by the atmosphere already created by the business world. If fee negotiations based on profit motives have become more and more routine, then surely ministry-motivated concerns to save money will fall on receptive ears. Plan to become a shrewd negotiator.

EIGHTH COMMANDMENT: USE MEDIATION
OR ARBITRATION IF AT ALL POSSIBLE

This commandment may sound like a restatement of the obvious, but civil litigation in the courts truly is the one place legal fees are more uncontrollable. Alternative measures to resolve legal disputes remain mysteriously underutilized. I say this because it is somewhat of a societal wonder that while Americans openly deplore the absurd growth in the number of lawsuits in this culture, at the same time they cannot seem to wait until it's their turn. People seem to rush to the courthouse cliffs like litigious lemmings.

When talking about staying out of court, I do not simplistically suggest that you succumb to every threat or demand out of a fear of the cost and turmoil of a legal confrontation. Rather, I suggest that you become shrewd in your affairs and take advantage of the many means available to stay out of civil lawsuits when an unavoidable legal dispute arises. To accomplish the goal of staying out of court, you need some advance planning and legal strategy in your organization's policies and practices. A commitment to resist litigation affirmatively will not only save immeasurable amounts of legal fees but might also keep your ministry away from the front pages of the local papers.

Effective Alternatives to the Traditional Lawsuit

First, let's look at the basic alternatives to resolving disputes outside of the traditional lawsuit. Then we will see exactly how your ministry can increase its chances of actually being able to use one or more of these avenues rather than the lawyer's gold mine known as the American right to have "my day in court."

Mediation. Many legal disputes are resolved by the protagonists through the use of some person or persons acting as a mediator. *Mediation* means to bring about a settlement, compromise, or reconciliation by the use of someone situated in the middle. What happens in the typical legal dispute is that the lawyers for each side will unsuccessfully attempt to mediate the differences between their clients.

The problem with this is threefold. First, lawyers are expensive, and having two lawyers negotiating a settlement can be twice as expensive as using another qualified mediator. Second, lawyers are not trained or skilled in mediation. Instead, they are purposely trained to advocate their client's position and only their client's position—remember Professor Kingsfield? Third, a mediation attempt by lawyers usually occurs only after enormous legal fees have been expended by the ministry or business involved. In some cases, it occurs when the lawyers are nearing trial and developing a bad case of cold feet. Unfortunately, many law firms openly say they will not begin settlement negotiations with the other side in a dispute until (1) all the legal issues have surfaced in the case and have been thoroughly researched, (2) all the facts have been ferreted out from careful review of all documents related to the dispute, and (3) all witnesses have been interviewed and/or depositions taken under oath.

This makes sense on the surface. How can you settle a dispute that you don't fully understand legally and factually? But this policy is often a red herring. In most legal disputes, the clients and their personnel know what happened and what the other side says happened. The parties normally have struggled with resolving the dispute long before they bring in the lawyers. So all the expensive document analysis and witness interrogation is for the lawyer's benefit for *trial* (fighting) preparation, not *settlement* (peacemaking) preparation.

The legal research that may come to bear on a dispute is not necessarily needed before settlements can be reached. If the law is clear on the subject of the dispute, the lawyers most likely already know what the research will confirm. In fact, when the law is black and white, disputes normally do not get very far with lawyer involvement because one party will recognize it has a dead loser of a case.

If the law is unclear, legal research will not necessarily tell the lawyer anything helpful for settlement. In gray areas, the library work lawyers do is primarily aimed at giving them an edge with the judge as the trial begins, so extensive (and expensive) legal research is not a reasonable prerequisite to talking settlement in most cases. Mediation of sorts may come out of the litigation system, but usually it is too late to save expensive fees.

The better approach to mediation is for the disputing parties to explore formal mediation avenues immediately after getting initial advice about the legal dispute they face. Your lawyer should be advised that you would prefer to mediate the problem right away. If any strong, unfounded resistance exists, you should then advise your lawyer that you *will* seek to mediate this dispute. Be prepared. Almost any lawyer might have a negative reaction because mediation and arbitration are competitors of the American system of lawsuits. Even the best lawyers who are secure in what they do might have some misgivings about mediation and arbitration because they do not find it as comfortable as the process with which they are familiar. Lawyers have traditionally known little about these alternatives. Their lack of knowledge creates unnecessary concern about how mediation will impact their client's legal position in court. Similarly, the lawyer's role in helping resolve your crisis is diminished significantly. Lawyers who need to control almost every aspect of their client's dealings will be very reluctant to applaud the desire to mediate the problem. So be forewarned.

Mediation, as distinguished from arbitration, is a process whereby the parties to the dispute come to an agreement on how to resolve their differences. The mediator helps restore communication between the parties. Arbitration, by comparison, is a process where a third person actually decides who is right and who is wrong. The third-party arbitrator is a decisionmaker, whereas the mediator only facilitates a mutually acceptable decision. Keeping these differences in mind will be helpful as you strategically plan to resolve existing disputes and to funnel future disputes away from the courthouse.

Mediation, unlike certain types of arbitration, is voluntary and consensual. It cannot be forced or compelled. Therefore, one side of the dispute may need to "sell" the idea to the other party or otherwise provide an incentive to participate. Often in disputes that have taken on emotional aspects, one or both sides will object to a proposition simply because their adversary desires it. So great care must be given to suggesting and implementing mediation by a third party.

To provide an incentive, one side may agree to pay all or a disproportionate (seventy-five—twenty-five) share of any costs associated with the mediation. To allay fears that you have something up your sleeve by suggesting mediation, it may be helpful to agree to allow both sides to be represented with their lawyers at the initial session or two to lay down the ground rules. In any event, thoughtful consideration of everything that can be done to overcome obstacles to commence and succeed at mediation will only benefit you and your ministry organization.

Many experts in dispute resolution outside of the court system, whether in a religious context or not, say that many legal disputes are resolved simply by letting each side be heard. To be given a chance finally to tell their side to the other is a large part of why people bring lawsuits. People who feel wronged can forget the wrong if they feel that they have been truly heard.

The experts also indicate that very often a straightforward, genuine "I'm sorry" is the key to unlocking a bitter legal battle. As people claiming faith in God, shouldn't Christians be the first to listen to complaints against ministry organizations? Shouldn't they be the first to seek forgiveness? "I'm sorry" should not be seen as an apology from God. Rather, His servants are imperfect and, on occasion, do cause harm. Mediation and arbitration are the places the Apostle Paul sends Christians to resolve their differences (1 Corinthians 6:1-8). This should be true whether the controversy is between two people or institutions of faith or involving a nonbeliever who claims to have been harmed. Clearly, Paul warns Christians to avoid having an ungodly legal system act as the place of final resolution.

If you are uncertain exactly how to explore the use of mediation and arbitration, any number of avenues are available. First, you should ask a trusted lawyer, one who has litigation experience, for a referral to what are commonly called "Alternative Dispute Resolution" (ADR) programs. If you are in or near a large metropolitan area, it is likely that there are ADR programs sponsored by the local bar association. As well, you will likely find some community-based or private ADR programs that you can consult about mediation and arbitration.

For example, in my home state the Colorado Bar Association has an extensive ADR program that even includes a fairly unique program called the "Colorado Pledge." This is a written commitment by participating businesses and organizations to, in all situations, turn to ADR techniques such as mediation and arbitration before filing lawsuits. The program has been somewhat successful, and the lawyers' bar association has been joined by the Greater Denver Chamber of Commerce, the Colorado Association of Commerce and Industry, the Colorado Society of Certified Public Accountants, and the National Federation of Independent Businesses in sponsoring the Colorado Pledge.[4] Your state will likely have a similar program in which you can learn about ADR.

On the ministry side of the equation there are several places to turn to learn about mediation from a scriptural perspective. The two most notable programs for Christians and their organizations are:

1. Association of Christian Conciliation Services, Inc., 1537 Avenue D, Suite 352, Billings, Montana 59102. (See appendix B for referral listings.)
2. Institute For Dispute Resolution, Pepperdine University School of Law, Malibu, California 90263.

Each of these programs provides written training materials, form agreements for mediation and arbitration, and educational seminars and conferences that provide ministries with the level of understanding they uniquely desire. A particularly excellent resource for your library on topics of Christian mediation and arbitration is the volume *Tell It to the Church* by Lynn Buzzard and Laurence Eck.[5]

Arbitration. As mentioned, arbitration is the process of involving a third party to decide, and thus resolve, a legal dispute. A civil suit is a form of involuntary arbitration. Once sued, the defendant has two basic choices: choose not to participate and lose by default, much like a team forfeits for not appearing at a game; or actively defend against the alleged claims.

Arbitration may come in two forms: binding or nonbinding. A lawsuit is binding, obviously. Once a final court order or judgment is reached in a settlement or as the result of a trial, it is binding on both sides. Abiding by a court decision is not optional. By comparison, a great number of the usual arbitrations used to resolve legal disputes are nonbinding. Either party may later reject the arbitrator's decision (sometimes at a price) and go back to the heat of battle. Why then would anyone want to pursue nonbinding arbitration if it could turn out to be a total waste of time?

The answer is found in the earlier point that many litigants are primarily seeking to be heard. They want a chance to convince someone that they are right. The mere process of telling their story to an impartial person or panel can often be sufficient satisfaction in and of itself. To hear that a fair and impartial decisionmaker does not agree with their perspective may be enough, even if that decisionmaker has no "binding" authority over them.

The key to success for most arbitrations is held within the phrase "fair and impartial decisionmaker." Confidence that these qualities are present in the arbitrator or panel of arbitrators is crucial for nonbinding arbitrations to resolve disputes successfully and avoid further proceedings. Often arbitrators can be selected from Christian or secular lists of trained people with particular areas of expertise. If the parties cannot agree on one arbitrator, they will usually each pick one and those two will select a third arbitrator, resulting in a three-member panel.

The Arbitration/Mediation Process

How can we be in a position to resolve a legal dispute by private arbitration or mediation? Remember, this method may be well worth our taking measures to avoid uncontrolled or irreparable media exposure. There are at least three ways to access arbitration and mediation.

Agree to arbitrate or mediate in advance of the development of a dispute. By inserting mandatory arbitration/mediation provisions in all your written contracts, you will find, in many states, that the courts will refuse jurisdiction to hear the controversy. Appendix A is an example of a clause from the association of Christian Conciliation Services. This is particularly true of binding and nonbinding arbitration in most states. You should ask your lawyer if your state has a statute to encourage and uphold arbitration clauses in contracts.

Mediation, being consensual, is a far less likely candidate for compelled participation by one side or the other. If one side can demonstrate the futility of mere talk, it is unlikely a judge will force mediation, regardless of what a contract says. But *arbitration*, agreed to in a written contract, is routinely enforced upon unwilling participants. An example of a mediation/arbitration agreement for use in secular contexts is found in appendix C. In addition, if binding arbitration has been selected in the contract, the decision of the arbitrators will be strictly enforced unless extenuating circumstances can be demonstrated.

So be sure all your written agreements contain arbitration provisions unless your lawyer has good reasons in your state to leave them out. I'd even go the next step to reduce more and more of your verbal (unwritten) agreements to written form and add arbitration clauses. For example, the relationship a church or ministry organization has with its staff (employees) is rarely memorialized in written form. With your lawyer's input, consider entering into simple employment agreements that contain appropriate mandatory arbitration terms if a dispute were ever to develop. As we have seen, disputes leading to lawsuits between employees and the church or ministry employing them are occurring much more frequently. A written contract requiring private arbitration before an impartial, unbiased person or panel should be in the employee's personal interest as well as his employer's.

Agree as soon as possible after a dispute has arisen to arbitrate or mediate. Similarly, most state laws encourage and accommodate mid-dispute desires to arbitrate or mediate. If a secular approach is necessary, most jurisdictions will have systems set up. Very often a quick "settlement conference" with an active judge other than the judge on your case will result in an end to the dispute.

In a Christian framework, the Association of Christian Conciliation Services has developed different types of mediation/arbitration agreements that can be helpful. Your lawyer may want to modify one to fit the circumstances of your dispute. These can also be altered for use in any contract to comply with state laws in your jurisdiction for compulsory arbitration to resolve contract squabbles.

Consider a private trial. Another related arbitration alternative growing in popularity is what I call the "private trial." It is very similar to traditional arbitration. A single arbitrator is used, and his or her decision is final and binding. But unlike arbitrations that are informally conducted, the private trial is conducted before a retired judge with all the same rules of procedure and evidence found in a state or federal court. In fact, a veritable cottage industry of former judges who perform such services has sprung up in nearly every state.

For a steep price, you and your antagonist can have the same trial you would have in a courtroom before a sitting judge, except your judge has left his position and now makes a living conducting trials for a fee. Your "courtroom" might be located in a hotel meeting room or in an office building rather than at a civil court. You can even assemble a paid jury if you like, but these are uncommon. Normally, the case is tried and presented to the judge alone, and he or she renders a decision. Because of the arbitration agreement you signed with the opposition, the judge's decision can be filed in your local court and will be enforced with the same effect as a civil judgment.

It should be noted that in most states binding arbitration awards can be appealed on only a handful of legal grounds. The challenger must establish that there was fraud, bias, or some other impropriety that affected the fairness of the proceeding. Merely being unhappy with the result won't get anywhere in an appeal of an arbitration award.

An excellent example within a religious context of a binding arbitration that withstood a later court challenge is the 1990 New Jersey case of *Elmora Hebrew Center, Inc. v. Yale M. Fishman*.[6] Both a trial-level court and a New Jersey appeals court agreed that a prearrangement to arbitrate a dispute before a rabbinical tribunal (Beth Din) should be enforced. This dispute concerned differences between a rabbi and his Jewish synagogue. Both parties entered into an agreement to submit the dispute to a Jewish tribunal and to abide by whatever decision the tribunal reached. In other words, both sides agreed to "binding arbitration." The synagogue, however, did not like the tribunal's ruling in favor of the rabbi, so it sought to challenge the arbitration award in the civil courts. Both New Jersey courts entertained the synagogue's arguments but refused to reopen the dispute and second-guess the arbitration panel. The appeals court cited the accepted rule of law concerning challenges to binding arbitrations:

> The scope of judicial (court) review of any arbitration award is extremely limited. Absent proof of fraud, partiality, misconduct on the part of the arbitrators . . . or that they exceeded their authority . . . the obligation of the court is to confirm and enforce the award. The law favors dispute resolution through consensual (by contract) arbitration, and so the award is presumed valid.[7]

As this case demonstrates, in most states a ministry can stay clear of court intervention if the following two things occur: (1) An agreement is freely and voluntarily entered into by the parties to submit an existing, or future, dispute to binding arbitration; and (2) the arbitration process and panel members are free from fraud, bias, or other inequitable misconduct. Unless the party resisting arbitration can show noncompliance with either of these two, it will not receive a sympathetic ear at the courthouse.

Ministries, therefore, can substantially minimize the role of the courts in any dispute simply by adding appropriate binding arbitration and/or mediation clauses in all written contracts. For disputes that come outside the scope of a contract, ministries must make every effort to negotiate an arbitration agreement to avoid court involvement. With an arbitration agreement before it, the court may only entertain issues concerning the two threshold criteria mentioned above. To arbitrate and mediate is essential to becoming shrewd.

In appendix B, you will find the Association of Christian Conciliation Services (ACCS), Inc., Referral Network. A sample clause for use in contracts between Christians as recommended by ACCS is found in appendix A. Other Christian arbitration programs include the Center for Conflict Studies and Peacemaking of Fresno Pacific College, Fresno, California; Lombard Mennonite Peace Center, Lombard, Illinois; and Zenas Ministries of Panama City Beach, Florida. Reputable secular programs include the Center for Public Resources, Inc., of New York City and the widely recognized American Arbitration Association (AAA), which is the national leader in secular dispute resolution in all fifty states.

NINTH COMMANDMENT: SETTLE, SETTLE, SETTLE!

Settlement is what you should seek from the first moment a dispute develops. After all, the end of every conflict and controversy is peace. A return to a state of equilibrium must be your and your lawyer's goal at all times. You must ask the question at every turn, "What can we do to get this conflict behind us as soon as possible?"

It is very true that defending yourself and your ministry at the point of attack is always warranted when legal counsel and your own wisdom say that your position is in the right. To some people, defending and seeking a settlement may seem to contradict each another. Many litigation attorneys agree. They view it as a sign of weakness and believe that only in strength can a palatable settlement be reached, if at all. Such thinking may be effective in secular disputes but is marginal even in that arena. Should you allow yourself to be thrust into a poker game of appearances? I don't believe so.

You must remember that the lawyer advising you to portray yourself as strong and invincible is not the one putting his or her assets and reputation on the line. The attorney will be paid for his or her time whether you win or lose in an unnecessary trial. In fact, the attorney will be paid far more if your case lasts all the way through a trial than if a mediated settlement is reached early in the process. If you doubt this, ask your lawyer to provide a budget on your next legal controversy that compares a three-day trial occurring two years later versus a settlement reached within sixty to ninety days. The dollars saved by a quick resolution could be used to pay a settlement and thereby save the toll on your staff, your reputation, and the effectiveness of your ministry.

In the Pastor Blair case in chapter 6, do you think the plaintiffs suing the church would have accepted $350,000 as a complete settlement at the beginning of the lawsuit? Your guess is as good as mine. Considering the $350,000 that was ultimately paid by Blair's church just in legal fees and expenses to its own lawyers and accountants, it would be a good bet they could have reached an early settlement.

Many a lawyer would counter that no one could have known that $350,000 in professional fees and expenses would be required to defend the case up to the eve of a trial. "Lawyers don't have a crystal ball either." Generally, this is nonsense, in my opinion.

If you have retained a law firm that cannot give you reasonable estimates of the legal fees that could be required to defend your case up to and through a trial (and even on to an appeal), you may have retained the wrong firm. Either the firm lacks sufficient experience in litigating cases of your magnitude, or it is being coy for fear of losing a big-fee case. In either circumstance, you are in the wrong place. Lawyers and law firms with trial experience can give you, based on that experience, a very good range of realistic legal fee projections.

Another factor in settling cases threatened or brought against ministries is the "should-versus-can" factor. All lawyers who are presented with a legal controversy to pursue or defend will focus upon what is possible, what *can* be done. For example, every contract *can* be broken if you are willing to pay the price for whatever harm is caused the other side. Lawyers emphasize the consideration of every possible claim or allegation that can be remotely supported in the law. Likewise, every possible defensive argument or measure must be thrown into the soup. The law of probabilities supports such thinking. If you make every argument and throw up every defense, maybe one will work.

Let me suggest that this is not something in which you *should* be involved. When your lawyer advises that you *can* follow a certain strategy in or out of court, you must consider whether such a tactic is compatible with your goal of a peaceful compromise or settlement. Before any legal action is taken, the Christian Legal Society suggests the following pertinent Biblical inquiries with their corresponding scriptural references:[8]

1. What action by me is likely to bring the most glory to God? (1 Corinthians 10:23-33)
2. If I had six months left to live, how much of my time would I spend in litigation? (Psalm 90:12)
3. What are my true motives for getting involved in litigation? Is my desire for revenge or security? (Matthew 5:38-48, 7:1-5; 1 Corinthians 13)
4. Is there a principle or issue at stake that is broader than my personal interests? (Acts 5:17-32)
5. Will the action I take compromise my witness before other Christians? Will I be a stumbling block? (Romans 14:13, 1 Timothy 4:12)
6. Will the action I take compromise my witness before nonChristians? Will I be a hindrance to their receiving the gospel? (1 Corinthians 6:1-8, 10:32-33)
7. Will the action I take compromise my witness before the other party, its counsel, or my counsel? (Romans 15:1-3)
8. Will the action I take compromise the testimony of the church or other Christians? (1 Corinthians 6:1-8, 10:32-33)
9. Will my action have potentially damaging consequences on "innocent" third parties? (Matthew 18:1-6, Mark 9:42, Luke 17:1-5)

10. Does Scripture expressly forbid the action I plan to take? (Matthew 5:31-32)
11. Does Scripture expressly endorse the action I plan to take? (Acts 25:1-12)
12. Does the dispute affect my obligations to my family and household? (1 Timothy 5:8)
13. Am I most concerned about my name, reputation, and feelings? (Matthew 5:38-42)
14. What are my other alternatives? (Matthew 5:23-26, 6:8-15, 18:15-18)
    a. Is forgiveness appropriate?
    b. Is settlement and compromise appropriate?
    c. Have I met with the person one-on-one to discuss my views and listen to his?
    d. Have I sought counselors or mediators to assist in reconciliation?
15. Am I as eager to forgive and be reconciled as I am to assert my rights? (Matthew 6:12-15)
16. In whom have I placed my real trust? (Matthew 6:19-34)

Do you trust that God's wisdom and instruction will lead to right relationships and reconciled adversaries? Settlement and compromise are synonymous with peace. For earthly, practical reasons as well as higher ends, you should measure every word and deed in your legal contexts to determine how they impact your chances of achieving peace through settlement. Remember, the three primary goals in a legal dispute should be to settle, settle, and settle.

TENTH COMMANDMENT: SPEAK UP IF YOU ARE NOT PLEASED

I often hear clients complain about their past or current relationships with lawyers, and the root cause of the problem is a lack of communication. The lawyer-client situation is not unlike most of our day-to-day relationships in which misunderstandings lead to hurt or hard feelings. Simple, honest communication or confrontation comes hard at times. Nonetheless, it usually results in a stronger working relationship and more respect than existed before.

Why is it hard to talk to your lawyer, and why is it difficult for him or her to hear what you are saying? The first question often finds its answer in the fact that the legal profession was once held in a lofty position in culture. The layperson was intimidated by the lawyer's level of education, unfamiliar legal terminology, and the high social esteem given attorneys due to their perceived power and wealth. A lawyer might have been the nicest person in town but still suffered from clients' feelings of inadequacy and fear in the relationship.

A true professional works hard to overcome these unproductive barriers. Unfortunately, some lawyers seem to enjoy the intimidating aspects of their profession. Stay away from these types. You don't have the time, energy, or budget to bring them down to earth. It is better to find a lawyer who already senses he or she is still a part of the human race. With this type of lawyer, an opportunity exists for you to be heard and valued as a client whose rightful participation is desired rather than thwarted at every turn.

Therefore, to lay the groundwork for communication with the lawyer of your choice, you must see yourself and your attorney as equals. Perhaps you are a professional in ministry for which you have been highly trained and educated. You are just as serious, committed, and sincere about your profession as a lawyer is about his. God has placed the two of you in different fields of endeavor, apart from which you are alike. So pick up that phone and walk into that office and speak with confidence and conviction. You're the client, the employer, the one directly or indirectly paying the fees. Neither you nor the lawyer should ever forget that basic fact. Good communication requires mutual respect. Insist on that with your lawyer.

If you are confused, ask questions. You must overcome personal feelings of embarrassment from not understanding legal terms or procedures if you are to become a shrewd client. By not asking questions, three things can happen to a client, and they are all bad: (1) the lawyer performs work or takes a position in a negotiation or controversy that the client did not want or need; (2) the client confronts a substantial legal bill for undesired or unnecessary work, or due to a counterproductive position that was put forward; or (3) the client loses a great opportunity to learn about the law and legal strategies and procedures that can minimize similar future debacles.

Whenever you receive an explanation from your lawyer about

your case or about a legal bill that seems excessive, the best thing to do is to call your other lawyer. Yes, you need access to at least two lawyers if you are going to become shrewd. In medicine, it is almost unheard of for a person to undergo any significant medical procedure or operation without the benefit of a second opinion. In law, the clients who advise their lawyer that they will be getting a second opinion are a fast-growing group. Some businesses do it only as a bluff to keep their lawyer honest. Even with the best of us, knowing that our work will be reviewed by an unknown colleague keeps us on our toes. It also keeps what we charge in line with appropriate marketplace standards. Finally, you will have the peace of mind that comes from knowing that an overall strategy makes sense to two independent lawyers before the "operation" is under way.

The last important element in professional communications is for you to speak up when you are unhappy about something your lawyer is about to do, is doing, or has done. As the counseling profession proclaims, keeping feelings of hurt, disappointment, or anger within only delays inevitable release. Usually, such feelings build up and a tremendous outburst finally occurs at such a late date that it does neither party any good.

As a Christian in ministry, you need to practice with your lawyers what you preach elsewhere. When your attorneys do not comply with your wishes, tell them how you feel right away. If they seem to make a mountain out of a molehill, tell them your perspective right then. Lawyers may fail to see how their behavior reflects poorly on the client's character and reputation. Remember, lawyers are trained in making war, not peace. If you want peace, dignity, and decency in your legal affairs, you must speak up early and often.

One last bit of wisdom, which may sound self-serving coming from a lawyer, yet is nonetheless a reminder of human nature: Before you confront your lawyer about any displeasure with his work or bring to his attention that your second opinion conflicts with his, it is a good practice to be current on your legal billing account. If you have not paid the legal fees you committed to pay, the lawyer probably will not hear you. He may appear to listen and dialogue with you; indeed, he may give every appearance of taking to heart everything you are saying. But he will listen without hearing; he will see without any perception. It is common in many businesses that the customer who has not paid for the product or service has no foundation on which to complain. "Pay me," the attorney will think, "and then I'll truly open my eyes and ears."

This, of course, is not how lawyers should behave. Their rules of ethics require otherwise. Regardless, if you want to have a meaningful relationship-building conversation with a lawyer that calls him on the carpet, be shrewd. Drop off your check before you make the phone call to schedule the meeting.

LEGAL STRATEGIES AND PRINCIPLES

◆ Sixth Commandment: Review your lawyer's invoices carefully, ask questions, and get second opinions concerning fees charged.

◆ Seventh Commandment: Negotiate the legal fee arrangement best for you.
   1. Billable hours, fixed fees, contingent fees, and monthly retainer fees.
   2. Negotiating fees has become commonplace.

◆ Eighth Commandment: Utilize mediation or arbitration if at all possible.
   1. Mediation—Making your own peace.
   2. Arbitration—Binding and nonbinding.
      —Voluntary and involuntary.
      —The private trial.
   3. Make arbitration and mediation requirements in your contracts.

◆ Ninth Commandment: Settle, settle, settle!
   —Sixteen questions Christians must ask before going to court.

◆ Tenth Commandment: Speak up if you are not pleased.
   1. See your lawyer and yourself as equals.
   2. Keep accounts current.

PART FOUR

Dodging Hailstones: Substantive Legal Ministry Issues

CHAPTER THIRTEEN

Corporate Law:
Structuring to Avoid
Personal Liability

If you are on the ministry staff or serve as a member of a governing board in your church, are you aware that you can be held personally liable for certain types of liabilities if your organization is not incorporated as a nonprofit corporation? You can be liable even if you are simply a member of an unincorporated church. This liability can include both personal injury and breach of contract damages. Exposure to serious liability risks are present in every unincorporated ministry and church.

For example, the music director at your church detected a problem in the sound system in the sanctuary. More specifically, a loudspeaker in the ceiling was not working properly, so the music director called an electrician to come out to make appropriate repairs. All of this occurred without your specific approval or even personal knowledge. While making the repairs in the ceiling, the electrician slipped and fell to the floor. He suffered serious injuries and made a claim against the church for medical expenses and lost income.

You must admit, this is the kind of accident that could easily happen to any church or ministry in the United States. The fact that you may be held liable as a church member or pastor is something that should be of great interest. Relatively easy legal steps can be taken to remove such a personal risk for nearly everyone involved in ministry in any fashion.

The beginning point in every legal matter or controversy must focus on the principal actors. In other words, you must ask two fundamental questions concerning your ministry involvements: (1) What *form* of ministry organization are you using, or should you be using, to accomplish your goals? and (2) What *forms* of business entities or nonprofit organizations are you dealing with along the way?

In every event or transaction your ministry encounters, you should determine at the outset the legal nature of the organization with whom you are dealing. Any nonprofit church or parachurch organization has several alternative forms of legal entities from which to choose. The success of what you do and the level of legal protection you may need will depend greatly on the answers to these fundamental inquiries.

HOW IS YOUR ORGANIZATION STRUCTURED?

In the United States, you will find three basic choices of organizational forms for your existing or future ministry. While each of the fifty states' laws are unique and terminology may differ, most ministries fall under one of these three umbrella categories. Since every rule of law has an exception, you should check with your organization's lawyer concerning the specific options existing in your particular state. The three types of formats are:

♦ The self-directed individual ministry
♦ The unincorporated association of persons/members
♦ The nonprofit corporation (the most common)

In the business world, these three essential forms are called the sole proprietorship, the partnership, and the (for profit) corporation. Later in this chapter we will take a closer look at these commercial forms, which have many similarities to charitable options.

Why is it important to know which of these categories your ministry is in and possibly should change to become? The answer takes us back to the issues of *liability*. Are *you* solely at risk to pay for damages caused to someone else by your ministry? Are you liable along with a group (small or large) of others participating in the ministry? Or, do you avoid all personal risk? Since the ability exists in one of these structure forms to insulate oneself from personal liability, these questions have tremendous legal consequences.

Self-Directed Personal Ministries

It is legally possible to conduct a church or parachurch ministry as an individual, one-man or one-woman show. Any other staff that may exist are merely employees or independent contractors of that individual. Ministry assets are owned by the person, and all contracts are entered into by and on behalf of that person. A name, referred to as a trade name or "dba" (doing business as) is permitted, but does not alter the legal fact that one person alone is behind the ministry being conducted. Essentially a benevolent dictatorship exists—a very effective and efficient form of operation.

With such power and control comes complete personal liability for any and all harms caused. One hundred percent control in a personal ministry means 100 percent liability. If ministry assets are not adequate to settle and pay a legal claim or if liability insurance is not available or applicable (chapter 16 will show why insurance is no absolute panacea), the leader's personal assets are on the line. One's home, all personal assets, personal investments, and future income are all fair game to a creditor or claimant harmed by the ministry. No legal barrier exists to protect personal assets if the self-directed ministry creates an unexpected financial obligation.

Unincorporated Associations

Quite frequently churches and non-church charitable and religious pursuits fall in the gap between the self-directed personal ministry and the formally incorporated nonprofit corporation. A group, small or large, has come together for a common purpose. They share both resources and the decisionmaking that goes on in the ministry.

Surprisingly, a substantial number of smaller churches fall in this category. No incorporation with the state has occurred to permit legitimate nonprofit corporate status. Typically in cases like this, little or no organizational paperwork or documents have been prepared to memorialize the association as a group. At any given moment, exactly who is in the association as a member or otherwise is very unclear. Few, if any, written rules exist telling how the association will be governed or how legally binding decisions will be made. Who has final authority to obligate the ministry to a contract obligation or debt is not certain.

Great risk of personal liability abounds in ministries and churches "organized" in this fashion. It might surprise many members or anyone officially affiliated with such an unincorporated association that they could be held financially responsible for the acts of the ministry and its staff.

No official ministry organization exists in this situation. No legal entity exists in the eyes of the law as separate and distinct from the members and others who have joined together unofficially and informally to form a church or other ministry. As with the personal ministry form, every member's home and other assets could ultimately be seized to pay for a liability or injury arising from a church or ministry activity or event. Many a church elder, trustee, and management committee member has learned the hard way that operating a church without incorporating was naive and imprudent on his or her part.

Nonprofit Corporations

Every state permits religious and nonreligious activities to incorporate, much like business corporations are created. The most distinguishing factor, however, is that these nonprofit corporations are not permitted to exist for the personal inurement or personal financial gain (profit) of any member, incorporator, director, or officer. While any of these individuals may earn a reasonable salary for services actually rendered, they may not receive any of the net income (monies received in excess of expenses) derived by the nonprofit corporation. While profits and income may be generated at Christmas tree lots, bake sales, auctions, and the sale of appreciated property, they may not legally be passed on to the corporation's members, directors, officers, and so forth as in a "dividend" to a shareholder in the business corporation.

HOW TO AVOID PERSONAL LIABILITY

The most serious reason to consider incorporating your church, school, food bank, or evangelistic ministry is to protect those who participate by what is referred to in legal language as "corporate limited liability." With a nonprofit corporation properly formed (preferably through legal counsel of a corporate lawyer), no member, director, officer, employee, trustee, or committee member is personally liable for the acts of the ministry. Unlike the previous two ministry forms, if you are a church member, a donor, an elder or trustee, a church or ministry officer, or someone else with decisionmaking authority in your organization, your home and personal assets cannot be used by a creditor or injured claimant to satisfy a legal obligation of your ministry.

Generally speaking, throughout the United States only a few understandable and obvious exceptions exist to this rule of limited personal liability. The exceptions primarily are twofold. First, no personal limitation of liability will apply to a person or persons who have used the corporation and its ministry to defraud people. Jim Bakker's jail sentence is an extreme example of how corporate limited liability protection will not shield someone proven to be involved in fraud.

Second, no personal limitation will apply to the person whose negligent conduct directly causes harm to another. For example, a church pastor or employee who drives a vehicle on church or ministry business (it doesn't matter who owns the vehicle) and negligently kills or injures a pedestrian cannot escape personal responsibility as a corporate agent of the nonprofit entity. To hold otherwise would give corporate employees and volunteers a license to cause harm intentionally and unintentionally, which public policy cannot condone. So, as with profitmaking corporate counterparts, the concept of corporate limited liability will not protect those in ministry individually for their personal car accidents, their own words of libel and slander, and their own breaches of trust and confidentiality.

On the other hand, peace of mind comes from knowing that you are not personally liable and that your home and personal savings for retirement are not on the line for the negligence of others in your organization. If you remain faithful to your responsibilities, you cannot be held financially at risk for your organization's actions and those of fellow directors, elders, members, officers, and employees over whom you have no direct personal control.

Being shrewd means giving strong consideration to incorporating your church or ministry (and as quickly as possible if you haven't done this yet). Furthermore, if you are not incorporated and are not planning to change, you should find out every reason why not from your lawyer. While there may be very good reasons not to incorporate as a nonprofit ministry, they are few and far between. I've found too many small churches and beginning ministries that take unnecessary risks and put families in jeopardy over this simple issue of incorporation. Why not spend $400 to $600 to avoid losing a $20,000 house equity? As we enter an era wrought with legal challenges never before experienced by ministries, let me suggest that you err on the side of incorporating.

The Expensive Real-Life Consequences of Not Incorporating

Let's look at a few real-life legal cases in which the type of organizational form created significant adverse legal consequences—in other words, cases in which having had the legal protection of being incorporated as a nonprofit organization could have made a big difference.

In an interesting case decided in January 1991, the Texas Court of Appeals (Houston, First District) had to resolve the question of whether an unincorporated church could be sued as a single entity or whether the *members* of the church were the proper parties to be sued by the plaintiff claiming an injury.[1] The court noted that the church argued creatively for the advantage of not being incorporated (therefore, no entity liability) while at the same time arguing as if it had been incorporated, thereby avoiding any personal liability for its members. Obviously, the court found that the church could not have it both ways, which would have left the plaintiff with no one to sue.

The Texas Court stated two principles that are typical of how any state court might react when confronted with a church or ministry that seeks to escape liability for itself and its members when no nonprofit corporation exists. First, unincorporated associations (as separate legal organizations) are not liable for their contracts. Rather, the members signing the contract along with those members who approved the contract, or those who otherwise did not take steps to prevent the contract from being signed on behalf of the church or ministry, are liable if the contract is not performed by the ministry.

Second, members of unincorporated associations are individually liable for negligent acts of agents and employees of the ministry if the negligence occurred while the agent or employee was performing services for the ministry. (In other words, church members can be sued personally for a staff member's car accident while driving church kids to a weekend church camp.)

So, in the case in Texas between a property owner and landlord against the Grace Tabernacle United Pentecostal Church, the church's members, both individually and as a group, were exposed to personal liability for approximately five years of unpaid rent and for other allegations of harm due to actions of church leadership. A Texas appellate court rejected the church's circuitous arguments and allowed the lawsuit to proceed toward a trial against the individual members. A simple, straightforward incorporation of the church as a nonprofit corporation under Texas law would have forced the plaintiff to sue only the church and its assets and not expose any member to personal liability for five years of rent. No doubt this was a sizable sum.

One chilling secular case overwhelmingly demonstrates the risks of ministries or other similar nonprofit organizations remaining unincorporated. In a case that was decided March 13, 1991, by the Indiana Court of Appeals, a member of a college fraternity was rendered a quadriplegic when he dove headfirst into a makeshift waterslide erected by his fraternity.[2] Clearly, if a court ever wants to allow the sympathies accompanying a plaintiff's severe condition to cloud its judgment, the instances of quadriplegia resulting from an injury provide the best opportunities.

In this instance, the young man sued his unincorporated fraternity association. This is a great example of how a court will treat an unincorporated organizational form even when facing severe emotional pressure to find assets adequate to compensate an injured party. The court stood up to the emotional challenge. It restated a fundamental rule that is the same around the country:

> The negligence of a single member of an unincorporated association is imputed (legally attributed to) to all other members of the association, *even including* an injured member who may himself have been free from negligence.[3] (emphasis added)

In this case, the injured fraternity brother had no suit against his fellow members of the unincorporated association because their negligence is attributed to him as well—a harsh, but necessary, rule. The result of this unique case is that the young man could not go forward with his lawsuit against the association because he himself was a member. However, you can readily see that if the injured man had been from another fraternity or belonged to no fraternity and had simply been invited to the party, the members of the fraternity would be accountable. Their negligence, imputed to every member, does not taint a nonmember—hence, no protection personally. Since one member was negligent, all members stand the risk of being deemed negligent as well. Shrewd thinking requires you to call your lawyer immediately to see if you are properly incorporated. If you are not, find out if a good reason exists not to be.

A real-life case similar to the one described at the beginning of this chapter demonstrates how a very unexpected event causing an injury can present legal exposure to liability for pastors and church members of unincorporated churches and ministries. In the 1991 case of *Crocker vs. Reverend Barr and the Calhoun Falls Pentecostal Holiness Church*, the injured plaintiff (Crocker) fell through the church ceiling from the attic while fixing an electrical wire at the request of the church pastor.[4] Crocker fell ten feet to a concrete floor and suffered serious injuries. His medical bills reached $36,850, and he missed ten months of work.

Crocker was permitted under South Carolina law to sue the unincorporated church and recover a maximum of $200,000 by a unique South Carolina statute. The state had implemented legislation to protect a charitable, nonprofit unincorporated organization *beyond* the first $200,000 in damages a court might award. As a result, every church, even if unincorporated, receives some financial protection in South Carolina. This is a unique limit on damages, applicable only in South Carolina. The statute is of no benefit to churches or ministries in other states unless a similar charitable immunity law exists in those states.

One thing, however, is certain in every state: Nonprofit corporation status will protect individual members from personal liability in every state in which the organization operates, with the only exception usually being when a church member himself was the careless perpetrator of the harm caused. When you personally cause harm to someone negligently or intentionally, you will always face personal liability exposure. The corporate form will protect you only from having to pay for liabilities caused by others, and this is still a great benefit.

KNOWING SECULAR BUSINESS ENTITIES

Now that we have learned some fundamentals about how ministries can be structured and why, it will be relatively easy to transfer our attention to the question, "What type of entity are you dealing with when you sign contracts with businesses to reroof the sanctuary, or to design a computer receipting system for donors, or to recarpet the seven classrooms in your private Christian school?" In the 1990s you need to be aware of the business forms of those whom you employ or otherwise do business with because limited liability concepts are a two-edged sword. Ministries can be prevented from seeking financial compensation because the business with whom they signed a contract is insolvent, legally preventing them from holding the principal owners liable.

In business, two basic forms or entity structures are available to give owners the protection of limited liability—the corporation (for-profit) and the "limited partnership." Limited partnerships, as opposed to general partnerships, allow partners to avoid risking personal assets, much like the stockholder in a corporation. Since it is unlikely you will confront a litigious situation with a limited partnership, we will focus on corporations.

In a typical case regarding a problem with a corporation, someone in a ministry organization trusts in the fact that some of the corporate owners, directors, officers, or employees are known to be very strong financially. Yet no one in the ministry realizes that the personal wealth of the principals of the corporation *cannot be tapped* by creditors to pay unsatisfied obligations of the business.

Even the secular business community remains largely confused in this area. It is not a pleasant task to explain to a new client that it is worthless to sue an insolvent, defunct corporation that breached a contract with the client, even though the client knows for a fact that many of the principals and shareholders of the insolvent corporation drove away from the bankruptcy proceedings in new Mercedes-Benzes and Cadillacs to homes in the city's finest neighborhoods. At first glance, corporate "separateness" seems inequitable, and it often creates unfair results. Nonetheless, American public policy, and that of most industrialized countries, concluded long ago that the benefits of freeing investors to put at risk only a portion of their personal holdings to start new businesses outweighs the smaller number of inequities. Limited liability concepts overcome investors' timidity by allowing only the assets invested in the corporation or limited partnership to be at risk. Thereby, the investor's liability is "limited" to what is represented by his or her ownership investment. Personal assets not put into the business (and thereby not owned by the business) are not at risk.

GETTING PERSONAL GUARANTEES

So how can you protect yourself from an inequitable result as described above? In other words, is there a way to ensure that the stockholder's personal Mercedes-Benz and other wealth is on the line to back up the roofing job, the computer system, and the carpet for which your ministry is paying tens of thousands of dollars out of precious ministry resources?

A very simple solution that you can borrow from the secular business community is the *personal guarantee*. In most commercial transactions, the shrewd businessperson requires the personal guarantees of the owners of a small or relatively new corporation as a matter of routine practice before a contract is signed. Essentially, the personal guarantee of an owner for his or her corporation means exactly what the phrase signifies. The owner personally guarantees performance of the contract being signed by his or her corporation. If the corporation does not perform properly under the requirements of the contract and this failure causes your organization to suffer economic hardship or loss, the owner giving the personal guarantee can be legally forced to stand behind that corporation. The owner's personal wealth can then be accessed if the corporation closes or goes legally bankrupt.

The next time your organization hires a small incorporated business to perform an important service or provide a significant product and the financial consequences if a problem develops are substantial, consider requiring that the business owner(s) guarantee the obligations of that company. Your lawyer can inexpensively assist you with contract language of a personal guarantee that will be appropriate under the laws of your state.

Quite often a very simple clause like this at the end of your written contract will suffice:

PERSONAL GUARANTEE
The undersigned individuals, for valuable consideration as the owners of ABC, Inc., do hereby personally guarantee the obligations of ABC, Inc., as set forth in the contract above. This personal guarantee is solely for the benefit of the other parties to this contract, and shall be considered to create joint and several liability on the part of the guarantors below if more than one is signing.

Another word of caution and one more reason to consult with your lawyer before signing an important contract: To be effective in almost every state, a personal guarantee must be in writing. The need for written agreements and undertakings will be addressed later, but for now be aware that a mere verbal promise "to stand behind my business" will in all likelihood be difficult to enforce if the need arises. Get it in writing as part of the contract with the help of your lawyer.

OVERLOOKED CORPORATE PROTECTIONS

Merely incorporating your church or ministry is not all there is to gaining corporate protections. There are rules to follow and some relatively minor corporate "red tape" with which you must comply. Chances are, however, that you have not been following these procedures. Since every state's corporate rules are different, consult with your lawyer to see where your nonprofit corporation currently stands and how you and your fellow staff can be sure your ministry stays within the lines.

Several common areas of oversight are illustrated by the following misfortunes taken from actual recent cases involving churches and ministries. It is imperative that all actions of your church or ministry conform to the procedural requirements of your nonprofit corporation's articles of incorporation, bylaws, and prior board and member resolutions. Each corporation, nonprofits included, has internal rules and regulations with which it must comply to ensure its activities are both legal under its state's laws and capable of withstanding a legal challenge by persons from outside, or even inside, the church or ministry.

The *Barnett* Case: A Handcuffed Church Board

Donald Barnett, a pastor in Washington state, sued both the board of directors and his church, the Community Chapel and Bible Training Center.[5] The lawsuit focused on whether the board's actions to remove the pastor were properly performed under the church's internal rules as set out in its original articles of incorporation and bylaws, which contained some very unique provisions. Is the governing body of your church or ministry adequately familiar with your articles and bylaws? Is the lawyer advising you familiar with and does he or she have access to your internal corporate rules? Procedural mixups can delay or totally thwart much-needed actions at critical junctures.

In 1967 Pastor Barnett and others incorporated Community Chapel and Bible Training Center (Community Chapel). According to the bylaws prior to March 4, 1988, the plaintiff was the "original pastor" who was "recognized as the Spiritual Overseer of the Church, ordained and appointed of God for the ministry and to shepherd the flock of Community Chapel and Bible Training Center." The bylaws further provided that the original pastor, "having established the original Church by the direction of God and with support of the congregation, shall have oversight of same until the Pastor agrees to change."[6]

The articles provided that the corporation should exist without members and that the affairs of the church were to be managed by a board of senior elders. The board was to consist of at least three members as well as the plaintiff pastor, who was designated as the original chairman and an ex officio board member. As long as the plaintiff was pastor of the church and chairman, the board was not to meet without his presence or permission, except to consider his salary. The board had no power to infringe upon the pastoral rights and authority listed in the bylaws.

For twenty years following its incorporation, Community Chapel apparently operated without untoward incident. In December 1987, however, allegations of sexual misconduct on the part of the plaintiff surfaced. In January 1988 the elders began a series of meetings and hearings regarding these allegations.

Hearings were conducted over several days in January and February 1988. On February 15, 1988, the elders wrote the plaintiff proposing restrictions on his pastoral role and putting him on a "special status." Pastor Barnett refused to accept the "special status" and to honor the board's resolution of the problem. He announced to the congregation that he was not under the authority of the senior elders and would continue in his role as pastor.

On March 4, 1988, a board meeting was called and the senior elders met with the plaintiff. The elders claimed they passed a resolution to amend the articles of incorporation. In response, the plaintiff asked the elders to leave his residence. It is undisputed that the elders continued the meeting at another site and that the plaintiff did not join them. At the continuing meeting, the elders amended the articles by striking the provisions requiring the concurrence of the plaintiff in any amendments to the articles and bylaws. They also voted to remove the plaintiff as a senior elder, pursuant to the amended articles. In addition, the senior elders amended the bylaws to remove those provisions that gave the original pastor the authority to veto actions of the board. The plaintiff in turn brought an action seeking a declaratory judgment that the senior elders had no authority to amend the articles without his concurrence. He also sought an order enjoining the elders from interfering with the performance of his duties on behalf of the church.

Isn't it amazing that a pastor and a board of elders are unable to resolve their differences without resorting to the civil courts? This case involves everyday, garden variety corporate legal issues. In small and large businesses across the United States, corporate struggles for power are a common occurrence. And such secular business disputes frequently and regularly end up in the courts. In the sense of its corporate law questions, this case is by no means noteworthy. For me, however, it is astonishing that a pastor, a church board, and a congregation somehow allowed themselves and their fellowship of believers to be open to such an act of Christian absurdity. But this is the way the wind is blowing these days.

In this case, the Washington Supreme Court put an end to part of the struggle by ruling in Pastor Barnett's favor. While the veto power given to the pastor in the church's articles and bylaws was unusual and, equitably speaking, handcuffed the church board, the court had no choice but to enforce the internal rules originally chosen by that congregation's board. Remember, this was a "nonmember" nonprofit corporation, which is permitted in most states. Thus, the board of directors held all legal power and was self-perpetuating. This means the board members themselves replaced departing members and filled vacancies without a vote from the congregation.

The board's meeting to change the church's articles and bylaws was deemed legally ineffective without the concurrence of Pastor Barnett regarding those changes. The Washington Supreme Court said, however, that its ruling upholding the church's corporate structure and its internal controls did not necessarily mean that Pastor Barnett could not be ousted on other legal grounds. In other words, if sexual misconduct was established, Barnett could be ousted for seriously failing to live up to his duties as a minister of the church, a decision over which Barnett did not have absolute control.

The case was sent back to the trial-level court in Washington for further proceedings on the sexual misconduct issue. It is probably obvious that the church board preferred to oust the pastor by adjusting the corporate structure rather than facing head-on the sexual misconduct issue. They then had no choice, and the board's predicament stemmed solely from the fact that it had permitted strange, old-fashioned corporate rules to collect dust without regular revision and updates to fit the needs of a growing church. By 1990 it was essentially no longer Pastor Barnett's church, it was the congregation's church. The board wanted to protect the body from what it perceived to be harmful conduct. The only problem was that the church's corporate charter (articles) and rules of operation (bylaws) were twenty years behind.

When a serious problem manifests itself, it is often too late to correct many years of legal neglect. Be shrewd, keep on top of your corporate structure, and be certain your actions are in compliance with those requirements. Overlooking the particular requirements of your nonprofit articles of incorporation and your bylaws, and failing to keep them current and in sync with the activities of your organization, can lead to serious trouble.

The *Banks* Case: Clarity of Ministry Governance Issues

In another similar lawsuit decided in November 1988, a Louisiana court of appeals was forced to decide on the authority of not one, but two rival boards to keep or remove a church pastor. The then-existing "board of trustees" took legal action to remove Pastor Freddie Banks from continuing as the pastor of First Union Baptist Church of Alexandria. Thereafter, another group naming itself the "board of directors and general membership" claimed to be the duly established governing body of the church corporation, and it entered the lawsuit to challenge the other "board."

The court's decision became complex because the church's corporate structure was a mess. In such a dispute, courts will look to a corporation's articles, bylaws, the prior board of record, and the minutes of board or membership meetings if the nonprofit corporation is legally structured to have voting members. In the best circumstances the corporate records are up-to-date and clearly drafted. In this case, the court found the church's records to be of no benefit. The Louisiana Court of Appeals stated in its written decision:

> The articles of incorporation and the bylaws are seriously deficient in not only meeting the requirements of law but also deficient in providing and directing the Directors, or the governing body, of the church as to how they should internally handle the affairs of the church. The bylaws are extremely vague and ambiguous outlining any specific authority for the removal of the pastor. One section states that "the church" has the authority to remove the pastor; another area impliedly gives the Board of Deacons such authority. The bylaws do not even provide for a Board of Directors, the usual corporation governing authority responsible for discharging employees. The Articles of Incorporation refer to a Board of Directors but fail to outline any authority for this Board. Testimony at the hearing indicated that the church has not had a "Board of Directors" since 1960, the year the church was incorporated.

The plaintiffs, whom all parties interchangeably referred to as the Board of Trustees/Directors were actually the Board of Trustees, who, in the bylaws, have authority to represent the legal affairs of the church, but, arguably, do not also have the power to remove the pastor. Therefore, in their capacity as either Directors or Trustees, the plaintiffs did not have specific authority in the bylaws or the articles of incorporation to remove the pastor. The Trial Court's ruling declaring such attempts on the plaintiffs' part as null and void and of no effect is affirmed.[7]

The court then exercised its broad powers and laid down very detailed orders for how the church's members would be notified of a court-ordered meeting to elect one board and to thereafter adopt bylaws, elect officers, and conduct other related, essential business. The court stepped in and ordered (not suggested, but ordered) that the church clean up its act. Even minutiae on dates, contents of written notices, and voting procedures were part of the court's order, indicating no spirit of cooperation on the part of the church had surfaced at such a late date.

I hope I'm stating the obvious: that great sums of ministry resources were expended in the church's legal battle, which encompassed legal proceedings at two different levels in Louisiana. The entire controversy could have been avoided if the quality of the church's charter, bylaws, board meetings, and minutes had been sustained over the years. Clarity in ministry governance is a must if Christians are to avoid internal controversies that lead to embarrassments like this. To find your ministry or church as the subject of what amounts to a judicial scolding is not my idea of exercising scriptural wisdom and prudence. All Christians must do better in these areas before it is too late.

SUMMARY

Shrewdness in ministry leadership means a clear understanding of the structural forms and fundamental bylaws and articles governing your organization or church. It also means understanding the consequences of ignoring those forms.

LEGAL STRATEGIES AND PRINCIPLES

◆ The single most effective means to protect against personal liabilities in ministry is to incorporate your organization as a nonprofit corporation under your state's laws. Otherwise, individual elders, volunteers, members, and committees stand a much higher level of legal exposure for any careless acts of others in the organization.

◆ The negligence of a single member of an unincorporated ministry can be legally attributed to all other members involved in the ministry. Incorporating protects against this danger of personal liability.

◆ When entering into contracts and other business transactions with small companies, obtain a written "personal guarantee" from the owners. This will prevent them from hiding, financially, behind the shield of corporate limited liability.

◆ If you are already incorporated as a nonprofit corporation, be sure your organization's articles of incorporation, bylaws, and other internal rules and regulations are legally up to date and are followed in every instance. Corporate benefits can readily be lost if we do not abide by the rules.

CHAPTER FOURTEEN

Real Estate Law: Commonly Overlooked Basics for Christian Organizations

The legal issues for anyone concerning real estate are rather dry and uninteresting. Since real property just sits there, it's not surprising that real estate law is not one of the more exciting legal topics to discuss. Ski accidents and cases of sexual misconduct are far more interesting to most people. Though the more prevalent legal concerns in real property arise from buying and selling property and are commonly handled by real estate brokers and sometimes real estate lawyers at the time of a sale, a handful of very important real estate legal traps need attention on a much more frequent basis. They deal with how you use property and what you place upon it in your ministry. Several routine danger zones can seriously harm ministry objectives.

For example, imagine your church spent months to plan and thousands of dollars to organize and publicize a new counseling center only to learn that your local zoning does not allow such an activity. We will look at a church in Massachusetts that suffered such a fate.

Another common disaster that befalls churches and other ministries that own property is the double payment for services resulting from mechanics' lien problems. Imagine being on the facilities committee at your church and having to explain to your congregation why the church paid a general contractor $6,400 for concrete work on the church parking lot and was later legally compelled to pay the $6,400 again, this time to the concrete subcontractor. Everyone's enthusiasm in serving on a church committee can easily be doused by the consequences of being legally unprepared.

OVERVIEW OF REAL ESTATE LAW

The American system contains a large, well-developed body of law known as real estate law or the law of real property. "Real" property law focuses on the ownership and use of parcels of ground along with the buildings and immovable fixtures (structures) placed thereon. Real property encompasses the ownership of the dirt, if you will, from the depths below to the heavens above.

Other forms of property obviously exist. They include what is called personal property, or those things people can own that are movable and can be taken from place to place. The most common examples of "personalty" (as opposed to realty) are cars, boats, televisions, furniture, and equipment. But personal property can also be intangible in nature, like stocks, bonds, accounts receivable, and contract rights. Real property, though, is the law governing how people purchase, transfer by gift, sell, use, lease, and mine the earth under their feet and everything that God and man has permanently affixed to it.

This area of the law requires concentrated specialization and expertise from a lawyer, except in the small number of simple real estate transactions like routine residential home purchases and straightforward apartment leases. Many states certify real estate specialists, and in other states I recommend that your church or ministry seek a real estate expert on any legal matters concerning your church's or parachurch organization's property.

Because of the sophisticated nature of most nonresidential real estate transactions today and due to the variety of planned uses for ministry properties, the current hot issue of state regulation of religious properties via zoning, land use, and related regulations comes into play. Because of the nonsecular character of the use of real estate for religious purposes, a number of First Amendment issues can impact the purchase, construction on, and use of real property. This is not a place to seek advice from a church member who happens to be a lawyer who specializes in litigation or adoptions. A mere recollection of real property from law school and study for the bar exam won't be adequate. Because of the law's multi-faceted nature for churches and Christian organizations, the need for expert real estate legal counsel will almost always be necessary regardless of the type of ministry.

A multi-volumed encyclopedia would be necessary to address the many technical issues concerning the ownership and use of real property. The scope of this chapter will be to highlight certain overlooked issues of common occurrence. Three major traps exist for the unwary acting on behalf of the typical church or religious organization in Any State, USA. They make up a significant number of lawsuits involving ministries:

◆ The need for written agreements
◆ Zoning violations
◆ Mechanics' lien problems

WRITTEN AGREEMENTS REQUIRED

As we will see in the next chapter, few agreements require written form to be valid and enforceable. Verbal promises and mutual oral commitments can be every bit as binding under the law as those reduced to writing and signed. Of course, proving to others later what was promised may be a fatal problem for a purely verbal agreement. But many types of agreements can be legally enforced as verbal contracts.

This flexibility in the law does not exist for agreements pertaining to ownership rights and usage of real property rights. Every state has its own version of what is called the "statute of frauds" dating back to English roots. These laws declare that any agreement to transfer any type of an interest in or concerning land must be in writing and signed by the person against whom enforcement of the agreement or promise was sought. A strictly verbal promise and a handshake are invalid when it comes to real property. Even if the verbal promise was made in front of a thousand honest witnesses, it remains unenforceable if it pertains to real property. The legacy of the statute of frauds remains in force in American law today.

This special rule for interests in land can affect a ministry in several ways, most of which will be adverse. Let me give a few examples that you may face someday.

For example, your church needed additional parking for Sunday services and rather than acquire nearby land at great expense, you casually asked the adjoining property owner whether it would be all right to park a few cars on his vacant lot for the next few months on Sunday mornings. In front of all your elders and deacons, the property owner gave assent, but no written agreement was prepared and signed. His promise is in all likelihood unenforceable. If the need arises, you probably cannot hold him to his word, simply because an interest in land is at stake (parking for a few hours a month is a right to use property) and no written contract is executed.

Similarly, you asked the same adjacent property owner if he would commit to not selling his property to anyone else before giving your organization the first chance to expand your property by adding his parcel to yours. He not only agreed to give you the first crack at negotiating a purchase before listing the property, but also stated that you will have a right to match any price offered by a prospective buyer so you can be sure that the land is not sold out from under you.

No matter how many credible witnesses you bring forward, the property owner's two promises are absolutely unenforceable, simply because he did not sign a written option. It seems harsh, but real property and its ownership and use have always been at the cornerstone of the American way of life. Real property has special status in a lot of ways in American law. Therefore, establish a relationship with a competent real estate lawyer and give him or her a call whenever you find yourself asking the question, "Does this need to be in writing?" If the question concerns real property in any way, shape, or form, the smart answer will be yes!

ZONING VIOLATIONS

Zoning issues are currently a hotbed of evolution in both the secular and religious realms. As local governments seek to expand their influence and power in regulating, and thereby controlling, the lands within their jurisdiction, they necessarily impose upon the corresponding rights and freedoms of private property owners. Even the secular commercial world finds itself butting heads much more often these days with local governments that have zoning and land use authority, as municipalities seek to create environmentally safe and aesthetically sound localities.

Ministries must learn to contend with these "uniformly" applied rules of protection, but also must be prepared to confront biases against religious beliefs and purposes. These biases are often acted out in the arenas of zoning and land use enforcement proceedings and may take on a decidedly political air, unfamiliar to many in ministry. Legal shrewdness dictates that Christians set aside their naiveté regarding such issues and become more sophisticated players (or at least more aware) concerning ownership and use of property. An entire book of this size (and more) could be spent unraveling religious zoning issues. But let me give the essence of zoning law in a nutshell, and then let's look at a few real examples of problems others have faced.

Zoning and land use laws originate at the city and county level in nearly every state. They find their constitutional empowerment under the "police power" inherently held by individual states to pass laws and regulations to protect the health, safety, and general welfare of their citizens. By regulating geographic areas (zones) that are suitable for one or more uses versus other areas that permit only other uses, local governments have been allowed by law to segregate incompatible activities. For example, it is universally accepted that factories and residential areas should be removed from one another for everyone's general welfare.

Zoning rules that permit the building of churches have historically centered in residential and semi-residential areas of a city. The evening and weekend aspects of traditional church activities fit well with residential districts. But this has changed of late as churches and parachurch organizations have taken on new societal roles that stretch the limits of traditional zoning principles.

Churches now commonly operate food or clothing banks for the needy. Churches also are moving into activities such as recycling centers and mental health counseling centers. Daycare and private schools have been added to many church campuses for a variety of reasons. Some motivations include making good use of an underutilized resource, namely church buildings that otherwise sit empty

Monday through Saturday. Churches also want to serve their church family creatively by offering various services. Others see a significant source of revenue available from daycare, private schools, and therapy clinics. All of these, and the many other new ways to minister, may or may not fit a zoning administrator's definition of a church activity.

Parachurch organizations that own or lease property also fall within the purview of local zoning and land use requirements. If you operate a private school on property zoned for a "school," you may find yourself in a legal bind if the school opens a recycling center to teach the students some business acumen.

Most state zoning laws anticipate and permit other nondesignated activities if they are *ancillary* (subsidiary) to the uses specifically prescribed in the zoning law. Each state and locality enforces these issues differently, so you must get detailed legal advice concerning the legality of what you contemplate doing. Is a daycare center ancillary to the operation of a church? If it is restricted to church members only, does that make a difference? If it is open to nonmembers and charges fees for services, is that any less ancillary? What about a fee-based professional Christian therapy clinic run out of church offices on weekday afternoons? Is that an ancillary, customary, accessorial use, legally embraced by the term *church* in a zoning law?

Most of us lawyers wish there were clear-cut answers to these tough questions. If we asked ten different city zoning administrators around the country, we would probably get ten varied answers, each based on different rationales suited to that community's approach to "public health, safety, and welfare."

However, we can offer some advice that would hold true throughout the United States without concern that it will cause harm. Zoning and land use legal questions are always better asked and resolved *before* the activity is commenced rather than after things are underway. The reasons are twofold. First, zoning laws are quasi-criminal in character at the least, or fully criminal at most, in nearly every jurisdiction. They are of the "thou shall not" variety, and they are packaged with fines and similar criminal punishments in nearly every instance. In other words, you cannot do what you please, violate a zoning prohibition, and when caught alter your organization's programs without further consequence. Minimum and maximum fines are commonplace, and they are calculated for each day the zoning violation existed. Substantial fines and public harm to a ministry's reputation in the community are at stake. Since quasi-criminal conduct is at issue, always see your lawyer before you make any contact with government officials.

Second, if you have any hope of working out a compromised version of your activity with zoning officials, my experience has been that they are far more cooperative when consulted in advance. Any sense they get, rightly or wrongly, that an existing violation was flagrant might close the doors to any middle-ground compromise. On the other hand, when consulted in advance, many zoning officials will bend over backwards to help a ministry find an alternative method to do what it wants without doing violence to that town's language in its zoning regulations. Treating officials as allies in the planning stages can be very shrewd. There's hardly a real estate developer in the United States who does not consult with local officials before a project is given the go-ahead and turned over to the developer's design staff. Will zoning, building, and land use rules let a ministry do what it wants to do, or can they be amended somehow to meet the ministry's needs? Ministry leaders need to ask these questions first, before a city official does.

Zoning for a Church Counseling Ministry

To see exactly how a church can run into zoning controversies, let's look at the experience of the Church of the Savior in Tredyffrin Township, Pennsylvania.[1] In this case, the church itself sought to modify the application of its current zoning restrictions to allow the church to conduct professional (nonpastoral) counseling by a church employee. A previous similar request to alter its zoning had been denied by the township zoning board because the church sought to conduct the professional counseling through a separate nonprofit corporation other than the church. The denial in the previous case was not appealed by the church presumably because the other corporation was not a church or part of the Church of the Savior. Therefore, the church could not argue that the counseling ministry was "ancillary" to or an "integral part" of its activities. "Religious" uses for activities like a "church, church school, or similar place of worship; convent, monastery or similar religious institution" were already approved by local zoning rules.

The court had to answer whether a professional, secular ("psychological" as opposed to "pastoral") fee-based counseling operation at the church's offices constituted a permitted use within the definition of a church function. In this instance, the church finally prevailed and was allowed to conduct the counseling activity it desired. However, one can only imagine what it cost this congregation in time and money to endure three levels of legal proceedings—two different hearings before the zoning board, the trial court, and the Pennsylvania appellate court. The process began in 1987 and did not end until 1990.

The church owned four contiguous tracts of land located in an R-1 residential (single family housing) zoning district. In addition to performing traditional religious services, the church sponsored a wide variety of programs, including a full range of *pastoral* counseling open to church members and the general public. Sixty percent of those who used the counseling service did so without paying; the remainder paid at a reduced rate in comparison to similar service rendered elsewhere in the community.

In November 1987 the church applied for a variance to conduct professional counseling by a nonprofit corporation. The zoning board denied the variance. On May 6, 1988, the church applied for a modification of its existing special exception to expand its pastoral counseling to include professional psychological counseling by a church employee. The zoning board also denied this application, so the church appealed. The trial court reversed the decision, and the township then appealed to the Pennsylvania appellate court.

The conceptual difficulty posed by this case is that while it is clear that the church's counseling services are conducted by the church, the definition of "church function" is far from objective or unequivocal. The zoning hearing board stated that the special exception provision of the zoning ordinance did not "envision" the church's professional counseling service because "the counseling sought to be offered was of a secular nature and not directly related to the church's functions."

The trial court found, as did the appellate court, that the evidence demonstrated that counseling is an integral part of the church's activities. In the absence of an objective definition of "church use," the remaining sources of definition are subjective. The court could not claim that counseling was not an objective church use. Accordingly, the order was affirmed.

Again, while a victory was finally obtained, is it possible that less expensive and less time-consuming alternatives existed in this situation? We do not know what steps at compromise may have been taken, but it does seem unusual that a local municipality would put up such a determined effort to prevent an activity that at face value seems harmless, or even beneficial, to the community.

It is my belief that an off-site alternative away from the church could have been implemented more quickly and with much less expense. Is it even such a good idea to run a counseling center for church members at a location that inherently impedes confidentiality? I'm sure there are some people who wouldn't want to meet a group of church acquaintances unexpectedly when leaving a counseling reception area. The stigma often attached to the idea of being involved in therapy, along with the lack of confidentiality, could be a barrier for some church members who genuinely need counseling. In an analogous situation, the large corporations that employ staff counselors and offer their employees such counseling benefits do not locate the counseling facility at company headquarters. At least the Pennsylvania parish properly sought the modification and did not go forward unaware. Instead of finding yourself confronted by a significant legal issue, take steps beforehand to avoid expensive mistakes.

Fee-Generating Counseling Not Religious

A Baptist church in Massachusetts and a Christian counseling center at the church suffered a different fate after several lengthy appeals. While Massachusetts law differs from Pennsylvania's because it uniquely provides a specific statewide exemption from zoning for all "religious purposes," the church's loss did not result from this fact. Looking at both cases objectively, they show the unpredictability any ministry could face if it tries to conduct business in the courtroom.

Needham Pastoral Counseling Center (NPCC), Inc., proposed to remodel 864 square feet of space in a church building into offices and counseling rooms for a psychological counseling center with a spiritual component. The courts considered whether the proposed use was for "religious purposes," which would have exempted the remodeling from zoning regulation. As mentioned, Massachusetts law specifically exempts "the use of land or structures for religious purposes or for education purposes." The church structure in which NPCC wished to locate was in a single residence B district that excluded businesses. When the city of Needham building inspector denied a building permit (he withheld approval because he thought "the proposed use is not unlike any other business use"), NPCC unsuccessfully went to the zoning board of appeals.[2]

To underscore the continuity between pastoral counseling and church activity, NPCC undertook to relocate in a church and made arrangements to that end with First Baptist Church in Needham. Six counselors and a director were employed by NPCC. The six counselors saw (as they did at the time of trial) approximately 120 clients per week. NPCC charged between thirty-five and fifty dollars per session. After deducting overhead costs, NPCC turned over the collected fees to the individual counselors, who were independent contractors, not employees.

The counselors treated such life problems as depression, grief, marital difficulties, substance abuse, job stress, loneliness, and absence of meaning, purpose, or direction in life. To those ills, they brought to bear psychological training with such therapeutic techniques as dream, intrapsychic conflict, and transference interpretations and clarification and confrontation therapy. The counselors saw themselves as "doing primarily long-term insight-oriented psychotherapy and shorter-term systems therapy." Folded into these secular psychological techniques was a layer of theological content. The counselors, who were ordained clergy or similarly trained in theology, believed that reconciliation with God, a minimum of relational separation from God, and a maximum of devotion to God's will are the means to alleviation of anxiety and internal conflict.

In the spirit of ecumenicity, NPCC was open to the general public. Its clientele was not limited to Baptists, Christians, or even believers in God. The counselors did not espouse to their clients any particular religious doctrine, and in accordance with the code of ethics of the American Association of Pastoral Counselors, they did not proselytize. Atheists and people with no religious beliefs were accepted as clients.

The trial judge found that NPCC's services and its method of delivering them were not significantly different from what a neutral observer who came on the scene might conclude was a mental health center applying standard psychological and psychiatric techniques. Some theological, inspirational, or spiritual content did not imbue an activity with religious purpose. An element of religion subsidiary to the dominant secular use does not convert that use to religious purposes. The court determined that NPCC's activity, although an extension of the ministry of the counselors, was not in its essential nature a religious use. Therefore, constitutional protection accorded religious use was academic—it did not exist.

The analysis the court used to unveil an otherwise generally accepted secular purpose that had been packaged with a religious institution is particularly interesting. In my opinion, it reveals clearly what we are going to see much more of in the next decade. If it serves someone else's interest, ministries will face more and more challenges in such governmentally regulated areas as zoning and tax exemptions on the basis that a portion of these activities are truly secular in nature.

National television news reports a few years ago showed secular amusement park owners claiming they suffered unfair business competition from Jim Bakker's Heritage Park because of its many exemptions as a religious, nonprofit enterprise. Such complaints fall on receptive governmental ears whenever a religious organization performs services or provides a product that in essence is nonreligious. There's a profound legal maxim that goes like this: "If it walks, talks, and looks like a duck, it must be a duck." Translated for churches and ministries: If what you do in a certain area walks, talks, and looks like a secular enterprise, you can expect to see your religious purpose shield challenged—or you may find that zoning for church or religious uses is not adequate.

Be prepared, if and when that time comes, to adjust in such a way that your calling to ministry is not impaired and that valuable monetary resources are not lost paying for lawyers, damage awards, fines, and penalties.

MECHANICS' LIENS

The area of law regarding improvements and repairs made to real estate and buildings contains a quirky mechanism that ministers and ministry staff persons should become keenly aware of as soon as possible if they have any authority over ministry property in their job. This legal offensive weapon that can put ministry properties at risk is called the "mechanics' lien." It has nothing to do with automobile mechanics. Instead, the term refers to a lien that can be imposed upon real estate if work performed on the property is not paid for as agreed.

A mechanics' lien is the right of every business and person who provides materials and work to a construction job, however big or small, to place a lien on that construction site or project for the amount the business or worker is not paid. Every mechanics' lien statute describes a very detailed procedure that the unpaid laborer or material provider must follow. It can ultimately lead to a forced sale of the entire real estate project to use the proceeds of that sale to finally compensate the contractor for the amounts owed but unpaid.

A hypothetical example may be helpful. Let's say your organization hired a small painting company, SOS (Started on a Shoestring) Painting, to paint the office building you own free and clear of any liens on two acres of land. You gave the painting firm's owner a $5,000 deposit toward a $10,000 total price for the paint job. When the project was done, you paid the owner of SOS the balance, and you were most pleased with the quality of the work SOS's six employees performed. This is true until you learned the painters were never paid for the two weeks of effort the six of them put in at your office building.

The six painters as a group claimed they were promised $400 a week, which is a reasonable wage. A total of $4,800 was due this group, they said. No problem, you thought, because you paid the owner of SOS all of the $10,000, which would amply cover these painters' wages. But you have the same problem the six workers have. You cannot make contact with the owner of SOS who, according to his neighbors, moved to Acapulco.

Under the law in every state, those painters likely have a right to file a mechanics' lien against your organization's building and probably the rest of the two acres to recoup their $4,800 collectively. If the lien is then "foreclosed" upon, meaning procedures are commenced in court to obtain a court-ordered sale of the property, your organization will have to choose between two unpleasant alternatives: (1) let your property go at a sheriff sale to pay off the lien; or (2) pay the $4,800 a second time.

Obviously, the mechanics' lien right is a powerful weapon. It can also be used just as effectively on a forty-eight dollar debt as a $48,000 debt arising out of materials and improvements to real property and buildings. So even the smallest repair and construction jobs require some care on your part.

As with much of the law concerning obligations placed on landowners, each state's laws differ from others. Sometimes the differences are quite substantial. Often they are minor. The laws in the locality where your ministry or church owns property will be the laws that govern how mechanics' liens affect what you do. Therefore, if your organization owns property in more than one state, it would be wise for those staff members overseeing particular property to become familiar with the nuances of mechanics' lien law in their state. It is possible only to generalize on this topic to a limited extent. A detailed "how to" memorandum for each state should be prepared by legal counsel to be given to the responsible staff managing each particular property. Such a quick reference legal memorandum, if followed, can save your organization great sums of money by limiting, or even totally avoiding, the dangers of an unexpected mechanics' lien imposed on valuable ministry assets.

The Hidden Dangers of Mechanics' Liens

Let's look to see what dangers a mechanics' lien can present and then how we can take steps to minimize those dangers. Mechanics' liens on real property have been in American law for quite some time. They are what is called "a creature of statute" in nearly every state. Therefore, a contractor's right to claim such a lien for nonpayment against your property is given by the state legislature to every unpaid contractor.

It is *not* a right of the contractor that comes as a result of the contract you sign with him or her. Herein lies the great danger. Since mechanics' lien rights do not arise by virtue of a negotiated contract between the subcontractor or laborer, they often seem like they come out of nowhere, and they cannot in most cases be eliminated by words in a contract. This is particularly true for subcontractors and laborers who have no contract at all with the property owner. In other words, a provision in a contract with the primary contractor on a construction project could state that the primary contractor waives (gives up) any right to claim a lien, and a court *might* find this enforceable to protect the property owner versus the contractor. To the contrary, however, such a provision will likely not be binding upon an unknowing sub-contractor of the prime contractor.

Since the lien's existence and power comes from a legal statute, many businesses, churches, and ministries learn about its existence the hard way. Many a property *owner* has had no choice but to pay twice for an unknown laborer's time and the load of lumber delivered to the construction site. Christians can do better.

These hypothetical figures of a 50 percent increase in the cost of a project were actually experienced by Ramseur Baptist Church in North Carolina. The church entered into a contract with a Willie Howell to construct a driveway and parking lot on church property. The total contract price was $12,450.85, inclusive of all labor and materials. The church paid Howell, but part of the money never found its way to a company named Concrete Supply. As you may have guessed, Concrete Supply provided the concrete. North Carolina's mechanics' lien statute forced Ramseur Baptist Church either to pay off the lien or lose the church at a forced lien sale. Two years of legal wrangling and appeals by the church had no effect.[3] The lien of $6,434.60 stood, and a parking lot that should have cost $12,450.85 ultimately cost $18,885.45 *plus* interest, court costs, and lawyers' fees for a trial and lengthy appeal that failed. A little more shrewd-ness might have been in order at Ramseur Baptist Church in early 1987, when the whole fiasco began.

Mechanics' Lien Protections

You will likely find that a handful of simple steps can bring some peace to the hiring of contractors for both big and small projects. But again, seek experienced legal advice in your state. First, see what statutory protections exist within your state's mechanics' lien statute. Many states now have mechanisms and procedures whereby certain property owners can post signs and notices in conspicuous places around the property *before* work commences and *during* a project. These signs warn unknown subcontractors, material suppliers, and laborers that you, the owner, will not be liable if they are not paid. Their compensation can then be taken up only with their employer or the firm that hired them, if your notices comply with your state's statute.

Second, property owners can pay contractors with two- or multiparty checks to ensure that the money gets into the hands of the subcontractors. For example, if Ramseur Baptist Church had asked Howell in advance for the names of his subcontractors and the amounts they were charging for their respective services and materials, the church could have issued a two-party check for $6,434.60 payable to "Willie Howell and Concrete Supply Company." That way, Howell could not cash the check without Concrete Supply's signature, and this endorsement of the church's check would have eliminated Concrete Supply's nonpayment claim. This procedure obviously requires knowledge of each and every subcontractor who works on the project and provides materials.

Third, property owners and managers can use "lien waiver" forms and lien release statements on the backs of their checks tendered to contractors and suppliers. A check endorsement form can simply state, "Endorsement of This Check Shall Constitute a Complete Release and Waiver of All Mechanics' Lien Rights of Payee." A lien waiver form could also be prepared by your legal counsel along the lines of appendix E.

Your task, therefore, is to be sure you receive a lien waiver from every subcontractor, sub-subcontractor, supplier, and even laborer to be fully protected before you issue checks to a general contractor for any completed stage of work. This assumes that you can accurately identify each and every one of these people, which might be difficult. At least take these steps because the increased significant costs could become a hardship, as in the Ramseur example.

Last, the best protection against mechanics' liens popping up on a project is to research and hire only financially strong, reputable firms. In connection with the three suggestions outlined above, the shrewd consumer of construction and building repair services (yes, repairs are also covered by most mechanics' lien statutes) will thoroughly research the final choice of a primary (general) contractor. The consumer will do the same for and require the use of specifically named subcontractors. For example, you can require in your contract with a roofing contractor that the roofer buy materials only from XYZ Roofing. This guards against strangers appearing on the site and allows you to write a two-party check upon presentation of an invoice from XYZ. The prime contractor is prevented from deviating from this procedure because you tied his hands in your contract with him.

Unless an organization's donors and directors are very forgiving when it comes to paying twice for a parking lot or carpet installation, a mechanics' lien strategy is necessary for each and every ministry that owns real property. Since the real estate owned and used by churches and parachurch organizations is often their most valuable and critical asset, don't overlook the fundamentals, and when legal issues are presented, always turn to a lawyer who is particularly experienced in real estate law matters. With so much at stake, this may not be the place to use a general practitioner.

LEGAL STRATEGIES AND PRINCIPLES

◆ Real property is legally unique property.
◆ Agreements and understandings concerning real estate always need to be in writing.
◆ Be certain local zoning allows your new ministry program before you start the program.
◆ Don't pay twice for repairs or improvements because of an unexpected mechanics' lien on your ministry's real estate.
◆ Get lien waivers upon payment.
◆ Use two-party checks.

CHAPTER FIFTEEN

Get It in Writing (and Keep a Copy)

Many clients lament the fact that they failed to get an important promise in writing from another company on a routine business deal. In the excitement of the moment or under everyday time pressures, it is not unusual to exchange promises without giving a thought to putting those mutual commitments into written, recorded form. Normally, the fact that these exchanged promises were executed verbally would not cause anyone a problem. The trust placed in the other person or organization typically proves warranted, and everything goes well according to both sides' expectations. But, as most people have probably experienced a time or two, expectations are not always met. It's sometimes amazing how two people's versions of the same undocumented agreement can become drastically different due to memory loss, pure confusion, or outright deceit. The small percentage of disputes over unrecorded contracts keep the courts and many lawyers quite busy.

While people should regret when an agreement goes without being memorialized in writing, they do not need to give up all hope about the contract's validity or whether a court can enforce its purpose. It comes as a surprise to many people that most contracts do not need to be in writing to be valid. Many agreements are enforceable in the courts and under American laws even though they were made verbally with or without any legal formalities of any kind. So the first lesson about contracts is that they are probably enforceable and valid although they may never have been written and signed by both parties. Before giving up or giving in on a legal dispute over a verbal contract or verbal promise from another party, contact your lawyer to see if your rights are enforceable nonetheless. In all likelihood, your position can be given some legal effect in the controversy.

WHY GET IT IN WRITING?

If many types of verbal agreements are just as valid as written contracts, why is there such a fetish among lawyers to "get it in writing"? There are several reasons that we will look at somewhat closely because they impact ministries fairly regularly.

Contracts That Must Be in Writing

First, certain types of contracts *must* be written and signed by the person or company that you want to hold to a particular contract. The so-called statute of frauds in every state (as discussed briefly in chapter 14) requires certain contracts to be written. Since there are other good reasons to get important agreements and understandings in writing, putting all contracts in written form means you won't need to memorize which contracts you *must* have in writing and which you *may* need in writing. For curiosity's sake, let's look at the handful of types of contracts that traditionally in the United States *must be in written form*, with the understanding that your lawyer should answer specific questions about laws in your state if your curiosity is not satisfied. The following contracts commonly must be in a written form and signed to be binding:

- ◆ Contracts pertaining to interests in land, such as purchase agreements, long-term (one year) leases and easements, sale or transfer of mineral rights, water rights, and the creation of a mortgage.
- ◆ Personal guarantees to answer for the debt of another person or business.
- ◆ Agreements that must under all circumstances take more than a year to complete.
- ◆ Generally, the purchase and sale of tangible goods or products having a price exceeding $500.

A few other less common contracts, such as an agreement to enter into marriage, require written formalities, but the previous contracts are those that traditionally have to be written to be valid. Almost all other contracts can be made orally and still be legally valid in all but extraordinary circumstances. But remember, it's easier in the long run if you just get all contracts and agreements in writing.

The Power of the Written Agreement

The second and most important reason to put every important agreement (exchange of promises) in writing is because of the uncompromising power of the clearly stated written word. When a written promise is made and signed by the person making the promise, it becomes next to impossible to explain away the clear meaning of the English language. The exact words used are recorded for future reference and exacting scrutiny by a court if necessary.

By comparison, verbal undertakings get people into difficulties in many of their relationships, including business, ministry, and even personal situations. We all recognize how easy it is in good faith to remember past events in a way favorable to our current needs. If we add some financially driven mischief or downright personal greed to the equation, it seems human memories become all the more frail.

A minister of the Mount Rainier Methodist Church, Ralph Minker, and the district superintendent of the United Methodist Church developed very different recollections when the minister filed a lawsuit in 1987.[1] They differed over the employment agreement made four years earlier concerning the minister's "temporary" assignment to the Mount Rainier church. Since no written memorandum was prepared and signed, the civil courts ultimately became the interpreters of the competing versions of what was or was not promised.

The Methodist church argued that the courts should not be allowed under the First Amendment to inquire into and interpret what the verbal agreement was. To do so would have been too much of an entanglement between church and state. The court ultimately disagreed, and because neither a written agreement nor written memorandum of what was discussed about the Mount Rainier appointment existed, the case went forward.

At the time he was hired, Minker was a sixty-three-year-old Methodist minister employed by the Baltimore Annual Conference of the United Methodist Church. After serving for ten years as a vocational counselor, Minker requested in 1982 that he be returned to a pastoral appointment. The following year, he assumed the pastorate of Mount Rainier Methodist Church on a temporary, emergency basis.

Minker alleged that the Mount Rainier assignment paid him less than what a pastor of his qualifications and experience would normally receive. Minker complained to the district superintendent, who, he claims, assured him that he would be "moved to a congregation more suited to his training and skills, and more appropriate in level of income, at the earliest appropriate time." Minker made repeated requests for reassignment thereafter, but as of June 1987 four years had elapsed without his being offered a new assignment.

In July 1987, Minker filed suit alleging that he had been denied a rightful "promotion" based solely on his age. The complaint alleged that the church violated the Age Discrimination in Employment Act (ADEA) and Minker's "contract" with the church. The contract claim was based on the district superintendent's oral promises to find him a more suitable congregation.[2]

The court ruled that a church is always free to burden its activities voluntarily through contracts, and such contracts are fully enforceable in civil court. The U.S. Court of Appeals specified that courts may always resolve contracts governing "the manner in which churches own property, hire employees, or purchase goods."[3] The church sought to extinguish these precedents on the ground that even proving the existence of a contract in this case would require the sort of inquiry into subjective, spiritual, and ecclesiastical matters that the First Amendment prohibits.

The church reportedly asserted that this case would produce the types of court inquiries and entanglements that might result from a protracted legal procedure involving subpoenas, discovery, and other tools designed to probe the mind of the church. The church further asserted that simply to permit a court to hear Minker's contract claims might distort church appointment decisions—causing churches to make only those choices that avoid the appearance of legal impropriety. The court acknowledged that the contract alleged by Minker threatened to touch the core of the rights protected by the free exercise clause:

> The relationship between an organized church and its ministers is its lifeblood. The minister is the chief instrument by which the church seeks to fulfill its purpose.[4]

The court agreed that any inquiry into the church's reasons for asserting that Minker was not suited for a particular pastorship would constitute an excessive entanglement in its affairs. Nevertheless, the court ruled that the First Amendment does not immunize the church from all temporal claims made against it. Thus, while the First Amendment forecloses any inquiry into the church's assessment of Minker's suitability for a pastorship, it does not prevent the court from determining whether the contract alleged by Minker in fact existed. In conclusion, the court held,

> The decision to appoint a minister is uniquely within a church's ecclesiastical discretion. We find the district court properly concluded that it may not interpret a church's spiritual policies without interfering with the free exercise of religion. But the first amendment does not afford defenses against promises made and contracts formed. A church, like any other employer, is bound to perform its promissory obligations in accord with contract law. Pastor Minker is entitled to rely upon his employer's representations and to enforce them in a secular court. It is possible that the first amendment's prohibition against proceedings that would create excessive entanglements with religious beliefs will make appellant's task at trial more difficult. But these difficulties do not eliminate appellant's right to enforce his employment contract.[5]

As we see from this case, courts will initially recognize the constitutional First Amendment restraints on delving into matters of faith and religious practice, but will readily go forward to adjudicate a controversy using secular principles. Unless you want to face a civil judge to explain hiring and firing practices that you made based on spiritual considerations, you had better reduce to writing what your employment relationships are truly based on with your ministry staff. This is true for parachurch organizations as well. Written employment memorandums and policy brochures, authored or approved by legal counsel, are the only way to avoid a future onslaught of *Minker*-type cases against churches and ministries.

THE ENFORCEMENT ADVANTAGE

American law has a number of helpful built-in rules of contract interpretation that courts apply to a written agreement. With rules such as these, you can see why a properly worded written contract can keep you out of court more often than not. The following few rules of contract interpretation (also called contract "construction") give written agreements a distinct advantage of enforcement over verbal commitments. You should also keep these rules in mind when asked to sign a written contract presented by someone else to your church or ministry.

Parol Evidence Rule
The single most important rule concerning written contracts is the *parol* evidence rule that is applied in every state. The rule can be stated as follows:

> Where the parties to a contract express their agreement in writing with the intent that it embodies the full and final expression of their agreement, any other oral statements or promises made prior to or contemporaneous with the signing will not be allowed in court to alter or modify the written terms of that contract.

In other words, once you sign a written contract that says that it is the "complete and final agreement between the parties" or "this agreement supersedes all prior agreements and understandings," you will not be allowed in court to present any evidence of a promise or guarantee made to you that contradicts the current agreement's provisions.

An excellent everyday example of how the parol evidence rule (a rule that bars parol/oral evidence) can be used effectively against ministries is in the area of warranties and guarantees. Not long ago, my law firm researched and purchased a computer word processing system. In its research, I met with quite a number of salespeople from a half-dozen computer firms. All of them spent hours puffing the myriad of tasks their computer products could perform. The literature from each hardware manufacturer was similarly extravagant in touting the wonders of each respective product. Every company was alike in these regards—and in one other.

When we made the selection and were tendered a final written contract to purchase the system, bold sections entitled *Disclaimer of Warranties* stood out. When we were ready to put our money down to buy the system, the manufacturer took a 180-degree turn. Its written agreement stated clearly that the product, for all the company knew, would perform very few functions. "It might not even turn on when you want it to" was the gist of the contract. Virtually nothing was guaranteed.

In this example, here's how the parol evidence rule works. If I bought the computer system and signed the contract without major changes concerning the capabilities and warranties for the product, I probably would not be allowed in court to testify about: (1) the salesman's numerous claims repeated in front of many witnesses; (2) the company representative's statement at the signing of the contract not to worry about the "disclaimer" section in the contract, that the company always "stands behind its product to the customer's complete satisfaction"; or (3) the company brochures given to me weeks before the contract signing that indicated that the computer was designed in a way to meet my needs.

To the extent any of this evidence contradicts, alters, or varies what the written agreement states without ambiguities, the judge would not allow me to open my mouth on the subject. When a contract is intended to be complete and final, covering every topic agreed upon, the courts will interpret it in just that way nine times out of ten.

So if you are worried about *Minker*-type lawsuits coming your way, implement a written employment agreement that states there are no future guarantees of continued employment and no expectations of any specific promotion or transfer of an employee. Such a written agreement might make the difference when the judge hears mention of the parol evidence rule in a similar case.

Ordinary Meaning to Words

This may seem ridiculously fundamental, but courts will interpret written contracts by giving ordinary and customary usage and meaning to words and phrases used. It is presumed in law that each word, each phrase, and each paragraph was chosen and inserted in the written agreement for some good reason. So nothing in a contract can be overlooked or given no effect unless it can be shown that a clear mistake had been made or that the overall purpose of the agreement forces a different interpretation of a word, phrase, or clause.

With verbal agreements, not only are there disputes over what was said, but it is usually impossible for the parties to recall specific terms and phrases. Hence, legal rules existing to help the courts resolve contract interpretation disputes are rarely of any benefit in oral agreements.

Let me give a quick example. Hypothetically, you verbally agreed with a paving contractor to repave the church parking lot by Easter weekend. Easter came and the lot was half completed, with equipment blocking the unfinished portion. You would like to deduct something from the price to compensate the church for the inconvenience on one of its busiest days of the year. The contractor is unwilling to agree to a reduction and claims that he only agreed to "make every effort" to complete the job by Easter. Your lawyer would likely advise you that without witnesses to your conversation with the paver, it is anyone's guess what a court would do. And without a probable courtroom victory on your side, the contractor would have little motivation to give in to your desired discount.

By comparison, a written contract or purchase order stating, "Work is to be 100 percent complete before Easter; time is of the essence," is a totally different matter. Giving ordinary meaning to the English language, the contractor blew it, pure and simple. Legal damages for delay in completing the job and for interim inconveniences are in your favor in this case. The negotiations take on a much different light. You are obviously in a strong legal posture when a written contract coincides with your stated position.

Written Evidence Always Wins

Much like the children's game of rock, paper, and scissors, in which rock breaks the scissors, scissors cut paper, and paper covers rock, a written piece of evidence presented to a judge or jury is given weight over strictly verbal testimony. The self-serving recollections of what was said and promised at an earlier time will lose their impact. The written word on paper cannot be denied or contradicted. Only vain attempts to explain it away are left for the party who finds itself out of line with the requirements of the written promises in the contract.

Even in matters outside conventional areas of written contracts, most lawyers recommend the use of a confirmation letter whenever doubts could arise in the future about one's own version of what has transpired. This is true solely because every lawyer wants to be able to wave a photocopy of the letter around the courtroom to let it work its magic. It will always draw more attention and be given more weight and credibility than the ever-changing and self-serving human memory of events. A picture is worth a thousand words, and a written confirmation of important events can be worth more than a thousand witnesses trying to recall the past.

Let me suggest that you begin to use confirmation letters with those outside your ministry when important, otherwise undocumented events transpire. For example, I recently became aware of a small Midwest church that almost got itself in quite a pickle in a building program designed to expand the church sanctuary and other facilities. After one year of raising monies and pledges from members, hiring architects, and even breaking ground for the foundation, the church realized that it had never received a firm written loan commitment from its bank to provide permanent financing for the project. Though dozens of meetings had been held and every word from the bank was positive, the church had nothing on paper from the bank to indicate even preliminary, informal approval.

While it may have had little binding legal effect on the bank at that time, I would have suggested that a church officer send a confirmation letter reciting the history of the meetings and the absence of anything thus far that would cause the bank to deny the loan. To document the prudent steps taken by the elders and officers to get to that stage, such a letter would be invaluable. Confirmation letters are powerful in that they can put the onus on the other person to articulate in writing a different perspective. Otherwise, the other person can be held accountable to (legally referred to as "estopped" from denying) your version of the facts as stated in your letter.

A confirmation letter can be very easy to draft. Essentially all confirmation letters go something like this:

> Dear Ralph,
>
> It was a pleasure talking/meeting with you today. This letter will confirm that we agreed to (fill in the blank). You agreed not to (fill in the blank). I agreed to (fill in the blank) once you have finished (fill in the blank).
>
> I will be proceeding on this basis and will be relying on you to do what you have said you'd do as outlined above. If you recall our conversation differently, please let me know right away.
>
> Best regards,
> Me

You can see how a confirmation letter creates an agenda for action and can put the other person in somewhat of a box if no written response is forthcoming within a reasonable time frame. Always remember to keep a photocopy of the letter in your files. Some letters that become very important later have a unique ability to disappear from the other side's records. A photocopy in your file of a confirmation letter is the next best thing to a written, signed contract. You'll get a lot more sleep down the road if you begin to use this simple legal tool. If high stakes are at issue or if you have the slightest reservation about what you have written, before you mail a confirmation letter to a client or business associate, show it, read it, or fax a copy to your lawyer for her input. A legally significant word here or there can tighten up this device commonly used in the business community.

One final word on confirmation letters. When you get one, do not let it go unanswered. Remember, the secular business community is often ahead of us in shrewdness. Letters such as this need attention when received, not after the other side has gone forward in reliance on what it believed were the facts.

Read It Before Signing

Finally, never sign any contract before reading it carefully. It would indeed be a shame to see an increase in ministry business acumen in the use of written contracts and then find that the same organizations have been hurt in another fashion. The failure to read an agreement presented to you, even by a member of your own church or organization, can lead to grave consequences. Just ask Pastor Wilhite of Calvary Baptist Church in Georgia.

According to the case report, on April 30, 1985, Pastor Wilhite signed an exclusive listing agreement with Kennon Realty Services, Inc., as broker and C. Robert Stacey as agent to sell certain church real property. The listing expired by its terms on September 1, 1985. After the contract expired, Stacey continued to assist with the sale of the church property. After Stacey left Kennon Realty and established his own company, the parties entered into another agreement by which Stacey would have an exclusive listing to sell the property. The original agreement, however, was misplaced, so Stacey offered to prepare another and leave it in his office for Pastor Wilhite to come by and sign. Wilhite signed the new contract without reading it.

The minister claimed that Stacey understood that the pastor could only enter into a three-month agreement on behalf of his church, which would have made the contract expire by March 1986. On June 13, 1986, a buyer presented the church with an offer to purchase the property. When Stacey called to congratulate Pastor Wilhite on the offer, he indicated that he expected 10 percent of the $195,000 sales price as commission under the listing agreement. Pastor Wilhite informed him that he believed the contract had expired in March and that the church owed him nothing. Stacey Realty filed suit against the church. The Georgia Court of Appeals finally ruled:

> Where one signs a contract without reading it, he is bound by its terms unless he can show that an emergency existed at the time that he signed it that would excuse his failure to read it, or the other party misled him by artifice or device to prevent him from reading it, or a fiduciary or confidential relationship existed upon which he relied in not reading the contract. Rev. Wilhite has not shown the existence of an emergency that would excuse his failure to read the contract. He cannot set

up a defense of fraud where he had the capacity and opportunity to read the contract. The defense of mutual mistake is not available to one who does not read a contract before signing it. He is likewise not entitled to equitable relief where, by exercising slight diligence, he could have prevented the fraud which he alleges to have been perpetrated upon him.[6]

As Pastor Wilhite's example shows, the courts give little or no sympathy to anyone who signs a contract without reading it and then complains about its contents. This really is not about shrewdness, it's about simple common sense.

The spoken word and traditional handshake are no longer adequate enough to protect an organizations' legal rights. Legal proof for the courtroom has sadly become the primary standard for whether commitments have meaning in most transactions. Christians need to continue to believe in the redemptive nature of men and women, but at the same time, they must get it in writing.

LEGAL STRATEGIES AND PRINCIPLES

◆ Verbal contracts are risky at best.

◆ Some contracts leave no choice but to put them in writing.

◆ Written commitments from others give better protection when needed.

◆ Include every aspect of an agreement in the written contract:

    1. Oral modifications are forbidden.

    2. Final means final and complete means complete.

◆ A picture is worth a thousand words, and a written contract is worth a thousand explanations.

◆ Don't forget to read what you sign, *carefully*.

CHAPTER SIXTEEN

Warnings About Insurance Coverage

For many in religious organizations, as well as other charitable and business pursuits, the proposed solution to the risks of unexpected claims and lawsuits is found in the purchase of liability insurance. It is quite true that liability insurance can provide much needed protection under the right set of circumstances. But as a basic shield to the ever-increasing onslaught of litigation, insurance is only one piece of the puzzle, and it is an expensive one at that.

Before looking at the pros and cons of purchasing liability insurance as it relates to Christian organizations and their exposures to legal claims, let's become familiar with some basics about liability insurance.

LIABILITY INSURANCE IN GENERAL

First, liability insurance is merely a means to place at risk someone else's money along with your own assets to allow you to pay for a liability that you fear may occur. If your assets were so large that any conceivable loss would not have a debilitating effect on your organization, you could run the risk alone, or "self-insure" against a loss with only your own assets. Most of the time in business, and probably all of the time in ministry, an organization's assets are not so plentiful. A successful lawsuit can ruin a ministry that took a lot of time and hard work to develop. So you need someone else's financial strength to become a partner of sorts in what you do. An insurance company is merely an enterprise that makes money by putting its assets on the line with yours and wagers that the dangers that you fear will never come to pass.

Liability insurance, as with all forms of insurance including life and health insurance, is a legalized form of gambling. When a forty-two-year-old man such as me purchases a $100,000 one-year term life insurance policy that has a $300 annual premium, a legal bet has been wagered in a very real sense. The insurance company is betting $100,000 to my $300 that I won't die in the next 365 days. If I die within the year, the insurance company loses big. As I get older, the premium cost for that same $100,000 of insurance begins to increase dramatically, because the chances of my dying also increase.

Liability insurance is no different. Utilizing past experience and sophisticated statistical data, the insurance company sets the odds for the bet on whether your church will be successfully sued, for example, for a bus accident with kids on their way to a Sunday school program. When the probabilities of a liability loss caused to some third person increase, the premiums to be waged go up along with them.

In some cases in which the ability to project the number of claims and lawsuits is very difficult and the amount of money that will be required to compensate for those injuries is also an unknown, insurance companies will refuse to bet. They either refuse to sell insurance for that kind of risk (bet) or they will close up shop and go out of business as illustrated in chapter 4. Churches and religious organizations are finding it extremely difficult to find insurance at all, let alone affordable insurance. A number of parachurch groups have found it necessary to band together to form their own insurance companies. These insurance companies are called "captives," because they are owned and controlled by a small number of organizations that they insure and no outsiders are allowed in on the bet.

When insurance company premiums quickly go through the ceiling for an industry or particular enterprise, it is always because the odds of a big loss or lots of small losses are perceived on the horizon. This is yet another harbinger of rough times ahead, because every

Christian organization already has outlandish liability insurance rates compared to twenty years ago.

Insurance policies are obviously more than a simple bet. They are now very sophisticated, complex contracts between you, the "insured," and the liability insurance company. As we have learned about contracts that are intended to be full and complete, insurance contracts cannot be altered or changed verbally in most cases. So, the next time your friendly insurance agent tells you, for example, "Don't worry, acts of sexual misconduct by volunteers are covered" under the policy that she is selling, I'd suggest that you ask her to point out *where* that is stated in the written policy. Maybe my experiences have been unusual, but it seems some insurance agents are just as willing to "puff" up the type of insurance coverage a policy provides as any other salesperson. But you need to be especially cautious because millions of dollars may be on the line in the future when a casual comment over coffee will not hold water in a court of law. Make absolutely sure in the *written* policy that your liability concerns are within the scope of coverages and are not an exclusion, as we will discuss shortly.

REVIEWING YOUR POLICY

Many people are very confused about how liability insurance policies operate before and after a loss is triggered. You should carefully review your existing insurance policies of all types with your lawyer and insurance broker for your own understanding. In addition, the following are a few helpful general insurance concepts to familiarize you better with this important area.

Claims-Made Versus Occurrence Policies

The liability insurance market offers two basic types of policies— *occurrence* policies and *claims-made* policies. Which one you purchase makes a big difference. An occurrence policy provides insurance protection *only* for losses that "occur" during that policy's time period. For example, if you purchase a typical occurrence type general liability policy for the year 1992, it will pay benefits for all covered losses that are caused during 1992 or take place due to events happening in that year. A youth group bus accident that occurs on

January 1, 1993, is not covered under that policy unless properly renewed for one more year. Likewise, a previously unknown injury or claim for a slip and fall on the church's sidewalk that took place on December 31, 1991, is also uncovered. Many general liability policies covering routine property damage and bodily injuries are occurrence policies.

Certain other policies and certain aspects of customized policies offer insurance coverage for a particular time period, but only for claims that are first made during that policy period. These types of liability policies are called "claims-made" policies. They focus both on when the accident or incident that caused harm occurs and when a claim is properly made to the insurance company. These policies will often have a "retroactive" date that extends the time period back earlier than the policy time period. Sometimes the retroactive date is many years past. Some claims-made policies have no retroactive date at all and cover any claim no matter when it occurred.

In the previous examples, a one-year claims-made policy for 1992 with a retroactive date of January 1, 1985, would pay for a slip-and-fall accident happening on the last day of 1991 so long as the claim is formally brought to the insurance company's attention before December 31, 1992. Most policies for professional counseling liability are claims-made policies.

Why is this difference important? There are a couple very serious reasons. First, it should be obvious that a ministry takes great risks in changing from claims-made coverages over a period of years to an occurrence form, thereby cutting off the chain of protection. Reinstitution of claims-made coverage may not be possible without a full and complete disclosure and investigation of prior activities. Second, if different amounts of coverages are acquired over time or if different insurance companies are involved from one period to the next, the type of policy you choose or are stuck with because you did not look more closely may result in inadequate insurance coverage. Worse yet, no coverage has been the result for the most unfortunate few who trusted a less than competent insurance salesperson.

Inclusion Versus Exclusion of Defense Costs
Another basic inquiry to make as you review or evaluate liability insurance is whether legal defense costs are counted toward policy

limits or whether they can be excluded from the calculation of when policy limits have been reached.

For example, your organization has a $100,000 liability limit for claims arising out of pastoral counseling. A lawsuit is filed against a pastoral staff person and the church. You vigorously defend the lawsuit. After a couple of years of pretrial legal maneuvering, the total of legal fees, deposition costs, and the like reaches $60,000. If legal defense costs are includable, you have only $40,000 of the insurance company's money left (remember, you supposedly won the bet here) for defense through a trial and payment of any judgment awarded at trial against the pastor and/or church.

On the other hand, if defense costs are not counted toward the policy limits, you still have $100,000 available to pay a loss at trial. Unfortunately, these latter kinds of policies are much more expensive and less readily available. Since legal fees can be very expensive these days, as I've tried to illustrate, you may need substantially higher policy limits than previously considered. Are you adequately covered?

Who controls the defense? The answer to this question is simple. If you are paying for the lawyers defending a lawsuit brought against you, you obviously have the right to direct them and disapprove strategies that are unacceptable to people claiming to follow Christ. But, if the insurance company is paying the lawyers' fare, they will have exclusive say over all defense and settlement decisions. The policy itself will even say so. Here's an example that is much like all others:

> We claim the right to defend any suit that seeks damages to which this insurance applies. We may investigate any claim or suit *at our discretion* and settle any such claim or suit *at our discretion*. The insured is required to cooperate with us in the investigation, settlement, or defense of the claim or suit.

As we move forward in the 1990s, you must be aware that your Christian witness may be held up to public scrutiny even in the way you litigate against the allegations brought against you. A harsh, badgering, sinister lawyer can cause you great harm, even if he's on your side. Insurance companies will necessarily always retain control over the lawyers and strategies used to defend their policy coverage obligations to pay if your organization is found liable. In fact, any significant interference or meddling in the defense strategies of a case can jeopardize the policy owner's rights to coverage.

At the time you purchase or review insurance, I'd suggest that you ask for references from leaders of other Christian ministries that the particular company has insured through litigation. See if the claim was handled in a dignified defensive posture. Inquire about the integrity of the insurance carrier when it comes to representing your ministry's best interests as well as the insurance company's own asset reserves. A little more paid in a settlement might cost the insurance company more money, but it can preserve your ministry by avoiding the potentially devastating limelight of the courtroom.

Likewise, when a highly revered principle is at stake in a case, such as the individual reputation of a pastor or staff member, ask whether the insurance carrier will go forward and take the inherent risks of a trial to clear the person's name. Or, will an expedient settlement that only serves your insurance carrier's bottom line be pushed upon your organization? There are fine insurance companies out there, but there are also those to avoid. Be shrewd and know the dividing lines between each group.

EXCLUSIONS: ARE YOU COVERED OR RUNNING NAKED?

A recent bold headline in a Colorado newspaper proclaimed, "Insurance Warning Issued: Methodist Churches Alerted on Sex-Misconduct Cases."[1] The article went on to report that the Rocky Mountain Conference of United Methodist Churches had formally warned all 275 congregations in a three-state region to make sure their liability insurance policies covered damages awarded in sexual misconduct and sexual harassment suits. The newspaper reported that church leaders believed that as many as 3,000 sexual miscon-duct lawsuits were pending at that time against all church workers and clergy.

If I could make my own warning about insurance coverages, it would go well beyond the obviously important area of claims for sexual misconduct and harassment. My headline warning to every minister and staff member in a Christian organization is this: "Be

Aware at All Times of the Beginning and End of Your Organization's Insurance," or as the business community says, "Know When You're Naked." The latter means to be aware when you are moving outside the comforting cloak of insurance coverage.

Reading an insurance policy is no fun task, and talking with an insurance salesperson is going to yield only vague results at best, so let me offer some help. To really learn what is or is not covered, carefully read the exclusions section of any policy you may consider. Every policy begins with a one-half page statement of what is covered that goes something like this: "We will pay *all* amounts up to the policy limits, for all damages because of *any* injury to which this insurance applies." You note, and your salesperson notes, that "all of any" is fairly comprehensive. You feel good and secure. You like those first few paragraphs on page one of the policy. It is the next ten to twelve pages of exclusions and conditions and requirements that are the real meat of every insurance policy.

We will examine a handful of typically excluded losses and injuries. Running naked on these is truly a great danger. Can you afford to insure these increasingly common risks? The real question in the nineties, I believe, is whether your organization can afford not to insure them. Get your policy; call your agent or broker; call your lawyer—don't linger in finding out if you're naked where it counts the most.

Exclusion 1: Officers and Directors

The typical liability policy will not include coverage of the organization's officers and directors as individuals from lawsuits claiming that they were negligent in their conduct as an officer, director, or elder of the church or parachurch corporate entity. The addition of coverage for directors and officers, called "D & O" coverage, may seem expensive unless you happen to be a director or officer.

Exclusion 2: Punitive Damages

Rarely does a policy include coverage for a court award for *punitive* or exemplary damages in addition to compensation for someone's injuries. Punitive, also called exemplary, damages are allowed in every state, usually when the judge or jury has determined that the defendant's conduct that harmed the plaintiff was accompanied by a willful, wanton, or reckless disregard for the rights and feelings of the injured victim. Punitive damages are not awarded to benefit the plaintiff but are given to make an example of the defendant and to punish him so others will wish not to be caught in a similar plight.

In most states, it is against declared public policy even to allow insurance to be issued to protect against punitive damage awards. The rationale for this is simple. The ability to buy such insurance would be tantamount to a license to cause harm intentionally, recklessly, and maliciously, knowing that an insurance company would pay.

Since punitive damage awards are almost universally excluded in insurance contracts, they present great risks to you and your organization because you are unprotected. Since punitive damages are often a multiple of what the judge or jury awards the victim for his compensatory (actual) damages, punitive damages usually come in large amounts.

They are also a favorite tool for plaintiff lawyers to drive a wedge between the opposing insurance company and the insured defendant. The organization or ministry being sued wants very much to see the case settled and dismissed, if for no other reason than to eliminate the risk of an uninsured punitive damage award. The insurance company, on the other hand, tends to look primarily at the actual damages portion of the lawsuit that *they* will have to pay and may not want to give in on a settlement that they think is unwarranted.

Keeping your organization's general or corporate counsel involved in monitoring any case like this is your best protection against permitting the will of the insurance company to be followed to the detriment of your organization's desires to reach a fair settlement. By the way, insurance companies all have a duty to enter into a fair settlement if one is presented. Their failure to accept a fair settlement on your behalf as the insured is actionable by you and arises as a result of the insurance carrier's "bad faith failure to settle."

Before leaving the area of punitive damages, I need to warn about another area of uninsured exposure for "fines, penalties, and similar administrative assessments." A common example of an uninsured risk due to these exclusions is a zoning violation proceeding as discussed in chapter 14. If your private Christian school on the church's property is claimed to violate zoning regulations and the city attorney comes after you, do not expect your liability insurance policy to pay for your legal defense or any fines or penalties ordered. The violation can happen as a result of innocent negligence, just like an unfortunate slip and fall on the sidewalk, but there is no insurance coverage for governmental fines and assessments under most policies.

Exclusion 3: Child Molestation and Sexual Misconduct
Many basic liability policies exclude coverage of any and all claims for damages that arise from molestation of minors or other forms of sexual misconduct by staff and volunteers. For example, one policy I have seen excludes damages resulting from "any actual or alleged erotic physical contact, or attempt thereat or proposal thereof."

Exclusion 4: Contractual Liability
Most liability policies exclude coverage and will not pay damages that arise from any type of contractual liability. For example, your church signed a contract with a painting contractor in which the church agreed to "indemnify" the painter from personal injuries caused by other contractors of the church. If the roofer dropped his hammer, causing the painter to fall from his ladder and suffer injuries, you may be exposed to a contract liability excluded by your insurance policy. True, the roofer was actually responsible for his negligence and should have paid for the painter's injuries. But what if the roofer let his liability insurance expire and does not have anything more than modest assets? Your church would be at risk to the painter and would probably not have backing from the insurance company. Be shrewd: make certain all contractors have substantial amounts of insurance as well as excellent safety records and procedures before you guarantee their behavior to others in a contract.

Exclusion 5: Libel, Slander, or Invasion of Privacy
Many policies routinely exclude damage awards for defamatory injuries and claims that one's privacy had been invaded. These kinds of lawsuits are further discussed in chapter 18. Obviously, great care needs to be exercised inherently at all levels of Christian ministries as they disseminate oral and written information about others in their midst. If your particular liability policy gives no protection, you have

one more important reason to be especially careful.

There is a fine line between genuine Christian concern for one another and gossip. You need always to check your conscience to be sure your "prayer requests" for poor so-and-so come from honorable motives. When derogatory information is communicated, you should first ask these libel/slander litmus test questions:

1. Is the information truthful?
2. Is the information complete?
3. Even if true, does the information cast the other person in a false or negative light or publicly disclose private information?
4. Does the recipient of the information have a legitimate need to know?
5. Do we stand to gain in any way by lowering the other person's reputation?

Exclusion 6: Personal Property of Staff
The exclusion of staff personal property may not cause the average ministry great concern, nonetheless it is an area where numerous, relatively small uninsured losses occur. It is also often the source of hard feelings between employee and employer. Nearly every property insurance policy that you see will protect only the property owned or leased by the ministry itself. Personal belongings and other property of employees and staff are not part of the coverage. It may seem irrational at first glance to make a distinction between the theft of a video camera owned by the youth organization and another owned by a volunteer when both are stolen from the same ski bus on a ministry ski weekend. But properly, the distinction is made this way.

When your organization buys insurance to insure against loss, damage, and theft to its property, the premium is based, for example, on the number of video cameras your organization owns. If it is one, a lower rate applies than if you desired to insure against the possible theft of forty-five cameras. This exaggeration assumes that every high school kid brings the family's video camera on the weekend and the thief strikes it rich. You can see how insuring a known, predictable amount of personal property is required over an unlimited, ever-fluctuating potential loss.

In all likelihood, then, the property owned by your employees, volunteers, and the people to whom you minister is uninsured even if lost, stolen, or damaged on your organization's premises. It is also likely you will not be able to afford the premium cost to add such coverage. To avoid having to face an unhappy employee or volunteer who "just assumed" the church's insurance would protect him, the best thing to do is remove that expectation.

Explain to all volunteers and employees or circulate a memo advising them that no insurance exists for their personal belongings and property, and they use their own property in connection with the ministry at their own risk. They may very well find their items are already insured under a standard homeowner's or renter's insurance policy if they have such insurance in place.

Take it from one who learned this lesson the hard way. My employee's hand-held recorder was taken from his desk overnight, and he expected me to pay for the $350 loss. I paid for the theft, because it seemed to be the only equitable thing to do, but I immediately circulated a memo and gave one to every new employee hired thereafter. It's said that when the donkey kicks you the first time, it's the donkey's fault. When he kicks you the second time, it's your fault. Maybe this will help you avoid being kicked at all.

A FINAL WORD ABOUT INSURANCE

Even though insurance companies are much needed friends in your ministry, you cannot forget they are businesses focused on financial preservation and gain as much as any other business. They are not interested in making charitable contributions to your ministry just to help you out in a time of need.

The insurance policy is a contract with requirements like any other contract. There are things you are required to do as the insured, and if you do them, the insurance company is then obligated to do certain things. If you do not hold up your end, then the insurance company does not have to hold up its end.

These are the cold realities of insurance. Every time an insurance carrier faces a very sizable claim, one that pushes or exceeds its policy limits, it will look carefully at every avenue available to avoid payment. This includes a vigorous defense of the lawsuit, and it also includes a review of every line of its policy to see if there is any legitimate reason to deny coverage at that point.

It makes sense, doesn't it, that before an insurance company writes a $500,000 or $1 million check it would be certain the insured has done every little thing required? On a very large claim, you need the insurance the most. But that's also the time the insurance company gives the most consideration to how it can legally and ethically leave you hanging.

Be shrewd. Give the insurance company no reason whatsoever to leave you alone in a time of your greatest need. Here are a few ways you, the insured, must hold up your end. (Check your policy to see what other unique requirements it may have.)

1. Pay your premiums, in full and on time.
2. Report to your insurance carrier in writing every accident or other serious occurrence that may even arguably be covered by your policy or develop into something that could be covered. The worst that can happen is you have wasted the postage expense.
3. Cooperate in the investigation and defense of any claims or lawsuits against you. If you do not appreciate how the insurance company is defending your case, tell the company about it and debate it, but never take the matter into your own hands by contacting the other party or opposing counsel without permission.
4. Tell the truth and the whole truth to your insurance company. Misrepresentation, concealment, and fraud are clear grounds for cancellation of any insurance policy. This is true about statements in the application and any follow-up correspondence concerning the policy. If you are not sure about some seemingly unimportant detail, do not make a lazy guess. Some day in the future, a million-dollar liability claim may be riding on the accuracy of every fact presented to your carrier.

LEGAL STRATEGIES AND PRINCIPLES

◆ Obtaining adequate liability insurance is an important element of every ministry's legal protection plan. Be careful to avoid gaps in coverage between "occurrence" and "claims-made" policies.

◆ Determine whether your insurance policy covers legal defense costs, and whether your policy's limits of coverage are high enough to pay for more than just your lawyer's fees.

◆ We must know in detail the nature and scope of the *exclusions* from coverage in our liability insurance program. Your organization may have a liability policy but, nonetheless, has activities that are excluded from insurance protection. Do you know where your ministry is "running naked"? Typical exclusions in the average policy do not cover negligence of officers and directors, punitive damage awards, sexual misconduct claims, breach of contract liabilities and libel, slander and invasion of privacy lawsuits.

CHAPTER SEVENTEEN

Counseling Liabilities 101

One of the great growth "industries" in society today is in the area of counseling. This is true not only if we look to secular forms of therapy and counseling traditionally performed by psychiatrists, psychologists, master's-level therapists, and social workers, but also if we look at pastoral and other forms of Christian counseling performed in and around churches and ministries. Twenty years ago Christian counseling clinics and lay counseling programs were merely dreams in the hearts and minds of most ministry leaders. Today, rarely does a community or church not have some form of counseling program or affiliation with a counseling clinic that emphasizes spiritual values to one degree or another.

The terms *counseling* and *therapy* have themselves become the victims of such divergent usage that trying to provide an all-encompassing definition of either is like trying to nail down a piece of Jello. Once you think you have it in place, it slips and shifts away.

The *American College Dictionary* defines *counsel* as "advice, opinion or instruction given in directing the judgment or conduct of another."[1] It defines *therapy* as "treatment of disease by some remedial or curative process."[2] But people can seek and receive career counseling and financial counseling, as well as hydrotherapy and dietetic therapy. With my license to practice law, even I am entitled to refer to my professional role as an attorney and "counselor" at law.

In the world of terminology lies the first fundamental psychological and spiritual counseling legal dilemma. Because these terms are used in so many contexts, lay people are often confused and uncertain about what to expect from a pastoral counselor as opposed to, for example, a secular social worker available through their employer's group medical plan. Sure, they know one is Christian and integrates faith, beliefs, and references to Scripture into the counseling process. They probably consider the other worldly and realize it will never consciously provide a meaningful connection to the religious motivations and implications in their lives. But beyond this very simplistic understanding of the differences between Christian and secular counseling, most, if not all, people who are the focus of Christian ministries have few clues to the mental, emotional, and psychological distinctions being brought to bear on their counseling needs. They don't appreciate the real difference between these two widely divergent fields of counseling practice.

If Christian *counselors* don't clear up this confusion with the people they counsel, the law says the courts will step in and end the ambiguity in favor of the person being counseled, especially when the person claims more was promised than received. Higher legal standards for counseling expertise are imposed on the Christian counselor than most counselors suspect. The jury foreman in the Bishop Frey case discussed previously was reported to have said after the trial, "The verdict should send a message to any entity that offers counseling. They darn well better be responsible people who are well-supervised and have definite guidelines."[3] Those being counseled can claim in a court of law that they were justified in believing that the unsuspecting Christian counselor was more capable than the counselor's training indicated.

THE EXPLOSIVE LEGAL RISKS OF COUNSELING

If you do not want to be held accountable in your counseling activities to the same standards imposed on licensed psychiatrists or licensed psychologists in the treatment of mental health problems, it is your responsibility to make clear your role. As we will see from several recent landmark legal cases, no other aspect of ministry currently presents as many explosive legal risks as do staff and lay counseling programs. While the dangers lurking about are menacing, this is not the time to hide your head in the sand. Ministries must face these mental health issues squarely and find responsible ways to provide the spiritual help for which they have been called, while at the same time avoiding the infliction of any harm due to an unwillingness to work alongside other professionals better equipped to handle serious mental health problems.

Disappearing Protections

For a long time, the law has held secular therapists and counselors liable for negative results that stem from careless and intentionally harmful counseling practices. In addition to licensing requirements for psychologists, psychiatrists, and certain other mental health practitioners, the law long allowed a victim of secular professional malpractice to obtain monetary compensation for physical and emotional damages suffered. On the other hand, religious counseling services until quite recently were not subject to lawsuits for two reasons that have begun to disappear.

Most states had charitable immunity laws that prevented lawsuits of all sorts against nonprofit operations. These charitable immunity laws have all but disappeared across the country in the last few decades, opening ministries up to litigation.

Second, the constitutional protections to religious organizations have become severely restricted to focus only on areas of faith and belief. To the extent a court is convinced that the counseling being performed went beyond religion in content, including general mental health issues, it is safe to say the counselor will not receive constitutional freedom of religion protections against litigation. The kinds of lawsuits now being upheld against pastoral and religious counselors include invasion of privacy, outrageous conduct, interference with contractual rights, infliction of emotional distress, defamation, fraud, and breach of trust responsibilities, also called breach of fiduciary duties. A highly creative laundry list of possible ways to be sued has been thrust upon ministries that do any sort of counseling.

Harms Caused by Bad Counseling

I hope people recognize that Christians cannot become too defensive on this topic. Incompetent counseling can be very damaging.

Sexual exploitation of a person being counseled is not only immoral, unethical, and dishonoring to God and Christian ministries, but it is also devastating to the damaged client. When serious harm is inflicted by careless and wrongful behavior, we should favor appropriate sanctions.

There may be some who believe that Christian counseling at its very worst could leave the client only at the same place where he or she started. Goals may not be attained, but how can inept counseling cause harm? Psychology professionals have long recognized that inexperienced and misguided counseling can often leave people worse off than before entering a therapy situation. The patient suffers what is called a "deterioration effect," which can result from the counselor's unconscious motivations, attitude, style, and personality traits. Inept counseling of all sorts is not a "neutral," valueless event to the person with true emotional and mental health needs or problems. If churches and Christian organizations fail to see the compelling need for only highly skilled and highly responsible actions in all "counseling" activities, they will likely share the guilt of increasing someone's suffering as a result. Therapy is not benign.

A New Professionalism
Another area of great confusion in Christian counseling today that leads to great legal problems revolves around culture's newest use of the term *professional*. In the past, professional has had two basic meanings. One common use of the term refers to a person belonging to or engaged in one of the learned or skilled professions. This is the older, more traditional usage that usually means the subject person is a doctor, lawyer, minister, or the like. A professional is one who has attained advanced levels of formal education and obtained any related licensing as required for that particular vocation.

The second common meaning is more broad and refers to anyone in a business, livelihood, or other pursuit for monetary gain. In other words, a professional is someone who is not an amateur. Thus, we have professional athletes, artists, and stamp collectors. The usage here means people make money at what they do, even if advanced formal education and licensing are not required for the activity.

More recent in origin than these two is a third usage. This new use of the word *professional* involves the person's belief that he takes what he does very seriously and responsibly. You hear a lot of businesspeople say such things as, "We are a highly professional organization," and "I consider what I do to be very professional." A self-proclaimed statement that "I'm a professional" might be nothing more than a subjective, wishful self-assessment. Or the person considers his job important even if he doesn't have any "fancy training or education," and even though he might not particularly excel at his "profession." In sum, if a person is proud of himself, he is a professional.

Herein lies the great danger for any church or ministry that performs any sort of counseling or advice-giving services. Are you saying one thing, when you really mean another? When you say you are "professional" in your counseling, do you realize the law says your clients are entitled to understand that the quality of your counseling is equal to that of the formally educated and state-licensed mental health professionals? Generally, the law holds the first definition of professional above, while when unlicensed and untrained volunteers call themselves professionals they mean only that they are honest, sincere, ethical, and serious.

If your organization does not feel comfortable having its counseling program held to the same level of accountability as secular counselors recognized by your state, you need to use different terminology to describe what you're doing and be clear about the level of counseling available. Rather than *professional* counseling, depending on what programs you provide, your lawyer might suggest that you use terms such as *lay counseling program, unlicensed lay counselors, church discipling program, volunteer counselor, pastoral counseling, spiritual advisors, biblical advisors, personal biblical counseling and discipleship*, or *mentoring ministry*. Any term that clearly discloses that you are not attempting to provide the equivalent of secular, professional, licensed counseling or therapy should be the goal.

Such an intentional recharacterization of your traditional counseling ministries may seem merely a game of semantics. But it was not so to the California Supreme Court in the landmark clergy malpractice case involving Kenneth Nally and the Grace Community Church of the Valley in Los Angeles, with its well-known pastor, Dr. John

MacArthur.[4] If sued, how you represent yourself and are perceived by others will dictate the standard of counseling liability you are held to in a court of law.

Of course, if your staff is trained, educated, licensed, and otherwise equipped to meet and exceed any mental health counseling standard that may be imposed, you have little to fear so long as you can prove that proposition to a jury by a preponderance of the evidence. But if you're concerned about your staff or rely to any degree on volunteer counselors who come and go in counseling ministries, you may want to become very familiar with the now-famous *Nally* case, which gives us a great overview of ministry counseling liability exposure.

THE FAMOUS *NALLY* CASE

Nally v. Grace Community Church has become a famous case because the California Supreme Court, the highest court in the country's largest and most visible state, decided that the law in California did not recognize a lawsuit for "clergy malpractice."[5] *Nally* is commonly regarded by Christian writers as a confidence booster to those in Christian counseling circles in which licensed mental health professionals are not used. In other words, *Nally* stands to many for the proposition that a "nontherapist counselor" or pastor will not be held to the same standards of mental health assistance as licensed psychotherapists, so long as the pastor or other religious counselor does not hold himself or herself out as more than just that, a religious, pastoral-type counselor.

Thus far, this limited assessment of *Nally* is true, but it is not the whole truth. Pastoral and other religious counselors in California and elsewhere must still exercise the highest levels of care. While two of the seven judges on the California Supreme Court agreed that the case should be dismissed in favor of John MacArthur's church, they reached this conclusion along a most contradictory and alarming path. These two judges *would have imposed a duty* of care very much like that of psychotherapists on the pastors of Grace Community Church had the facts been different in the case. These two judges, in other words, favored California recognizing a claim that would be tantamount to a clergy malpractice lawsuit had a clergy malpractice claim been founded. They concurred nonetheless in the dismissal against MacArthur's church simply because the evidence at the trial clearly demonstrated MacArthur and his colleagues fulfilled their duties as clergy and did not commit negligence.

Therefore, these two judges may likely recognize clergy malpractice in California in the future against others in ministry under differing factual circumstances. As we will see next, their concurring opinion in the *Nally* decision articulates what I personally believe is the philosophical wave of the future in this area. I'd suggest churches and ministries should give more heed to the concurring judges' logic than the fact that a temporary victory in one state was won. A close look at all facets of *Nally* is warranted.

Facts of the *Nally* Case as Reported by the California Supreme Court[6]

According to the record of the case, on April 1, 1979, twenty-four-year-old Kenneth Nally committed suicide by shooting himself in the head with a shotgun. His parents filed a wrongful death action against Grace Community Church of the Valley, a Protestant Christian congregation located in Sun Valley, California. The suit also named four church pastors, MacArthur, Thomson, Cory, and Rea, alleging "clergyman malpractice"—specifically, negligence in failing to prevent the suicide. Nally, a member of the church since 1974, had participated in the defendants' pastoral counseling program prior to his death.

At the close of the plaintiffs' evidence at the trial, the court granted the defendants' motion for nonsuit on all counts. The appellate court granted review to address whether it should impose a duty on the defendants and other "nontherapist counselors" (i.e., persons other than licensed psychotherapists who counsel others concerning emotional and spiritual problems) to refer persons to licensed mental health professionals once suicide becomes a foreseeable risk.

In 1973, while attending the University of California at Los Angeles (UCLA), the case reports that Nally became depressed after breaking up with his girlfriend. He had talked often to his friends about the absurdity of life, the problems he had with women and his family, and occasionally the possibility of suicide. Although Nally had been raised in a Roman Catholic household, he converted to

Protestantism while he was a student at UCLA, and in 1974 he began attending Grace Community Church, the largest Protestant church in Los Angeles County. Nally's conversion apparently became a source of controversy with his family. During this time, Nally developed a close friendship with defendant Pastor Cory, who was responsible for overseeing the ministry to the collegians attending the church. On occasion, Nally discussed his problems with Cory, but the two never established a formal counseling relationship. Between 1974 and 1979 Nally was active in the defendants' various church programs and ministries.

The church offered pastoral counseling to church members in matters of faith, doctrine, and the application of Christian principles. During 1979 the church had approximately thirty counselors on its staff, serving a congregation of more than 10,000 persons. The court found that the church had no professional or clinical counseling ministry, and its pastoral counseling was essentially religious in nature. Such counseling was often received through instruction, study, prayer, guidance, and mentoring relationships called "discipleships." According to Pastor MacArthur's trial testimony, "Grace Community Church does not have a professional or clinical counseling ministry. We don't run a counseling center as such. We aren't paid for that, and we don't solicit that. We just respond as pastors, so what we do is on a spiritual level, and a biblical level, or a prayer level." In essence, the defendants portrayed themselves as pastoral counselors able to deal with a variety of problems—not as professional, medical, or psychiatric counselors.

Following the breakup with his girlfriend in December 1978, Nally became increasingly despondent. In February 1979, Nally told his mother he could not "cope." She arranged for him to see a general medical practitioner, who prescribed Elavil, a strong antidepressant drug, to relieve his depression. The record reveals that the doctor never referred Nally to a psychiatrist. Nally's depression did not appear to subside, so he was examined by a physician, who did not prescribe medication or refer him to a psychiatrist but suggested he undergo a physical examination.

On March 11, 1979, Nally took an overdose of the antidepressant prescribed by the doctor. The record indicates that Nally's parents, concerned about their friends' reaction to their son's suicide attempt, asked the doctor to inform other persons that Nally had been hospitalized only for the pneumonia he suffered after the drug overdose rendered him unconscious.

On the afternoon of March 12, Pastors MacArthur and Rea visited Nally at the hospital. Nally, who was still drowsy from the drug overdose, separately told both pastors that he was sorry he did not succeed in committing suicide. Apparently, MacArthur and Rea assumed the entire hospital staff was aware of Nally's unstable mental condition, so they did not discuss Nally's death-wish comment with anyone else.

Four days later, a staff psychiatrist at the hospital examined Nally and recommended he commit himself to a psychiatric hospital. When both Nally and his father expressed reluctance at the thought of formal commitment, the psychiatrist agreed to release Nally for outpatient treatment, but warned Nally's father that it would not be unusual for a suicidal patient to repeat his suicide attempt.

After his release from the hospital on March 17, 1979, Nally arranged to stay with Pastor MacArthur because he did not want to return home. MacArthur encouraged Nally to keep his appointments with a Dr. Hall and arranged for him to see Dr. John Parker, a physician and church deacon, for a physical examination. Dr. Parker's testimony revealed that Nally told him that he was depressed, had entertained thoughts of suicide, and had recently taken an overdose of Elavil. After examining Nally, Dr. Parker believed he was a continuing threat to himself and recommended he commit himself to a psychiatric hospital. Nally, however, immediately rejected the advice.

Dr. Parker then informed Nally's father that Nally needed acute psychiatric care and that he should contact Glendale Adventist Hospital for information concerning the psychiatric facilities. The record shows that Mrs. Nally strongly opposed psychiatric hospitalization for her son, saying, "No, that's a crazy hospital. He's not crazy."

Eleven days before his suicide, Nally met with Pastor Thomson for spiritual counseling. According to the record, Nally asked Thomson whether Christians who commit suicide would nonetheless be "saved." Thomson referred to his training as a seminary student and acknowledged "a person who is once saved is always saved," but told Nally that "it would be wrong to be thinking in such terms." Following their discussion, Thomson made an appointment for Nally to see Dr. Bullock for a physical examination but did not refer Nally to a psychiatrist.

Several days later, Nally moved back home. At the end of the week, he met with a former girlfriend. She turned down an apparent marriage proposal by telling him, "I can't marry you when you are like this. You have to pull yourself together. You have to put God first in your life." The next day, Nally left home after a family disagreement. Two days later, he was found in a friend's apartment dead of a self-inflicted gunshot wound.

The Course of the *Nally* Trial
At trial, four experts testified for Nally's parents regarding the general standard of care to be followed by the counseling community when dealing with a suicidal person. Each witness testified that although standards varied among secular and denominational counselors, a counselor has a duty to investigate the counseled person's suicidal tendencies and to encourage that person to seek professional help once suicide becomes foreseeable. Although the parents attempted to show that the defendants violated these standards, the court found that the suggested standards were vague and dependent on the personal predilections of the individual counselor or denomination. The court also found that the standards had not been officially or formally adopted by any organized body of counselors.

The parents introduced several counseling manuals that were apparently sold in the church bookstore as support for an inference that the defendants advertised that their counselors were competent to treat a myriad of emotional problems and as evidence of the defendants' inadequate training as counselors.

At different points in its opinion, the lower court referred to the duty imposed on nontherapist counselors as a duty "to take steps to place (a suicidal person) in the hands of those to whom society has given the authority and who by education and experience are in the best position to prevent the suicidal individual from succeeding in killing himself"; "informing those in a position to prevent the counselee's suicide about the factors"; and "to insure their counselees also are under the care of psychotherapists, psychiatric facilities, or others authorized and equipped to forestall imminent suicide."

The California Supreme Court recognized that under traditional negligence law principles, one is ordinarily not liable for the actions of another and is under no duty to protect another from harm in the absence of a special relationship of custody or control. Because liability for negligence turns on whether a duty of care is owed, the court's first task was to determine whether a duty existed in this case.

Although the court had not previously addressed the issue, it had imposed a duty to prevent a foreseeable suicide only when a special relationship existed between the suicidal individual and the defendant or its agents. For example, two cases imposed such a duty in wrongful death actions after plaintiffs proved that the deceased committed suicide in a hospital or other inpatient facility that had accepted the responsibility to care for and attend to the needs of the suicidal patient.

The California court had in previous cases recognized that a lawsuit may exist for professional malpractice when a psychiatrist's treatment of a suicidal patient falls below the standard of care for the profession, thus giving rise to a traditional malpractice action. But none of these cases supported the finding of a special relationship between Nally and the defendants, or the imposition of a duty to refer a suicidal person to a professional therapist as urged by the parents' lawyer.

The court noted that the closeness of connection between the defendants' conduct and Nally's suicide was tenuous at best. As the defendants argued, Nally was examined by five physicians and a psychiatrist during the weeks following his first suicide attempt. The court noted that the pastors "arranged or encouraged many of these visits and encouraged Nally to continue to cooperate with all doctors."

Nevertheless, the plaintiffs argued that mere knowledge that Nally may have been suicidal at various stages in his life should give rise to a duty to refer. Imposition of a duty to refer Nally necessarily would imply a general duty on all nontherapists to refer all potentially suicidal persons to licensed medical practitioners. The California court specifically rejected this notion.

Based on the foregoing analysis, California does not recognize "clergy malpractice," in this context at least. The judges' final words were:

> The suicide of a young man in the prime of his life is a profound tragedy. After considering plaintiffs' arguments and evidence, however, we hold that defendants had no duty to Nally on which to base liability for his unfortunate death.

Analysis of the Minority Opinion

Two of the seven California Supreme Court judges wrote that they concurred in the judgment that nonsuit was properly granted, but disagreed with the majority's holding that the defendants owed no duty of care to the plaintiffs. They stated that while the majority appears to reject the proposition that "nontherapist counselors in general" have a duty to advise potentially suicidal counselees to seek competent medical care, the majority does not purport to "foreclose imposing liability on nontherapist counselors, who hold themselves out as professionals, for injuries related to their counseling activities."

In light of the factual background, the concurring judges believed the conclusion is inescapable that *the defendants owed a duty of care to Nally*. That duty, in the judges' view, was simply to recognize the limits of the defendants' own competence to treat a person, such as Nally, who exhibited suicidal tendencies and, once having recognized such symptoms, to advise that particular individual to seek competent professional medical care. The two judges found that the record demonstrated that the defendants neither breached their duty to Nally nor contributed in any legally significant respect to his suicide. Here's what these two judges had to say:

> In the special case of determining the existence of an affirmative duty to protect another, courts have traditionally looked to relationships where "the plaintiff is typically in some respect particularly vulnerable and dependent upon the defendant who, correspondingly, holds considerable power over the plaintiff's welfare."
>
> The special relationship that arises between a patient and his doctor or psychotherapist creates an affirmative duty

to see that the patient does no harm either to himself or to others. The relation of the nontherapist or pastoral counselor to his counselee contains elements of trust and dependence which closely resemble those that exist in the therapist-patient context. *Defendants here patently held themselves out as competent to counsel the mentally ill,* and Nally responded to these inducements, placing his psychological and ultimately his physical well-being in defendants' care. In each instance, the adequacy of the nontherapist counselor's conduct must be judged according to what is reasonable under the circumstances. Where, as here, defendants have invited and engaged in an extensive and ongoing pastoral counseling relationship with an individual whom they perceive to be suicidal, both reason and sound public policy dictate that defendants be required to advise that individual to seek professional medical care. . . .

It has been suggested that both public policy and the constitutional right to the "free exercise" of religion militate against the recognition of a duty of care in these circumstances.

The governmental intrusion in this case (i.e., the duty to advise a suicidal counselee to seek medical care) is religiously neutral. Defendants are not exposed to liability for refusing to counsel contrary to their religious beliefs or for affirmatively counseling in conformity with their beliefs. Thus, the burden on religion is relatively minimal.

The governmental interest, on the other hand, is compelling: society's interest in preserving the life of a would-be suicide is as profound as its interest in preserving life generally. To this end, society surely may require a pastoral counselor who invited and undertakes a counseling relationship with an individual in whom he recognizes suicidal tendencies, to advise that individual to seek competent medical care.

Thus, we are persuaded, on the facts presented, that defendants owed a minimal duty of care to Nally. We are equally persuaded, however, that defendants fulfilled their duty.[7] (emphasis added)

These words have much moral weight behind them, and likely will become persuasive in other jurisdictions in the future. We must remember, however, that while the Supreme Court of California is often considered a highly influential, prestigious court in judicial circles of other states, it does not establish what the law is, or suggest what the law should be, in any other state. In your state, you should get an up-to-date legal opinion on your particular pastoral counseling responsibilities and risks. But as we will see in the next chapter about a Colorado case, the effects of *Nally* and the concurring judges' logic are going to reverberate throughout the country as more and more states answer for themselves whether clergy and others in Christian counseling ministries can be sued for malpractice, or "professional negligence" as some label it.

As you and your legal advisor consider the warnings that the *Nally* case provides, you must confront and answer the following questions:

1. Are we representing in some way, directly or indirectly, that we are professional counselors, therapists, or other- wise rendering psychological help? Are we "holding ourselves out" to be more than we can legally live up to?
2. Is the person we are "counseling" suffering from or manifesting symptoms of a serious mental or emotional illness that may need to be diagnosed by a qualified state licensed mental health professional, i.e., a psychiatrist or psychologist? For example, is there any indication of a chemical dependency or abnormal family behavioral pat- tern that may cover a much more serious situation?
3. Do we objectively and subjectively know the limits of our own abilities in recognizing and dealing with the range of emotional and mental health issues we are likely to confront?
4. Are we creating relationships with the people our min- istries counsel that include unique elements of trust and confidence being placed in our abilities to help people with their problems? As we answer this and other simi- lar questions, we must remember that the law would look at the relationship through the eyes of the client

and his or her family, not through ours.

5. In all honesty, are we utilizing undertrained and inexperienced staff and volunteers? It may be true that the magnitude of the problems in our communities require many bodies to meet the challenge, but we may find we do as much harm as good with this approach, while asking for a serious lawsuit in the process.

6. Have we engaged the resources of Christian licensed therapists to the greatest extent possible, and do we utilize secular therapy alternatives where appropriate? It may be more prudent to trust God by making a referral to a competent secular psychologist for a person with a drinking problem than to allow a well-meaning, but unprepared lay counselor to waste precious time without unearthing the person's real issues.

7. Has our counseling program, pastoral and volunteer, been reviewed and is it routinely supervised by a Christian or secular state-licensed mental health professional?

LEGAL STRATEGIES AND PRINCIPLES

◆ In our pastoral and lay counseling activities, we must be very careful to explain (preferably in writing) the fundamental limits of what we can and cannot do for people. Unrealistic expectations can often be the springboard to a lawsuit when the results of counseling have fallen short of the mark.

◆ The loss of "charitable immunity" laws and the severe restrictions being imposed by the courts on previously protected religious freedoms mean that our Christian counseling programs need to be legally prepared to meet professional standards similar to licensed mental health practitioners.

◆ Unlicensed Christian counselors, pastoral and otherwise, should avoid any representations implying that they are rendering emotional, psychological, or mental therapy.

◆ Counselors of every type should be carefully screened and qualified, preferably by a mental health professional, for the specific kinds of counseling activities they will be doing.

◆ Engaging competent Christian, and even secular, licensed mental health professionals to "audit" and regularly supervise counseling activities is probably the best model for having a program that most properly cares for people's problems while imposing a formidable barrier to legal claims of counseling negligence.

CHAPTER EIGHTEEN

Protecting Counseling Ministries from Legal Attack

The *Nally* case has essentially set the stage around the country for individual states' responses to the clergy malpractice controversy. Colorado simultaneously came to the same conclusion as California in another nationally notable case. Colorado went further, however, and acknowledged a handful of other legal theories for certain plaintiff lawyers to get exactly what they wanted anyway—a vulnerable group of Christians in counseling-type ministries.

The Colorado Supreme Court case involved the sexual misconduct of a Catholic priest with the wife in a couple whom he had been counseling. In 1979, Robert and Edna Destefano were having marital problems that led them to seek marriage counseling from their Catholic priest, Grabrian. The Destefanos were both Catholics who had "faith and confidence in their parish priest." To comply with church doctrine regarding marriage and divorce, the diocese encouraged its parishioners to participate in marriage counseling.

According to reports on the case, during the course of counseling, Grabrian developed a relationship with Edna that "Grabrian knew or should have known would lead to additional marital problems."[1] Grabrian knew that his intimate relationship with Edna probably would cause the dissolution of the Destefanos' marriage. Grabrian told the Destefanos that he would act as their marriage counselor and that they could trust him. The court noted that the diocese owed a continuing duty to train, interview, and supervise priests engaged in marriage counseling.

THRESHOLD ISSUES

First Amendment Protection

The threshold issue that the court had to resolve first is whether a member of the clergy who represents himself as being trained and capable of conducting marital counseling is immune from any liability for harm caused by his counseling by virtue of the First Amendment of the U.S. Constitution.

If Grabrian's alleged conduct was dictated by his sincerely held religious beliefs or was consistent with the practice of his religion, the court would have had to resolve the First Amendment issue. But the court noted that "every Catholic is well aware of the vow of celibacy required of a priest at the time of his ordination." As such, the conduct upon which the lawsuit is premised is, by definition, "not an expression of a sincerely held religious belief."[2]

Members of the clergy cannot in all circumstances use the shield of the First Amendment as protection and as a basis for immunity from civil suit. When the alleged wrongdoing of a cleric clearly falls outside the beliefs and doctrine of his religion, he cannot avail himself of the protection afforded by the First Amendment.

Fiduciary Duties of Counselors

The lawsuit alleged that Grabrian, in his position as a priest and as one who held himself out to the community as a professional or trained marriage counselor, breached his fiduciary duty to Edna Destefano. A fiduciary is a person who has a duty created by his undertaking to act primarily for the benefit of another in matters connected with the undertaking. A fiduciary has a duty to deal "with utmost good faith and solely for the benefit" of the beneficiary. A fiduciary's obligations to the beneficiary include, among other things, a duty of loyalty and a duty to exercise reasonable care and skill.

A person standing in a fiduciary relationship with another is subject to liability to the other for harm resulting from a breach of the duty imposed by the relationship. The court had no difficulty in finding that Grabrian as a marriage counselor owed a fiduciary duty to the couple. His duty was "created by his undertaking" to counsel. Grabrian had a duty, given the nature of the counseling relationship, to engage in conduct designed to improve the Destefanos' marital relationship. As a fiduciary, he was obligated not to engage in conduct that might harm the Destefanos' relationship. The court held that Grabrian breached his duty and obligation when he had sexual intercourse with Edna Destefano.

Potential Clergy Malpractice

Secondly, the lawsuit alleged that Grabrian "negligently performed his duty as a marital counselor" and that a member of the clergy who represents himself as a competent marital counselor has a duty to employ the degree of knowledge, skill, and judgment ordinarily possessed by members of that profession in the community. This claim of professional negligence is a claim for malpractice. Malpractice consists of any professional misconduct, unreasonable lack of skill or fidelity in professional or fiduciary duties, evil practice, or illegal or immoral conduct.

Since Grabrian is a Catholic priest, the malpractice claim allegedly falls within the realm of "clergy malpractice." The Colorado Supreme Court stated, "To date, no court has acknowledged the existence of such a tort. Since the claim for clergy malpractice is not supported by precedent and raises serious first amendment issues, we have concluded that Edna's second claim for relief was properly dismissed. We do not recognize the claim of 'clergy malpractice.' "[3]

Outrageous Conduct

Courts have generally recognized that when a professional counselor engages in sexual relations with a patient or client, he may be held liable for damages. The lawsuit alleged that Grabrian engaged in outrageous conduct. The test for outrageous conduct in Colorado is, "One who by extreme and outrageous conduct intentionally or recklessly causes severe emotional distress to another is subject to liability for such emotional distress to another, and if bodily harm to the other results from it, for such bodily harm."[4] Other states call the same claim intentional infliction of emotional distress.

The court found that the priest's actions could be determined by a jury to be outrageous conduct.

Church's Duty to Supervise Counselors

Lastly, it was argued that the diocese breached its duty to supervise Grabrian, and the actions of Grabrian should be imputed to the diocese. An employer may be held responsible for negligent or intentional conduct by an employee only if the tort is committed by the employee within the course and scope of employment. An employee acts within the scope of his employment if he is engaged in the work that has been assigned to him by his employer or he is doing what is necessarily incidental to the work that has been assigned to him or that is customary within the business in which the employee is engaged.

A priest's violation of his vow of celibacy is contrary to the instruction and doctrines of the Catholic church. When a priest has sexual intercourse with a parishioner, it is not part of the priest's duties nor customary within the business of the church. Such conduct is contrary to the principles of Catholicism and is not incidental to the tasks assigned a priest by the diocese. Under the facts of this case, the Colorado court held that there was no basis for imputing vicarious liability to the diocese for the alleged conduct of Grabrian.[5]

Direct Liability from Careless Supervision

Even though Grabrian's actions did not create a basis for holding the diocese vicariously liable, the diocese could have been held directly liable for negligently supervising Grabrian. A person conducting an activity through employees or other agents is subject to liability for harm resulting from the employees' conduct if the employer is negligent or reckless in the supervision of the activity.

Employers can be considered negligent if they have reason to believe that the agent, because of certain character qualities, is likely to harm others in view of the work entrusted to him. If the dangerous quality of the agent causes harm, the employer may be liable. Employers are not liable merely because the employee is incompetent, vicious, or careless. Liability results only under circumstances in which the employer has not taken the care that a prudent man would take in selecting the person for the business at hand. Precautions that must be taken depend upon the situation. If, therefore, the risk exists because of the quality of the employee, liability exists only to the extent that the harm is caused by that same quality of the employee who the employer had reason to know could be likely to cause harm. To the extent the priest's conduct was known or foreseeable, the Catholic church could be liable.

Accordingly, the Colorado Supreme Court in this case held that a person who knows or should have known that an employee's conduct would subject third parties to an unreasonable risk of harm may be directly liable to those parties for harm caused by the person being supervised.

Battle Won, But Not the War

Although the Colorado court rejected the concept of professional clergy malpractice, just as the California court did, the Colorado court, much like the concurring minority opinion justices in *Nally*, fully recognized that a clergyman, his organization, or others in Christian counseling ministries can be successfully sued for:

1. Violation of any special obligations ("fiduciary" duties) of loyalty, failure to exercise reasonable care and skill, and failure to deal with impartiality toward anyone with whom a special counseling relationship has been formed.
2. Conduct that is deemed extreme and outrageous and either intentionally or recklessly causes severe emotional distress to someone in a person's care. (The conscience of the entire secular community is the sounding board to be used, not the subjective values of one's religious group or denomination.)
3. Negligent hiring and supervision of staff for whom the organization knew, or should have known, would present a risk to others.

A rose by any other name is still a rose, and clergy malpractice under the guise of breaches of fiduciary duty, outrageous reckless conduct, or negligent supervision of counseling staff are still professional acts of negligence. Obviously, those in Christian counseling ministries of every sort must be discerning and take every precautionary step available for their legal protection. *Nally* and *Destefano* may give false confidence to the extent that Christian counselors may believe the issue of clergy malpractice is a battle already won.

STEPS TO AVOID NEGLIGENT COUNSELING LAWSUITS

Now that you recognize the ever-increasing exposures to a lawsuit based on personal and organizational negligence in counseling ministries, you need to look at steps that can be taken to act more competently and shrewdly. You should consider with your lawyer the following eight defensive protections.

Step 1: Conduct an In-Depth Analysis
Have an objective, independent mental health professional in consultation with your lawyer conduct an in-depth analysis of your organization's counseling program.

Step 2: Consider Cutting or Dropping Counseling
It may sound drastic, but many churches and other groups have ceased to render any counseling at all or have seriously curtailed the types and quantity of their counseling. If an in-depth analysis of your ministry's counseling program by a mental health professional and your lawyer indicates the risks are too great, it may be wise to eliminate all counseling per se, especially what you cannot closely control and supervise. Counseling by inexperienced, unsupervised staff and lay volunteers is potentially an area of high risk in which real harm and indefensible appearances of impropriety can occur.

Step 3: Eliminate Indicated Risks
If a total ban is not feasible or would cut out the heart of your ministry, develop specific parameters for your counseling program that carefully take into consideration the areas of legal liability mentioned in your analysis.

For example, one large denomination is seriously considering limiting each pastor's counseling time with any one church member to three to five sessions. The purpose is to allow the person to be heard to some degree on a spiritual level and to instill some scriptural perspectives and religious goals to the person's counseling agenda.

Then the person is referred to a competent mental health professional, preferably one of compatible personal beliefs, for ongoing long-term therapy. The pastor's role can continue in a limited, spiritual advisory role that runs parallel to the therapy received outside the church setting.

Other churches are limiting their counselors to a narrow range of personal and spiritual growth issues that avoid the more serious psychological categories that are beyond a minister's or lay counselor's abilities. For example, ministerial or lay counseling might be limited to such areas as clarification of one's spiritual pilgrimage (evangelism or discipleship), grief from the death of a family member, divorce recovery groups, or the loss of meaning in one's career. By comparison, one-on-one marriage counseling, depression, chemical addictions, and anger control would necessitate referrals to Christian psychologists.

These referrals must be made to protect the pastor and the organization when clearly extenuating circumstances indicate that a mental health problem may exist. Pastoral counseling may certainly continue alongside more in-depth therapy or medical treatment when organic problems are diagnosed (those requiring dietary or chemical treatment). As a minimum, your church and organization should get a counseling liability "audit" by your insurance broker, your lawyer, and a Christian (or secular) psychologist to determine what limits should be placed on the pastor, his staff, and volunteer lay counselors.

Step 4: Screen Your Counselors
To the extent your ministry continues any form of counseling activities, you should perform a personal interview and background check of every counseling staff member and volunteer. In particular, I recommend that every person working with young children, and even teenagers, be screened in some formal fashion. Many secular youth organizations now require volunteers to provide character references and to certify that they have never been charged with a crime of sexual misconduct or abuse of a minor. You should call references and carefully handle any confidential information that you receive from these calls. Your lawyer can help in this regard.

The *Destefano* case and similar lawsuits that focus on negligent hiring (in which no background information was reviewed) and negligent supervision make it abundantly clear that ministries today face grave risks by readily accepting every volunteer who crosses their path and representing volunteers in any capacity, counseling or otherwise, as people who can be trusted. Those days of throwing any willing warm body into the junior high youth department are over.

Step 5: Administer Psychological Testing

Before leaving the obligation to carefully and prudently hire staff and recruit capable volunteers, I need to mention a new, evolving aspect of staffing ministries toward which several groups are moving—psychological testing. It may seem like going overboard to some, but not to certain Episcopalian, Methodist, and Catholic churches, among others.

For example, a Denver newspaper reported that the five finalists for the Episcopalian bishop position in Colorado had to undergo psychological tests before church members chose from among them in the fall of 1990. The article noted, "Most major Protestant denominations, the Catholic church and some Jewish synagogues give psychological tests to potential clergy members, either before seminary, before ordination, or both."[6]

Depending on the complexity of the issues and demands upon your ministry's staff, you may want to look into some form of formal psychological review. You may also want to explore how to make psychological testing an ongoing aspect of your organization's periodic assessment of staff. Legally speaking, having any mechanism in place that could uncover a potential problem before it manifests itself should appeal to any legal advisor and insurance carrier with whom you deal. In any event, every step you can take to demonstrate the highest care in the selection and supervision of staff and volunteers will serve your organization well.

Step 6: Refer Clients to Competent Professionals

Develop a list of licensed, competent mental health professionals who share your spiritual values and to whom you can refer clients for evaluation and therapy. Such referrals protect you, even if you continue in a pastoral, spiritual counseling role. Essentially, this may enable your organization to shift the major liability risk to other professionals who, in the eyes of the law, are more qualified to handle emotional problems and mental illness. The *Nally* case was a victory for John MacArthur and Grace Community Church in my opinion *solely* because Ken Nally was surrounded by a large number of physicians, psychiatrists, and other professionals who could share any blame. MacArthur and his colleagues met their obligations by referring and continuing to refer Nally to those other health professionals.

Let me make one final point about referrals to licensed therapists before everyone views them as the cure-all to counseling liability. In counseling, as well as other professional areas, it is possible to make a *negligent* referral and be liable for that carelessness as well. If the professional to whom you send your church members is deemed incompetent and you should have known better, your liability is different, but still there.

Make every referral a matter of serious consequences to you and your client. I find it comforting to give the names of at least two other lawyers when I make a legal referral. By doing so, I am not pushing one over another. The client makes the final choice after an initial meeting with each. Your ability to recommend two or three qualified licensed practitioners may be your strongest defense to any claim that you made a negligent referral in a situation when the person being counseled trusted you implicitly as his or her minister or spiritual mentor. Furthermore, you and your organization have an obligation to your clients or parishioners who seek help in line with their own spiritual values. If you have interviewed these professionals to ascertain their values, you've met an obligation to those whom you care for that is just as important as that of taking care to protect yourself and your own organization.

Step 7: Use a Legal Advisement Form
Use a legal advisement form at all times. The best way to eliminate having people assert that you or your staff misled them about counseling abilities is to get their signature on a form that acknowledges what they have been told at the beginning of your counseling activities. Your lawyer and, again, a mental health professional should help you prepare a standard form for you and your ministry's use with everyone being "counseled." The legal advisement form will necessarily need to be drafted to fit the laws in your state as well as the characteristics of your counseling efforts. Every advisement should at least address the following issues as does this simplistic example:

DISCIPLESHIP ADVISEMENT AND WAIVER

I _____ the undersigned member of ABC Church hereby understand and acknowledge that I have been advised to my satisfaction concerning the following issues about this discipleship, mentoring program:

A. The church staff are not licensed as psychiatrists, psychologists, nor mental health therapists in this or any state. Rather, this discipling program is staffed by pastors and church volunteers solely trained as follows: _____.

B. The church staff and volunteers are not trained in, nor experienced in, evaluating, diagnosing, or treating any forms of physical, emotional, or mental illness or psychological problem.

C. A referral list of Christian and secular licensed mental health professionals in the community has been provided to me, and it is the recommendation of the church and its staff that I seek the professional services of such a licensed therapist whether from that list or from other sources.

D. The church and its employees and volunteers participating in this church discipleship program shall not be liable under any circumstances, and I hereby waive all rights against the church and its staff for any claims and damages arising directly or indirectly from any physical, emotional, or mental illness or psychological problem I may now have or may develop in the future.

E. Only limited rights of confidentiality exist, and what I say may be required to be divulged at some future date under state law.

Church Member _____

Dated _____

While this example gives an idea of what an advisement and waiver could look like, your lawyer can do a much better job in tailoring such a document for your state's particular needs.

Before leaving the advisement and waiver form idea, be mindful that the legal ability of these forms to ward off a legal attack is never guaranteed. They may or may not be enforced by a judge in the final analysis. As a minimum, they demonstrate your efforts to dispel any notions that your ministry "held itself out to be more than it is." In a *Nally*-type case, that evidence can be crucial.

Step 8: Train Your Counselors

Finally, there is probably no better protection against negligent counseling lawsuits than training, and more training, of your counseling staff. Allowing Christian and secular psychologists, psychiatrists, clinical social workers, and master's-level therapists to come and address your staff and volunteers is an essential aspect of any legal protection plan. The more varied the input, the more likely you and your staff can detect a high-risk client.

Formal supervision of your counselors and regular case review by a licensed practitioner may also be needed. In some states, secular therapists with only master's-level degrees are permitted to counsel clients for a fee so long as they are under the protective wing of a supervising licensed psychologist. The counselor under supervision meets regularly, often several times a month, with his or her supervisor to go over each client's case, diagnosis, treatment plan, and the like.

If your church counseling program can affiliate with a state-licensed Christian therapist for regular, behind-the-scenes supervision, the quality of your ministry could not help but improve. Future allegations of negligent supervision would also ring false.

SUMMARY

We are not finished seeing the courts deal with accusations of clergy malpractice. The courts have so far protected those churches who could have been found liable had the circumstances been only slightly different. Fortunately, in the *Nally* and *Destefano* cases, each church had performed its obligations according to legal guidelines.

People involved in ministries must learn how to protect themselves against the potential of lawsuits and the growing possibility of a change in the courts regarding treatment of the legalities of clergy malpractice. But remember, following the guidelines set forth in this chapter provides not only increased protection but also a more careful, more thorough, and more effective counseling ministry. The goal is still to point people toward God and a relationship that glorifies Him and edifies the Body of Christ.

LEGAL STRATEGIES AND PRINCIPLES

◆ The First Amendment offers no protection for sexual misconduct in counseling.

◆ Counselors have legal duties of trust known as "fiduciary duties."

◆ Be aware that clergy malpractice theories continue to surface.

◆ Counseling misconduct may be termed "outrageous" by the courts, resulting in serious liability.

◆ Thorough and ongoing supervision of staff and volunteer counselors is a must.

1. Liability can be indirect (vicarious) for all employees and volunteers.
2. Liability can be direct for the supervisor who fails to act.

◆ Ministries can take eight proactive steps to avoid negligent counseling lawsuits.

1. Have an in-depth analysis of their organization's counseling program done by a mental health professional in consultation with their lawyer.
2. Consider cutting back on or dropping their counseling programs altogether.
3. Develop specific parameters for their counseling program to eliminate risks indicated in the analysis report.
4. Perform a personal interview and background check of every counseling staff member and volunteer.
5. Administer psychological testing to those staff and volunteers they consider hiring for their ministry.

---

6. Develop a list of licensed, competent mental health professionals who share the ministry's spiritual values and to whom the ministry can refer clients for evaluation and therapy.
7. Use a legal advisement form at all times.
8. Conduct training, and more training, for their counseling staff.

CHAPTER NINETEEN

Counseling Confidentiality and Transference

Confidentiality in counseling settings is essential to the counseling process. Obviously, people who enter counseling could not feel a sense of trust and confidence in their pastor or counselor if they thought the subject matter of their sessions might be communicated beyond that relationship without their permission. Confidentiality and privacy are essential to any spiritual or psychological interaction that effectively deal with serious, personal matters.

Because of the important role of privacy in counseling, nearly every state has enacted laws both acknowledging the need for confidentiality and mandating adherence to strict standards for members of the clergy and professional therapists of varying levels. Since each state's requirements differ in significant ways, remember to consult with a competent attorney to sort out the exact legal requirements that may be imposed by state statutes and precedent-setting cases that may affect personal counseling activities as well as those of any counseling program your church or ministry has established. The requirements of confidentiality are more than just helpful to the counseling process, they are also civil legal duties to the people whom you are counseling.

Careless or intentional disregard of the confidentiality laws in your state could ultimately cause serious legal consequences to you and your organization.

CONFIDENTIALITY REQUIREMENTS

In a nutshell, the legal duty to keep confidences sacred requires the following to be present:

1. Any written, verbal, express, or implied communication made by the client to the counselor within the context of the counseling relationship is considered confidential. Generally, anything that falls within the scope of the counseling relationship is given great leeway by the courts. Even a whispered comment in your ear at a social barbecue attended by hundreds of others would probably still qualify. In other words, the confidential relationship goes far beyond just the statements made in your office during a formal counseling session.
2. The information provided must be of a confidential nature and given in a context that manifests its secret characteristics. Statements made openly in a public setting would not fit this requirement. However, statements made in a group, such as a therapy group, where the person expects his secrets will be kept in confidentiality, would fit this requirement. Therefore, always presume that confidentiality obligations apply to statements made in a group therapy situation in which an expectation of secrecy has been expressed or is implicit.
3. The confidential statement must be made to the counselor for use in the counseling process, and the counselor must be in the class of people in his or her state that comes under the legal obligations of confidentiality. For example, if you are an ordained minister who comes within the state's rules for secrecy, but the person speaking secrets to you does not know you are a clergyman, no confidentiality expectation exists. On the other hand, if you do not fall within your state's confidentiality rules and are involved in lay counseling of some sort, I suggest you warn each person in writing that it is a remote possibility that you could be forced to disclose what they tell you at some future point, possibly against your will,

because your status does not fall within the confidentiality provisions of state law.

Once the duty of confidentiality is found to exist in the relationship under state laws, there are two basic consequences under those laws. First, the confidences must be forever maintained unless the person being counseled consents to a disclosure, or a more compelling state law creates an exception, such as child abuse reporting statutes. If there is no legal exception nor a free and informed consent given by the patient, liability is created for disclosure of a confidence that can result in imposed monetary damages in a lawsuit. The liability is both personal against the pastor or counselor violating the confidence and corporate against the church or parachurch organization that employs him. As in all areas, the acts of an organization's staff and volunteers are the acts of the organization. So as an individual counselor, you could be sued successfully along with the organization or church to which you belong. Even board or committee members who were guilty of negligent supervision in the face of obvious prior abuses of these obligations could find themselves exposed under the laws of their particular state. Confidentiality is serious business.

Exceptions
Once the duty to hold confidences is clearly applicable, a person must consider whether any exceptions exist if a disclosure of confidential information for some reason becomes necessary or is desired. There are very few exceptions in most states, and since the legal consequences are severe if you guess wrong on whether an exception applies, I suggest that you call your lawyer in every instance before you disclose a confidence. These kinds of dilemmas should occur only infrequently, and you won't incur expensive lawyer time on a weekly or even monthly basis. The following kinds of exceptions typically permit or require disclosures of confidences.

The duty to warn of imminent harm. In every state there is a duty imposed on licensed mental health practitioners to *warn* others and *report* to authorities whenever a client is considered to be in real, imminent danger of committing physical harm to himself or to others. Under some rules, the "other" person needs to be a specific, ascertainable person (i.e., spouse, boss, opposing litigant). Some state standards suggest disclosure is also required when the danger to others is real but the person or persons that may be the target of harm are not known or even ascertainable (e.g., a dangerous anger toward all politicians).

Whether this duty to warn and report applies also to you as a pastor, unlicensed therapist, board or committee member, or lay volunteer can be answered only under the specific requirements of your particular state's laws. Since this is a "damned if you do, damned if you don't" area, you must become especially sophisticated in your Christian counseling programs. In fact, it can be readily argued that Christian counselors' levels of training and supervision should exceed all secular counseling standards.

The duty to report child abuse. Like the general duty to warn of imminent harm, every state has enacted some form of child abuse reporting law. These laws can cover both physical and emotional abuse, although they vary from state to state. These laws typically cover only a limited number of designated types of professionals. For example, many apply only to the activities of doctors, teachers, psychologists, and police personnel. Often clergy are not specifically included, although at least one state, Texas, does have language in its law that seems to cover "any person" who has reasons to believe a child has been or may be abused. My sense is that we will see a nationwide broadening in these laws to include more people, such as the Texas law has done.

These statutes are not optional for people whose roles fit within the specific requirements of a particular state's law. Other duties of confidentiality give way. Serious legal consequences apply, and the defense of "I didn't know" is never allowed. Thankfully, many states recognized the dilemma of competing legal obligations for those who fall under these rules—namely, the duty of confidentiality versus the duty to report child abuse. The relief from this serious problem will be found in either "immunity" statutes or precedent-setting court opinions that recognized a "qualified privilege to breach a duty of confidentiality."

For example, many child abuse reporting statutes also include a provision that the person reporting the abuse will be totally protected from any legal liability resulting from the disclosure to the appropriate officials. Obviously, the reporting of the suspected abuse must be made only to the officials designated in the statute and protection comes only when there is a good faith, reasonable basis to suspect abuse. Whether your state provides statutory immunity for reporting and warning is something with which your ministry should become very knowledgeable.

Another protection for a compelling disclosure may come in the form of precedent-setting appellate court opinions that recognize a qualified privilege to warn others and report a dangerous situation to the police. Every state acknowledges that in unique circumstances the protection of a life and/or prevention of a serious crime will override a duty of confidentiality. Your lawyer is best suited to give a specific answer whenever you are faced with any such dilemma and a reporting immunity statute does not exist or seem to be of benefit.

Formal supervision exception. Another exception to the duties of confidentiality that may apply to counseling is the clinical advice or supervision exception. Many states allow certain unlicensed and lay counselors to perform some levels of counseling only if they are under the formal supervisory wing of a more highly trained, licensed professional. For the strict purposes of any such formal supervision, the actual counselor is permitted to discuss the confidences of his or her clients. Mental health policy favors such professional discussions for the benefit of the client. Similarly, most states recognize an exception that, in one way or another, allows a licensed professional to discuss a client's circumstances with other licensed mental health professionals to get advice and input as to the best therapy strategies. Essentially, certain limited conversations between two state-recognized professionals (clergy included) who are both by law required to maintain confidences will not be deemed a violation of a confidence per se. Similarly, a conversation with a lawyer, who is also obligated under an attorney-client duty to maintain divulged confidences, is also permitted under strict, limited scenarios.

Consent to disclose confidences. Lastly, a commonly used exception to the requirement to maintain confidences is the client's consent or permission to the disclosure. If practical, always get the written consent of the person who you are counseling *before* any disclosure takes place. For example, disclosures of even the existence or nature of the counseling to a spouse or insurance company should be made only upon receiving written permission.

The primary legal problem with written consents, as is true in all areas of the law (i.e., waivers of liability for personal injury), is whether the consents were given freely and upon adequate information at the time. If the person giving the consent was pressured or coerced in any way, the permission may not be effective. Coercion and pressure can come in many forms, including prior physical threats by a spouse or parent. Coercion and pressure can also be emotional or financial.

Likewise, if the decision to give consent was based on a misunderstanding of the consequences of the consent, it could also be challenged. A full and fair explanation of what will happen and what could foreseeably happen is essential to getting a reliable consent in any area. The same is true of a consent to a confidential disclosure. Again, ask your lawyer for help in the preparation and use of any consent forms.

INVASION OF PRIVACY

Another aspect of one's duty to keep confidences extends well beyond the role as a counselor in Christian ministry. The obligation to avoid public dissemination of confidential information concerning others is the duty that can give rise to liability for "invasion of privacy" if the duty is breached. This obligation to not invade the privacy of another arises in much of what is done in Christian ministry. It is present in hiring and firing paid staff, screening volunteer leaders, and the far-reaching activity of sharing prayer requests with one another within the context of organized church and parachurch work.

As touched on earlier, those in organized Christian ministry run the risk of legally invading the privacy rights of another person far more than persons in secular involvements. This is true because Christians intentionally and consistently encourage each other to share burdens and difficulties so as to foster closeness and commitment in groups. Christians are also living out God's commandment to His followers to love one another.

The reason I see greater legal risks for people in ministry is the fact that they happen to carry around more potentially harmful information about those with whom they work. My friends outside the church do not share their fears and personal struggles among themselves to anywhere near the degree that Christians are accustomed. Therefore, the information about one another that Christians possess can be a loaded gun of legal liability if people are careless with their tongues or succumb to the temptations of gossip disguised in the cloak of Christian concern.

Liability for invasion of the right to privacy can come in several different forms. For example, an appropriation of a person's name or picture for a promotional advertising benefit is an invasion of that person's privacy if his or her consent is not in hand. You need to be very careful how you use the names of the celebrity members of your congregation. It is so easy to just "assume" they wouldn't mind that you are promoting the fact that they support your ministry.

The most common exposure to liability that Christian ministries can face is the public disclosure of private facts about someone else. The information you pass on into the public realm must be found to be objectionable to the average reasonable person, and even if the information is true, liability can still attach. Unlike lawsuits for libel or slander, the truth of what is being said to others is no defense. You may be telling the absolute truth and yet find yourself sued for substantial damages because of the harm caused to the reputation of the other person.

Let me give a unique example, but one that could become a more prevalent dilemma for Christian ministries in the future. Someone involved in your church or parachurch ministry approached you with an interest in working in your youth program. The person is forty-eight years old, married, has two children, and is a certified public accountant by profession. The person seems to be an ideal role model for teenagers, until you are told that the individual had one experimental homosexual encounter six years ago. The person further insisted that there has never been another such experience because the individual is happily married, and you believe this person to be totally honest. You alone have knowledge of this information and the person did not say the information could be publicly discussed.

From what we have just learned, a "public" disclosure of these obviously private facts would be harmful to the person's reputation in the community. A qualified legal privilege would allow you to privately seek counsel from a high-level supervisor in your church or ministry. Such a privilege under your state's laws would also protect you if you consulted a lawyer and probably a doctor or licensed psychologist, if their expertise was needed for your resolution of the issue of whether to let the person work with your kids or not.

On the other hand, sharing a prayer request in a group setting or from the pulpit is clearly going to expose you to an invasion of privacy lawsuit. Who is told, how many people are told, and for what purpose the information is revealed are all factors you and your legal advisor should explore.

A homosexuality incident is the kind of privacy matter I trust everyone in Christian ministry would be sensitive to and could recognize as being legally dangerous. But what if the information divulged by this same person involved a recent careless driving accusation that was quickly dismissed? Or that a personal tax return was being audited by the IRS? Or this person and his or her spouse were beginning marital counseling? These are much more likely hypothetical situations because the apparent severity of the harmful information is much less than the severity of an alleged homosexual encounter.

Nonetheless, you must remember that the answer to the questions of what is public or private and what is harmful or not is not your personal decision to make. The law will use an objective "average reasonable person" test to answer those questions. Maybe because you had a serious traffic violation at one time, went through a successful audit, or even expound the benefits and virtues of counseling in what you do every day, these revelations may not seem particularly sensitive. Remember, your background and subjective personal perspective are no defense when you pass on a casual comment over lunch to a few friends. If any doubt exists about whether it is proper to divulge information, there is only one good rule to follow: Always resolve your feelings of uncertainty on the side of holding personal information confidential.

TRANSFERENCE

Are you familiar with the term *transference*? If you are involved in any form of counseling or oversee a counseling program as a board or committee member in your organization, allow me to mostly strongly encourage you to become particularly aware of this psychological concept. It is considered by many mental health specialists to be at the root of most, if not all, of the sexual affairs that are becoming commonplace in many church circles. Legally as well, it is being used as a weapon to win sexual misconduct cases. While not trained or educated in psychology, I still need to discuss transference and the legal consequences that can be created by a counselor's misuse of this phenomenon. Most trained professionals in the field of psychology describe transference as follows:

> Transference is the unconscious tendency to shift our emotional interest and investment toward new persons in the hopes of reexperiencing old persons or in the hopes of succeeding where formerly we failed.[1]

To illustrate,

> When a young man begins college and first meets his professors, he bears toward them a basic emotional perspective that is a compilation of past experiences with parents and other important educators. Perhaps he idolizes them quickly, and as time goes on and he sorts out reality from fantasy (transference) he may change his opinion accordingly. To the degree reality does not alter this basic emotional frame of reference, he is caught up in an unconscious transference.[2]

A highly regarded expert described transference in this way:

> Transference is a specific form of interpersonal perceptual distortion. In individual psychotherapy, the recognition and the working through of this distortion is of paramount importance. For many patients, perhaps the majority, it is the most important relationship [the therapy relationship] to work through since the therapist is the living personification of parental images, of teachers, of authority, of established tradition.[3]

As you can see, the person in therapy and counseling can readily adopt a fantasy relationship with the counselor or therapist at an unconscious level. If the real world does not contradict the transference fantasy as time in counseling progresses, the unreal world becomes more and more a significant part of the person's life. If the therapist or counselor is not on guard and fully cognizant of what is taking place (a fantasy becoming securely imbedded as reality), an inadvertent one-way love affair may result.

Countertransference and Manipulation

Sadly, counselors and therapists sometimes intentionally and manipulatively get involved in love affairs with patients. Of even greater danger is when the counselor begins unconsciously to experience a countertransference to the person being counseled. An unconscious fantasy and transference can go both ways. No one is immune.

When these two fantasy worlds collide at the wrong time and place, a front page, headline-making lawsuit is right around the corner. Pastoral careers are easily thrown aside. Wives and families are recklessly disregarded, and a minister's high esteem among close friends and the congregation is amazingly reduced to no personal value whatsoever. Much of this happens at an unconscious level, but it may be led along the path by a series of conscious choices by the counselor. The great danger lies in the fact that in making these little choices, the counselor overlooks the forest to focus on the trees.

Many experts would say that for any therapy relationship to be effective, repressed feelings must be brought to the surface. The relationship between therapist and patient may be used effectively as an emotional release of unresolved inner problems. As the person being counseled confronts these repressed thoughts and emotions with the therapist or counselor and as the therapist or counselor responds in a different manner than in the patient's prior experiences, a gradual emotional reeducation takes place.

As a typical example, a female seeking pastoral counseling with her minister may fantasize at an unconscious level (transference) that her minister is a spouse, father, divine authority figure, or even all three. In the counseling process, she will carefully watch the pastor's reactions as she reviews prior experiences. If the pastor's reaction is positive, the woman may obviously see the pastor as the caring, listening, sensitive husband she always yearned for, as the forgiving father she never had, or as the representative of God the Father who truly brings acceptance and a closeness she never before experienced.

At a conscious level, an unscrupulous pastor can most likely lead this woman into any sexually motivated relationship he desires. At an unconscious level, the pastoral counselor may experience an attentive wife or lover that finds him attractive. The two together become like fire and gasoline with an explosion to follow that rocks the foundations of the Christian community.

The *Garvin* Case Revisited

In the Alaska Supreme Court case discussed in chapter 4, the lawsuit concerned a reported sexual affair between an ordained counselor, Pastor Garvin, at a Christian counseling center and a woman who was referred there by her church minister.[4] The woman began seeing Garvin for emotional and spiritual therapy in September 1984. She had attended approximately thirty-four sessions with Garvin by June 1985. In an affidavit presented to the court, she recapped her experience in her own words:

> In mid-June, 1985, Reverend Garvin announced suddenly that I was in need of no more therapy. This confused and upset me as I felt that I was still in turmoil and needed to resolve some issues. At the end of the session, I was feeling very vulnerable and asked him to hold me. He did, but began touching and fondling other parts of my body. Shortly thereafter, I had another session with Dr. Garvin at the Samaritan Counseling Center during which he fondled and kissed me.
>
> Dr. Garvin convinced me that we should meet outside his office. I did not want to lose him as a counselor so I continued to see him outside the office. I believed he still had my best interest at heart and would not do anything to harm me.
>
> As I continued to meet with him, Reverend Garvin became more aggressive sexually. I confronted him about his conduct and he agreed he was wrong. However, the sexual contact continued until mid-July when sexual intercourse occurred.

In December 1985, the woman began seeing another counselor, who testified that "the woman comes from an extremely unstable background. Any reasonable practitioner would have been able to see that she was easy prey for the kind of conduct reportedly engaged in by Dr. Garvin." She also testified that Garvin negligently handled the "transference phenomenon—a type of parent-dependent relationship which developed during counseling."[5]

The Alaska Supreme Court went on to recognize a unique tort (negligence) liability theory as it concluded that the trial of the case should go forward rather than be dismissed:

> A trier of fact [jury] might reasonably conclude that the sexual intercourse which occurred roughly one month after counseling, was connected with the *tortious misuse of the transference phenomenon during counseling*.[6] (emphasis added)

This Alaska case is by no means unusual in its recognition of the transference process as an aspect of a legal claim for sexual misconduct by a minister or any other counselor or therapist. Far too often, the lawsuits and headlines tell that men in ministry are not helping women in counseling differentiate fantasy from reality. Whether it is intentional or at an unconscious level, every ministry needs to become hypersensitive to transference and countertransference issues.

AVOIDING TRANSFERENCE LIABILITY

The following are a few practical suggestions that will help immensely in avoiding the devastating allegations experienced by the Samaritan Counseling Center in Alaska:

1. As mentioned before, there is no substitute for well-trained, experienced counselors. When well-understood, transference can often be used as a tool for promoting health rather than creating more emotional trauma.
2. Supervision by trained psychotherapists who can readily spot transference phenomena is essential to any counseling setting. If an expense is required, can you

afford not to pay for such an important precaution?

3. Practical limitations on male-female counseling relationships must be set. For example, many churches are moving toward less private counseling visits. Doors are left open whenever possible if windows on doors do not exist. One church spent a large sum to install pastoral office doors equipped with large windows to eliminate even the appearance of any impropriety.

4. Again, client referrals to licensed mental health professionals may also be a must for anyone looking at long-term counseling. The Samaritan Counseling Center example of more than thirty-four sessions is probably going to become the rare exception in programs that use unlicensed counselors. This is particularly true when liability insurance policies do not cover sexual misconduct claims.

Unfortunately, the long-term, one-on-one counseling relationship appears to be wrought inherently with psychological traps and unique sexual temptations between counselor and client. Ministries or churches that plow ahead using ill-prepared novices who are unaware of the power of transference and countertransference will risk both harming people and suffering costly legal proceedings that otherwise could be avoided.

Of all the many controversies over which Christian ministries are being sued, the misconduct in the counseling relationship is causing the greatest alarm. This is true financially and in terms of the reputation of the church. Ministry organizations as a group must reverse this trend. Counseling programs must be legally sound, and the best way to accomplish this task is to make them professionally above reproach. If Christians are truly to honor God in this aspect of ministry, every secular counseling standard must be exceeded.

LEGAL STRATEGIES AND PRINCIPLES

◆ Keeping confidences and preserving privacy are essential elements of a legally sound counseling ministry.

◆ A duty of confidentiality exists under the following conditions:

1. The subject communicated is made within the counseling relationship.
2. The information communicated is of a private, confidential nature.
3. The information is communicated in a private, non-public way.
4. Under the law of your state, no exception requiring disclosure is applicable.

◆ Exceptions requiring and permitting disclosure include:

1. The duty to warn others of imminent and real danger of physical harm.
2. The duty to report child abuse to proper authorities.
3. Discussions within the context of formal supervision by a licensed mental health professional.
4. Informed, voluntary consent to disclosure by the client.

◆ Preserving the personal privacy rights of others is not an option in ministry, it is a legal obligation.

1. An unjustified public disclosure of private facts can lead to liability.
2. Rights to privacy issues extend well beyond counseling relationships and encompass every aspect of ministry.

◆ Transference: "The unconscious tendency to shift our emotional interest toward new persons in the hopes of succeeding where formerly we failed."

◆ The ever-present dangers of countertransference and emotional manipulation in counseling require every counselor, from top to bottom, to subject themselves to some formal supervision on a regular basis. The unconscious aspects of countertransference are the root cause of most sexual misconduct lawsuits against ministries.

◆ To avoid transference or countertransference liabilities, every program should consider the following:

1. Set and follow strict standards to employ only well-trained, experienced counselors.
2. Establish a formal supervision component using a licensed psychologist, psychiatrist, or other licensed mental health practitioner with appropriate qualifications to be supervising others.
3. Place clear limitations on the scope of the counseling the ministry performs, e.g., limiting lay counseling to small-group settings.
4. Offer routine written referrals to licensed mental health professionals to coincide with the purely spiritual counseling the ministry provides.

Epilogue

I want to make one final comment for any person in ministry, especially as we consider a coming decade of perhaps unimaginable legal crises. Many will say after reading this book that we cannot ultimately place our trust in legal defense principles and strategies. They might be surprised to hear that I agree.

God's will and His divine providence will surely prevail in all things. In Psalm 127:1-2 we are warned, "Unless the LORD builds the house, its builders labor in vain. Unless the LORD watches over the city, the watchmen stand guard in vain." Surely this is the case with churches and ministries today.

Further, it is quite certain that Jesus taught us to turn the other cheek. Jesus Himself, when presented with the numerous legal arguments and accusations that led to His crucifixion, gave no answer. He was silent as a lamb.

Clearly, then, I cannot fault those people who, in their given legal circumstances, choose to turn the other cheek or to give no answer if that is what they believe God is asking them to do.

What I must suggest, in trying to be a good steward of the

education and professional experience God has allowed me to have, is that all those in ministry takes their legal rights and responsibilities seriously. This means becoming informed in the areas covered in this book. That way God can use our legal preparedness when He so chooses.

If you look at the example of the Apostle Paul, on two different occasions he specifically and purposely used the unique legal privileges of being a Roman citizen from birth to his advantage and to serve God's will (Acts 16:37-40, 22:25-29). As you study these passages, you will see that Paul did not accidentally stumble upon the fact that he was being mistreated as a citizen of the Roman empire. He knew full well that his legal rights were being disregarded and he boldly pronounced the particulars of his jailers' errors. We too must learn the particulars of our own legal rights and responsibilities. If we do, I think it will allow God to use us and protect us more effectively.

There will be times when God calls us to suffer quietly for His sake. But there may also be times ahead when He calls us to protect our ministries with legal defenses and shrewd strategies. My personal hope is that we're prepared for either occasion.

Association of Christian Conciliation Services Recommended Conciliation Clauses

The parties to this agreement are Christians and believe that the Bible commands them to make every effort to live at peace and to resolve disputes with each other in private or within the Christian church (see Matthew 18:15-20, 1 Corinthians 6:1-8). Therefore, the parties agree that any claim or dispute arising from or related to this agreement shall be settled by biblically based mediation and, if necessary, legally binding arbitration in accordance with the *Rules of Procedure for Christian Conciliation* of the Association of Christian Conciliation Services (ACCS). The parties agree that these methods shall be the sole remedy for any controversy or claim arising out of this agreement and expressly waive their right to file a lawsuit in any civil court against one another for such disputes, except to enforce an arbitration decision.

✻ ✻ ✻

Association of Christian Conciliation Services Referral List

The Association of Christian Conciliation Services (ACCS) has members located throughout the United States. The following list includes regional contacts who can provide you with conciliation assistance or refer you to other members in their regions. In order to be included on this list, an individual must be enrolled in the ACCS Conciliator Training Program. You may also contact the national office of the ACCS for referrals or materials: 1537 Ave. D, Suite 352, Billings, MT 59102, (406)256-1583.

ARKANSAS
  ◆ Little Rock. Robert Gross, P.O. Box 68, 72203. (501)376-0669.

CALIFORNIA
  ◆ Hollywood. CCS of Los Angeles, Bryan Hance, 1800 N. Highland #507, 90028. (213)467-3331.

◆ Malibu. Pepperdine School of Law, Peter Robinson, I.D.R., 90265. (213)456-4655.

◆ Novato. Bay Area CCS, Tim Arensmeier, P.O. Box 617, 94948. (415)382-9162.

COLORADO

◆ Lakewood. CCS of Denver, Richard Wise, 1545 S. Kline Ct., 80232. (303)988-3230.

FLORIDA

◆ Lake Worth. Larry Durham, 1302 - 13th Ln., 33463. (407)642-3113.

◆ Melbourne. CCS of Brevard, Francis Bradley, 427 Timberlake Dr., 32940. (407)242-1421.

ILLINOIS

◆ Chicago. C. Frederick LeBaron, 233 S. Wacker Dr. #8300, 60606. (312)993-5335.

◆ Elmhurst. CCS of Northern Illinois, John Steven Cole, P.O. Box 54, 60126. (708)834-4740.

KANSAS

◆ Overland Park. CCS of Kansas City, Blaine Robison, 6405 Metcalf #307, 66202. (913)362-2102.

MICHIGAN

◆ Lansing. CCS of Central Michigan, Anne Bachle, 1710 E. Michigan, 48912. (517)485-2270.

◆ Redford. CCS of Southeast Michigan, Donald Remillard, 26847 Grand River, 48240. (313)533-9140.

MISSISSIPPI

◆ Jackson. CCS of Central Mississippi, Angela Simpkins, P.O. Box 55552, 39296. (601)366-5497.

MONTANA

◆ Billings. CCS of Montana, Ken Sande, 1537 Ave. D #352, 59102. (406)256-1583.

◆ Bozeman. Mark Bryan, P.O. Box 1371, 59715. (406)586-8565.

◆ Helena. Michael Becker, 428 N. Benton, 59601. (406)442-7450.

NEW YORK

◆ Commack. Matthew Radin, 861 Larkfield Rd., 11725. (516)462-9335.

◆ Hopewell Junction. Dewey Lee, 4 Regent Dr., 12533. (914)223-7890.

NORTH CAROLINA
- Blowing Rock. Lynn Pace, Rt. 1 Box 273, 28605. (704)295-9404.
- Trinity. Trinity CCS, Forrest Horn Sr., P.O. Box 1009, 27370. (919)434-5449.

OHIO
- Circleville. John Bowen, 218 N. Scioto, 43113. (614)477-1688.

OKLAHOMA
- Edmond. CCS of Oklahoma City, Robert Raftery, 1813 Running Branch Rd., 73013. (405)341-2253.

OREGON
- Portland. CCS of Portland/Vancouver, Will Wright, P.O. Box 9070, 97207. (503)231-1624.

PENNSYLVANIA
- Allentown. Everett Forner, 2460 Lisa Ln., 18104. (215)398-7887.

TENNESSEE
- Memphis. J. Maxwell Williams, 2374 Holly Grove Dr., 38119. (901)522-2083.

TEXAS
- Austin. Barbara Horan, Christian Reconciliation Ctr., P.O. Box 202133, 78720. (512)328-3662.
- San Antonio. CCS of San Antonio, Jobeth McLeod, P.O. Box 15717, 78212. (512)227-0638.

VIRGINIA
- Annandale. Christian Legal Society, George Newitt, President, 4208 Evergreen Ln. #222, 22003. (703)642-1070.
- Fairfax. F. Mather Archer, P.O. Box 396, 22030. (703)642-1070.

WASHINGTON
- Seattle. CCS of Puget Sound, Mark Albertson, 424 N. 130th, 98133. (206)367-2245.

WYOMING
- Gillette. Frank Stevens, P.O. Box 1148, 82717. (307)682-1444.
- Powell. Dick Kahl, 207 E. First, 82435. (307)754-2603.

Agreement to Resolve Disputes by Mediation and/or Arbitration

The undersigned parties hereby agree and knowingly consent to submit to mediation any controversy or claim between them caused by or related to any alleged act, error, or omission.

Mediation is an informal settlement process to try to negotiate disputes. It is nonbinding on either party and does not involve testimony from witnesses or use of exhibits as evidence. Arbitration is a formal procedure like a trial where witnesses testify under oath and exhibits are utilized. The arbitrator makes a decision after the conclusion of the arbitration as to which party's position is correct and whether either party is entitled to a damage award.

If, within ten days after service of a written demand for mediation, the undersigned cannot agree as to a mediator or mediation organization, then the undersigned consent to submit to mediation through the American Arbitration Association. If the parties agree to mediate, but the mediation does not within ninety days result in settlement of the dispute, then, at the sole option of either party the dispute may be submitted to binding arbitration. Such submission to binding arbitration shall be through an arbitrator(s) or arbitration organization of the parties' choice. If, within ten days after service of the written demand for arbitration, the undersigned cannot agree as to an arbitrator(s) or arbitration organization, then the dispute shall be submitted to binding arbitration by the American Arbitration Association.

Judgment upon the award rendered by the arbitrator may be entered in any court having appropriate jurisdiction.

The undersigned are each entitled to, and encouraged to, seek the advice of independent counsel with regard to the terms and condition of this agreement. The signatures below indicate that the undersigned have sought such advice or that they are waiving their right to do so.

Signature: _____   Signature: _____

Date: _____   Date: _____

Affidavit and Waiver of Lien

STATE OF   )
)   SS.
COUNTY OF   )

_____, being first duly sworn upon oath, deposes and says:

(Complete only if signed by a corporation.)
That he is the _____ of _____ and makes this Affidavit for and on its behalf, being authorized so to do.

That in consideration of the sum of _____ (amount being paid) Dollars ($ _____) the receipt of which is hereby acknowledged, the undersigned does hereby waive, release, and relinquish any and all claims or right of lien that the undersigned now has upon the premises known as and described as (insert the legal description of property involved)

and also known as _____ (insert street address of property) for labor or material, or both, furnished or which may be furnished by the undersigned pursuant to that certain contract dated the _____ day of _____, 19_____ , whereby the undersigned was to supply the following materials or perform the following services:

That for valuable consideration paid to the undersigned, the receipt of which is hereby acknowledged, the undersigned does hereby warrant, represent, state, swear, and certify that it has paid in full any person who has labored or furnished materials, machinery, fixtures, or tools in connection with the above construction contract, and the undersigned does further warrant, represent, state, swear, and certify that any and all liens for labor or materials that were created by the undersigned as an agent of _____ in connection with said contract above mentioned have been extinguished through payment, and the undersigned further agrees to furnish any and all waivers of liens from said laborers and material suppliers as may be required.

Date: _____   By: _____
                                     Title: _____

SUBSCRIBED AND SWORN to before me, this _____ day of _____ , 19_____.
My Commission Expires: _____
                                       Notary Public

Notes

Chapter 1: The Changing Legal Winds for Ministries

1. Bob Dylan, *Subterranean Homesick Blues*.
2. *Natal v. Christian and Missionary Alliance*, 878 F.2d 1575 (1st Cir. 1989).
3. *Minker v. Baltimore Annual Conf. United Methodist Church*, 894 F.2d 1354 (D.C. Cir. 1990).
4. *Alicea v. New Brunswick Theological Seminary, et al.*, 581 A.2d 900 (N.J. Super. A.D. 1990).
5. *Barnett v. Community Chapel and Bible Training Center, et al.*, 792 P.2d 150 (Wash. 1990).
6. *Kennedy v. Gray*, 807 P.2d 670 (Kans. 1991).
7. *First Union Baptist Church v. Banks*, 533 So.2d 1305 (La. App. 3d Cir. 1988).
8. *Charles Blair, et al., v. Charles Blair, Jr., et al., as Trustees for the Peoples Baptist Church*, 396 S.E.2d 374 (S.C. App. 1990).
9. *Logan v. Old Enterprise Farms, Ltd.*, 564 N.E.2d 778 (Ill. 1990).
10. *Tollefson v. Roman Catholic Bishop*, 268 Cal. Rptr. 550 (Calif. App. 4th Dist. 1990).

Chapter 2: The Litigation Avalanche Hits Ministries

1. California Board of Bar Examiners, Colorado Bar Association, New York Attorney Registration, Illinois Supreme Court and Attorney Registration.
2. Weston D. Darby, Jr., "Are You Keeping Up Financially?" *American Bar Association Journal,* December 1985; quoted by Richard L. Abel, *American Lawyers* (New York: Oxford University Press, 1989), pages 160-61.
3. Ken Myers, "Despite Worsening Job Outlook, Applications Hit Record High," *National Law Journal,* October 7, 1991.
4. Committee of Bar Examiners of the State Bar of California, January 15, 1992.
5. Myers, "Despite Worsening Job Outlook, Applications Hit Record High."
6. Myers, "Despite Worsening Job Outlook, Applications Hit Record High."
7. *Black's Law Dictionary* (St. Paul, MN: West Publishing Co., 1968), page 200.

Chapter 4: Enterprise Liability Theory: Opening Deep Pockets

1. Reporter's Study, "Enterprise Responsibility for Personal Injury," *American Law Institute*, vol. 1, April 15, 1991, page 28.
2. Reporter's Study, page 19.
3. Reporter's Study, page 19.
4. Colorado Jury Instructions 3d, Civil, 9:34.
5. John F. Cleary, "Special Problems: Tort Liability for Churches," *American Bar Association National Institute on Tort and Religion*, Boston, Massachusetts, June 14-15, 1990, page 9.
6. Cleary, page 9.
7. Cleary, page 9.
8. *Doe v. Samaritan Counseling Center*, 791 P.2d 344 (Alaska 1990).
9. *Doe* at 344.
10. *Doe* at 349.

Chapter 5: The Christian Response Thus Far: In the World But Not of It

1. *American Bar Association National Institute on Tort and Religion*, Boston, Massachusetts, June 14-15, 1990, and American Bar Association Annual Meeting, "Tort and Religion Seminar," San Francisco, California, May 4-5, 1989.
2. D. A. Carson, "Matthew," *The Expositor's Bible Commentary* (Grand Rapids, MI: Zondervan, 1984), vol. 8, pages 246-247.
3. Walter L. Liefeld, "Luke," *The Expositor's Bible Commentary* (Grand Rapids, MI: Zondervan, 1984), vol. 8, pages 985-988.
4. Geldenhuys, *The New International Commentary on the New Testament: The Gospel of Luke* (Grand Rapids, MI: Eerdmans, 1979), page 415.
5. Colin Brown, ed., *The New International Dictionary of New Testament Theology* (Grand Rapids, MI: Zondervan, 1979), vol. 2, page 619.
6. Fred B. Craddock, "Interpretation," *Luke: A Bible Commentary for Teaching and Preaching* (Louisville, KY: John Knox Press, 1990), pages 190-191.
7. *Alicea v. New Brunswick Theological Seminary, et al.*, 581 A.2d 900 (N.J. Super. A.D. 1990).
8. *Corporation of Presiding Bishop v. Amos*, 483 U.S. 327 (1987).
9. Candler School of Theology at Emory University, Dallas Theological Seminary, Denver Seminary, Fuller Theological Seminary, Gordon Conwell Theological Seminary, Perkins School of Theology at Southern Methodist University, Princeton Theological Seminary, Southwestern Baptist Theological Seminary, Trinity Evangelical Divinity School, and Yale Divinity School.

Chapter 6: Could a Killer Lawsuit Happen to You?

1. "Jury Awards Woman $1.2 Million," *Denver Post*, September 6, 1991.
2. Calvary Temple literature and press releases.

Chapter 7: The Legal Playing Field
1. Gary Schoener, Walk-In Counseling Center, Minneapolis, Minnesota.
2. Uniform Commercial Code 2-302.

Chapter 8: "L.A. Law" Is Not the Law
1. Law Firm Listings, *National Law Journal,* November 18, 1991, page S4.

Chapter 9: Lawyers: Friend or Foe?
1. Richard L. Abel, *American Lawyers* (New York: Oxford University Press, 1989), page 283.
2. Abel, page 283.
3. Abel, page 283.
4. Gail Diane Cox, "New Lawyers: White Men Are in the Minority," *National Law Journal,* September 30, 1991.
5. Abel, page 280.
6. George Silvestri and John Lukasiewicz, "Projections of Occupational Employment, 1988–2000," *Monthly Labor Review,* November 1989, page 45.
7. "American Bar Association Membership Report," July 1991.
8. "American Bar Association Membership Report."
9. Mark Hansen, "Quayle Raps Lawyers," *American Bar Association Journal,* October 1991, page 36.
10. Hansen, page 36.
11. Hansen, page 36.
12. Robert D. Yates, "Smell the Roses," *American Bar Association Journal,* October 1991, page 42.

Chapter 10: Professor Kingsfield Revisited: Lawyers' Education and Ethics
1. *American Bar Association Specialization State Plan Book,* August 1990, Standing Committee on Specialization.
2. *American Bar Association Specialization State Plan Book.*
3. Code of Professional Responsibility, Disciplinary Rule 7-101.
4. Code of Professional Responsibility, Disciplinary Rule 2-106.
5. Code of Professional Responsibility, Disciplinary Rule 4-101.
6. Code of Professional Responsibility, Disciplinary Rule 5-105.
7. Code of Professional Responsibility, Ethical Considerations, 7-7 and 7-8.

Chapter 11: Ten Commandments for Working with Lawyers, Part I
1. "101 Ways to Cut Legal Fees and Manage Your Lawyer," National Chamber Litigation Center, 1615 H Street NW, Washington, DC 20062.
2. The American Bar Association has created The National Discipline Data Bank, which functions as a national clearinghouse for lawyer discipline information. The National Discipline Data Bank, American Bar Association, Center for Professional Responsibility, 750 North Lake Shore Drive, Chicago, IL 60611, (312)988-5000.

Chapter 12: Ten Commandments for Working with Lawyers, Part II

1. "101 Ways to Cut Legal Fees and Manage Your Lawyer," National Chamber Litigation Center, 1615 H Street NW, Washington, DC 20062.
2. Mark McCormack, *What I Should Have Learned at Yale Law School: The Terrible Truth About Lawyers* (New York: Avon Books, 1987).
3. "Battles to Control Counsel Costs Are Won, Lost," *National Law Journal,* September 9, 1991, page S7.
4. Colorado Bar Association, 1900 Grant Street, Suite 950, Denver, Colorado 80203.
5. Lynn R. Buzzard and Laurence Eck, *Tell It to the Church* (Wheaton, IL: Tyndale, 1985).
6. *Elmora Hebrew Center, Inc., v. Yale M. Fishman,* 570 A.2d 1297 (N.J. Super. A.D. 1990).
7. *Elmora* at 1300.
8. Samuel E. Ericson, *16 Questions a Christian Should Ask Before Going to Court* (Christian Legal Society, 1987). Used by permission.

Chapter 13: Corporate Law: Structuring to Avoid Personal Liability

1. *Hutchins v. Grace Tabernacle United Pentecostal Church,* 804 S.W.2d 598 (Tex. App. 1991).
2. *Foster v. Purdue University, Beta Theta Pi Fraternity,* 567 N.E.2d 865 (Ind. App. 3 Dist. 1991).
3. *Foster* at 871.
4. *Crocker v. Reverend Barr and the Calhoun Falls Pentecostal Holiness Church,* 409 S.E.2d 368 (S.C. 1991).
5. *Barnett v. Community Chapel and Bible Training Center, et al.,* 792 P.2d 150 (1990).
6. *Barnett* at 150.
7. *First Union Baptist Church v. Banks,* 533 So.2d 1305 (La. App. 3d Cir. 1988).

Chapter 14: Real Estate Law: Commonly Overlooked Basics for Christian Organizations

1. *Church of the Savior v. Zoning Hearing Board of Tredyffrin Township,* 568 A.2d 1336 (Pa. Cmwlth. 1989).
2. *Needham Pastoral Counseling Center v. Board of Appeals of Needham,* 557 N.E.2d 43 (Mass. App. Ct. 1990).
3. *Concrete Supply v. Ramseur Baptist Church,* 383 S.E.2d 222 (N.C. App. 1989).

Chapter 15: Get It in Writing (and Keep a Copy)

1. *Minker v. Baltimore Annual Conf. United Methodist Church,* 894 F.2d 1354 (D.C. Cir. 1990).
2. *Minker* at 1359.

3. *Minker* at 1360.
4. *Minker* at 1361.
5. *Minker* at 1361.
6. *Stacey Realty v. Calvary Baptist Church,* 374 S.E.2d 537 (Ga. App., 1988).

Chapter 16: Warnings About Insurance Coverage

1. Virginia Culver, "Insurance Warning Issued Methodist Churches Alerted on Sex-misconduct Cases," *Denver Post,* January 4, 1992.

Chapter 17: Counseling Liabilities 101

1. *American College Dictionary* (New York: Random House, 1964), s.v. "counsel."
2. *American College Dictionary,* s.v. "therapy."
3. "Jury Awards Woman $1.2 Million," *Denver Post,* September 6, 1991.
4. *Nally v. Grace Community Church,* 763 P.2d 948 (Calif. 1988).
5. *Nally* at 960.
6. *Nally* at 950-952, 955, 964, 967.
7. *Nally* at 968, 970.

Chapter 18: Protecting Counseling Ministries from Legal Attack

1. *Destefano v. Diocese of Colorado Springs, et al.,* 763 P.2d 275 (Colo. 1988).
2. *Destefano* at 284.
3. *Destefano* at 285.
4. *Destefano* at 286.
5. *Destefano* at 287.
6. Virginia Culver, "Scandals Spark Clergy—Screening Changes," *Denver Post,* April 28, 1991.

Chapter 19: Counseling Confidentiality and Transference

1. Sheldon Roth, *Psychotherapy: The Art of Wooing Nature* (North Vale, NJ: Jason Aronson, Inc., 1987), page 18.
2. Roth, page 18.
3. Irvin D. Yalom, "The Theory and Practice of Group Psychotherapy," 3rd edition (New York: Basic Books, 1985).
4. *Doe v. Samaritan Counseling Center,* 791 P.2d 344 (Alaska 1990).
5. *Doe* at 345.
6. *Doe* at 349.

Glossary of Legal Terms

ALLEGATION. The argument, factual position, assertion, or statement of one party to a lawsuit. In other words, when we say something, it's the truth, but when the other side says something, it's an allegation.

AMICUS CURIAE. Technically means a "friend of the court"; someone who is not directly involved in a lawsuit but who volunteers written information in the form of a brief upon some matter of law.

ANSWER. A court filing in which the defendant admits or denies the PLAINTIFF'S ALLEGATION of facts found in the plaintiff's complaint.

APPEARANCE. The formal process by which a defendant or a lawyer submits himself to the jurisdiction of the court in a particular case.

APPELLANT. The party appealing a decision or judgment to a higher court because it believes the lower court committed a significant error.

APPELLATE COURT. A court having jurisdiction to hear and decide an appeal; not a "trial court."

APPELLEE. The winning party against whom an appeal is taken.

BRIEF. A written argument prepared by legal counsel to file in court, setting forth both facts and law in support of the client's position in a case.

BURDEN OF PROOF. The legal duty of a party to prove affirmatively a pertinent fact or facts at a trial of a lawsuit.

CHAMBERS. Private office or room of a judge.

CHANGE OF VENUE. The removal of a lawsuit started in one district to another district for trial because the original location would result in an unfair trial.

CODE. A collection of laws enacted by a state legislature, by Congress at the federal level, or by a local legislative authority.

COMMON LAW. Law that derives its authority from traditional usage and customs or from the precedent-setting decisions of APPELLATE COURTS. Also called "case law."

COMPLAINT. The initial written filing or pleading on the part of the PLAINTIFF in a civil action that begins the lawsuit and states why the defendant is liable to the plaintiff.

CORROBORATING EVIDENCE. Evidence given that tends to strengthen or confirm previously offered evidence.

COUNTERCLAIM. A claim of liability presented by a defendant in response to the claims of a PLAINTIFF. Essentially, the defendant argues that the plaintiff is liable to the defendant, not the other way around.

COURT REPORTER. Person who records oral argument and testimony of witnesses during court proceedings.

CROSS-EXAMINATION. The questioning of a witness in a trial or the taking of a DEPOSITION by the lawyer opposed to the one who produced the witness. Its purpose is to discredit the witness's testimony.

DAMAGES. Financial compensation that may be awarded by the court to any person who has suffered loss or injury to his person, property, or rights through the unlawful act or NEGLIGENCE of another.

DECREE. A decision, judgment, or order of the court. A final decree is one that fully and finally disposes of the litigation; an interlocutory decree is a preliminary decree which is not final.

DEFAULT. When a party fails to respond within the time allowed by legal rules or fails to appear at the trial, the party is said to lose by default, much like a forfeit in a sport event.

DEPOSITION. The recorded testimony of a witness not taken in open court but under oath, usually with lawyers for both sides present to allow for fair questioning by both.

DISCOVERY. The investigation and exploratory process under legal rules whereby each party may become informed as to the facts known by the other parties and their witnesses.

ESTOPPEL. A person's own act or acceptance of facts that preclude his later making claims to the contrary.

ET AL. An abbreviation of *et alii*, meaning "and others."

ET SEQ. An abbreviation for *et sequentes* or *et sequentia*, meaning "and the following."

EXHIBIT. A paper, document, or other article produced to a court during a trial or hearing.

EX PARTE. By or for one party; done for, in behalf of, or on the application of one party only.

EXPERT EVIDENCE. Testimony given in relation to some scientific, technical, or professional matter by persons qualified to speak authoritatively by reason of special training, skill, or familiarity with the subject. Testimony in the nature of giving an opinion rather than a mere recitation of factual occurrences.

FIDUCIARY. A person having the character of a trustee, a relationship requiring scrupulous good faith and candor.

FRAUD. An intentional perversion of truth. Deceitful practice or device resorted to with intent to deprive another of property or other right, or in some manner to do him injury.

GARNISHMENT. A proceeding whereby property or money of a debtor, in possession of another (the garnishee), is applied to the debts of the debtor.

HARMLESS ERROR. In APPELLATE practice, an error committed by a lower court during a trial, but not prejudicial to the rights of the party and for which the court will not reverse the judgment.

HEARSAY. Evidence not proceeding from the personal knowledge of the witness.

HYPOTHETICAL QUESTION. A combination of facts and circumstances presented to an expert witness to obtain his opinion at trial.

IMPEACHMENT OF WITNESS. An attack on the credibility of a witness, usually by the testimony of other witnesses.

IMPLIED CONTRACT. A contract in which the promise made by the obligor is not stated expressly but is inferred from conduct.

IMPUTED NEGLIGENCE. Negligence that is not directly attributable to the person himself but which is the negligence of another over whom he has direction and control.

INADMISSIBLE. Evidence that under legal rules cannot be admitted or received at trial.

IN CAMERA. In the judge's chambers; in private.

INJUNCTION. A mandatory or prohibitive order issued by a court requiring someone to do a specific action or refrain from doing a specific act.

INTERROGATORIES. Written questions presented by one party in a lawsuit to an adversary who must provide written answers under oath.

IRRELEVANT. Evidence not relating or applicable to the matter in issue; not supporting the issue.

JURY. A certain number of persons, selected according to law and sworn to decide certain matters of fact and to determine the truth of evidence before them at a trial.

LEADING QUESTION. A question that puts into a witness's mouth words to be echoed back; a question that suggests to the witness the answer desired.

LIBEL. A method of defamation expressed by print, writing, pictures, or signs. Any publication that is injurious to the reputation of another.

MISTRIAL. An erroneous or invalid trial that cannot stand in law because of the absence of some fundamental legal requirement.

MITIGATING CIRCUMSTANCE. This is a circumstance that does not constitute a justification or excuse for an offense, but which may reduce the degree of one's responsibility.

NEGLIGENCE. The failure to do something that a reasonable person guided by ordinary considerations would do; the doing of something that a reasonable and prudent person would not do.

OPINION EVIDENCE. Evidence of what the witness thinks or believes regarding a fact in dispute, as distinguished from personal knowledge of the facts; not admissible except in the case of experts.

PARTIES. The persons who are actively concerned in the prosecution or defense of a legal proceeding; also the persons who have signed a written contract or entered into a verbal agreement.

PLAINTIFF. A person who starts a lawsuit.

PLEADING. The process by which the parties in a suit or action alternately present written statements of their contentions.

PREPONDERANCE OF EVIDENCE. Greater weight of evidence or evidence that is more credible and convincing to the fact-finder's mind, not necessarily the greater number of witnesses.

QUID PRO QUO. "This for that"; something of value or consideration given to each party in a contract.

RETAINER. The act of a client employing an attorney; the initial deposit toward legal fees that clients pay when they first hire an attorney.

SLANDER. Defamatory spoken words that tend to harm another's reputation, business, or means of livelihood. Both "LIBEL" and "slander" are methods of defamation; the former being expressed in physically tangible forms and the latter verbally.

STARE DECISIS. The legal doctrine from a higher court that pronounces a principle of law applicable to certain circumstances; it must be adhered to by lower courts and applied to future cases where the facts are substantially the same.

STATUTE. The written law enacted by legislative bodies.

STIPULATION. An agreement by attorneys on opposite sides of a case as to any matter pertaining to the trial.

SUBPOENA. A court process of serving papers to cause a witness to appear and give testimony before a court or at a deposition.

SUBPOENA DUCES TECUM. A court process of serving papers by which the court commands a witness to produce certain documents or records in a trial or at a deposition.

SUMMONS. A writ directing the sheriff or other officer to notify the named person that an action has been commenced against him in court and that he is required to appear on the day named and answer the complaint in such action.

TORT. An injury or wrong committed to the person or property of another. A tort can be the result of intentional or negligent conduct.

TRANSCRIPT. The official record of proceedings in a trial or hearing.

UNDUE INFLUENCE. A pressure brought against people that destroys their free will and causes them to do something they would not otherwise do.

VENUE. The particular county, city, or geographical area in which a court with jurisdiction may conduct a trial and determine a case.

VOIR DIRE. The phrase denotes the preliminary questions asked of witnesses or jurors as to their qualifications to be witnesses at trial or to serve as jurors.

WEIGHT OF EVIDENCE. The greater amount of credible evidence offered in a trial to support one side rather than the other.

WILLFUL. An act done intentionally, as distinguished from an act done carelessly or inadvertently.

WITHOUT PREJUDICE. A dismissal "without prejudices" allows a new suit to be brought on the same circumstances. A dismissal of a lawsuit "with prejudice" means it can never be filed again.

AUTHOR

Carl F. Lansing is an attorney in the private practice of law in Denver, Colorado. In his fifteen years as a lawyer, he has emphasized business law and litigation. Mr. Lansing serves as corporate legal counsel to a diverse group of public and private companies and nonprofit ministries, as well as professional practices, including psychologists and Christian psychotherapists. He has taught the Law of Corporations at the University of Denver School of Law and Business Law at the college level and speaks to professional and industry groups on legal topics. In addition to writing about legal issues confronting workers in Christian ministry, he directs Young Life's nationwide resource program for local-area fund-raising committees.

Mr. Lansing has been an active professional member of the American Bar Association, the Colorado Bar Association, and the Christian Legal Society. He is a certified mediator and has served as a court-appointed arbitrator in commercial litigation.

Mr. Lansing earned his Juris Doctorate from Pepperdine University School of Law in Malibu, California, and his B.A. in Political Science from Westmont College in Santa Barbara, California.